NORTHERN STORM RISING

RON RHODES

HARVEST HOUSE PUBLISHERS

EUGENE, OREGON

Unless otherwise indicated, all Scripture quotations are taken from the New American Standard Bible®, ©1960, 1962, 1963, 1968, 1971, 1972, 1973, 1975, 1977, 1995 by The Lockman Foundation. Used by permission. (www.Lockman.org)

Verses marked NIV are taken from the HOLY BIBLE, NEW INTERNATIONAL VERSION®. NIV®. Copyright ©1973, 1978, 1984 by the International Bible Society. Used by permission of Zondervan. All rights reserved.

Verses marked NLT are taken from the *Holy Bible*, New Living Translation, copyright ©1996. Used by permission of Tyndale House Publishers, Inc., Wheaton, IL 60189 USA. All rights reserved.

Verses marked NKJV are taken from the New King James Version. Copyright ©1982 by Thomas Nelson, Inc. Used by permission. All rights reserved.

Verses marked KJV are taken from the King James Version of the Bible.

Cover by Dugan Design Group, Bloomington, Minnesota

NORTHERN STORM RISING

Published by Harvest House Publishers
Eugene, Oregon 97402
www.harvesthousepublishers.com

Library of Congress Cataloging-in-Publication Data

Rhodes, Ron.
Northern storm rising / Ron Rhodes.
p. cm.
Includes bibliographical references.
ISBN-13: 978-0-7369-2174-9

1. Bible. O.T. Ezekiel XXXVIII-XXXIX–Prophecies–Israel. 2. Bible. O.T. Ezekiel XXXVIII-XXXIX–Prophecies–Islamic countries. 3. Bible. O.T. Ezekiel XXXVIII-XXXIX–Prophecies–Russia (Federation) I. Title.
BS1545.6.P26R46 2008
236'.9–dc22

2007028424

Printed in the United States of America

13 14 15 16 / LB-NI / 10 9 8 7

Acknowledgments

Someone said that writers are not home even when they are home. I wouldn't go that far, but a writer's time is consumed like few other jobs and occupations. Writing is hard work, and doing it right involves a lengthy, drawn-out process. For this reason, I never tire of giving a special heartfelt thanks to my wife, Kerri, and two children, David and Kylie. I appreciate their sacrificial attitude more than I can put into words.

Target: Israel

Hitler revealed in *Mein Kampf* that he intended to commit genocide on the Jews of Germany...He communicated his true intentions, even if only those who knew how to listen to disturbed personalities believed him at the time. So, too, the mad mullahs who rule Iran have been clearly telling the world that they intend to use their missiles and, when they have them, their nuclear weapons.

Jerome Corsi
author of *Atomic Iran*

At the apocalyptic end of days, mainstream Muslims envision that a great, armed jihad will result in the subjugation of the entire world to Islam.

Dore Gold
author of *The Fight for Jerusalem*
former Israeli ambassador to the United Nations

The country in most immediate danger would be Israel. After decades of vowing to destroy the Jewish state—albeit failing to do so with both conventional war and guerrilla tactics—the Islamic world would have the means to create a new Holocaust simply by pressing a few buttons.

Al Venter
author of *Iran's Nuclear Option*

Over the past several years, Israeli military planners have viewed Iran's burgeoning strategic arsenal with mounting alarm. According to top Israeli intelligence officials, Iran's nuclear program now constitutes the single greatest "threat to the existence of Israel" since the Jewish state's founding in 1948.

Ilan Berman
author of *Tehran Rising*
vice president for policy, American Foreign Policy Council

Putin's Russia has shown itself willing to facilitate Iranian nuclear ambitions...Especially in light of the mullahs' stated willingness to "share" their nuclear technology with other Islamic countries, the threat from Iran and its activities must be viewed as a ticking time bomb—and perhaps a mortal danger.

FRANK GAFFNEY
author of *War Footing*

They ask, "Is it possible for us to witness a world without America and Zionism?" But you had best know that this slogan and this goal are altogether attainable, and surely can be achieved. This regime that is occupying Jerusalem must be wiped from the map.

MAHMOUD AHMADINEJAD
president of Iran

The Iranians see themselves as being at the forefront of the battle against the "heretics"...They believe in their connection to Allah and that salvation will come only when the war of Gog and Magog begins—and now is the time for it.

"No One Can Prevent Nuclear Iran, Top Defense Official Says"
Ynetnews.com, February 12, 2007

Is nuclear mega-terrorism inevitable? Harvard professors are known for being subtle or ambiguous, but I'll try to be clear. "Is the worst yet to come?" My answer: "Bet on it. Yes."

GRAHAM ALLISON
director of Harvard University's Belfer Center for
Science and International Affairs

In memory of Dr. John F. Walvoord,
my mentor in biblical prophecy
at Dallas Theological Seminary.
His legacy lives on in those he taught.

Pray for the peace of Jerusalem.

Contents

Part One

ESCALATING WORLD TENSIONS

1

The Threat from the North

The sports arena at Southern Methodist University in Dallas erupted into spontaneous applause as Ronald Reagan walked in. I was sitting on a bleacher and had a perfect view of him. He flashed that famous smile of his and walked down the aisle, looking left and right, waving to the enthusiastic crowd, making his way to the podium. After hearing his dynamic speech, I was confident he would be elected president of the United States—and he soon was!

Reagan was a big fan of the biblical prophet Ezekiel. In fact, Ezekiel was Reagan's favorite book of prophecy. Like many other Christians, Reagan believed that the fierce Old Testament prophet foretold that God would one day gather the children of Israel who were scattered among heathen nations back to the promised land. He also believed, based on his reading of Ezekiel 38 and 39, that atheistic Russia—along with various Arab nations of the Middle East—would one day lead an invasion into Israel from the north and that God would intervene and utterly destroy this military coalition. He understood that not everything had fallen precisely into place, but he nevertheless believed the stage was being set for the fulfillment of end-time prophecies. Reagan believed he might even witness the second coming of Jesus Christ in his own lifetime.[1]

I have stood at the foot of the gravesites of men like John F. Kennedy and Richard Nixon who themselves had encounters with the leaders of Russia and various Arab nations. Scripture is clear that powerful human leaders come into power for a while and then die, but in the end, our eternal God will fulfill His sovereign purposes in human history. An overwhelming northern military coalition may attack Israel, but God is always watchful—"He who keeps Israel will neither slumber nor sleep" (Psalm 121:4)—and He will be Israel's defender.

Perpetual Threats and Insecurity

My family and I could have been blown to smithereens!

I will never forget it. We were vacationing in England in 2005. We spent the first week in London and the second week traveling throughout England's gorgeous countryside.

During the first week, our primary means of transportation was London's famous network of underground trains. With its various "tubes," one could travel just about anywhere of significance in the London area. We could walk out the front door of the Capital Hotel, stroll down to the nearby Knightsbridge station, and go anywhere in London. Perfect! The Underground—supplemented by an occasional ride on London's double-decker buses—made travel convenient and easy.

One morning during our second week in the English countryside, we toured a beautiful grand old castle. Before long, one of the tour guides walked up to us with a somber look on her face and told us that if we had plans to go into London that day, we should cancel those plans because the city had been locked down by the police. She informed us that a number of bombs had exploded in the Underground and on a double-decker bus.

I grieved for the people who lost their lives that day and for the hundreds who were injured, and I was thankful to God that our family was spared. We had been on those very Underground trains and double-decker buses the entire previous week! We may have passed right by some of the Islamic terrorists preparing to execute their horrific plan.

The following day, I thought of the Londoners who would continue to work in the city and use the Underground. Surely they would feel some insecurity, not knowing for sure whether they would be safe. What a tragic way to have to live.

Sometime later, during my personal time of Bible study, I contemplated how this is true for the entire nation of Israel. Israel is surrounded by Muslim nations intent on seeing the Jewish nation destroyed—pushed into the sea, never to reemerge. Iran's current president—Mahmoud Ahmadinejad, who is seeking nuclear weaponry as I write—assures the world that humanity will soon live in a world free of Israel and the United States. Talk about insecurity! No wonder Israel has worked so steadfastly to build up its powerful military.

Whether we are wrestling with individual insecurity or national insecurity, the Bible comforts us that God is in control not only of our individual lives—including the timing and circumstances of our deaths—but also of human history. And through biblical prophecy, God has given us a portrait of what things will look like on this planet during the last days. If biblical prophecy teaches us anything, it is that God is in complete control of human history and its culmination.

As a student at Dallas Theological Seminary in the early 1980s, I was privileged to study under Dr. John F. Walvoord, my primary professor in prophecy courses. This was a fascinating time for me. I know that Dr. Walvoord, in his old age, was truly holding out for the rapture, but the Lord had other plans. Dr. Walvoord is now in the direct presence of the Lord in heaven, and this book is written in his memory.

Those who have followed my career know that my primary writings—more than 40 books—have dealt with Christian apologetics. So why am I writing a book on biblical prophecy? I have several reasons:

- A large percentage of the Bible is prophetic. Explaining the correct meaning of prophetic passages is an important task.

- Incorrect views on biblical prophecy abound, and as an apologist, I write to defend what I believe to be the correct view.*

- Biblical prophecy motivates Christians to live righteously and in purity (see, for example, 1 Timothy 6:14; Titus 2:11-14). Understanding prophecy is beneficial to our spiritual lives.

- Events transpiring on the world scene today may be setting the stage for the specific fulfillment of prophecies uttered thousands of years ago by the Hebrew prophets. I will always continue to warn people against the folly of date-setting (Acts 1:7), but I will also urge people to be thoughtful observers of the times (see Matthew 16:1-3; Luke 21:29-33) who seek to understand how certain current events may relate to the fulfillment of end-time prophecies. For example, the current events in Russia, Iran, and other Muslim nations may be setting the stage for an eventual invasion into Israel by a northern military coalition, as predicted by the prophet Ezekiel 2600 years ago.

Understanding Our Terms

My primary goal in this book will be to discuss Ezekiel's prophecy of an end-times military coalition that will one day invade Israel, but I will also need to mention the rapture, the tribulation, the Antichrist, Armageddon, the second coming, and the millennial kingdom. I have learned never to assume that all my readers know what such Christian terms mean. I will use these terms throughout the rest of this book, so I will briefly define them at the outset. I hope those who are already

---

* For example, preterism espouses the idea that most if not all Bible prophecy was fulfilled by the time of the destruction of Jerusalem in AD 70. For an extensive listing of articles that critique this unbiblical position, see "The Problem with Preterism" at my website: www.ronrhodes.org. One preterist makes a bizarre case for the idea that the invasion of Ezekiel 38–39 was fulfilled in the events of Esther 9. Such a view ignores the biblical teaching that the invasion takes place in the "latter years" and "last days" (Ezekiel 38:8,16) by a specific coalition of nations nowhere even remotely found in the book of Esther (see Ezekiel 38:1-6).

familiar with these terms will indulge me. A little review never hurt anyone!

The Rapture

The rapture is that glorious event in which the dead in Christ will be resurrected and living Christians will be instantly translated into their resurrection bodies—and both groups will be caught up to meet Christ in the air and taken back to heaven (John 14:1-3; 1 Corinthians 15:51-54; 1 Thessalonians 4:13-17). This means one generation of Christians will never pass through death's door. They will be alive on earth one moment; the next moment they will be instantly translated into their resurrection bodies and caught up to meet Christ in the air. What a moment that will be!

Christians seem to love to debate end-time issues. Perhaps the hottest debate relates to when the rapture occurs. Four primary views are popular:

- Partial rapturism is the view that only spiritual Christians will be raptured when Christ returns. Carnal Christians will be left behind. Throughout the tribulation period, as more Christians become spiritual, they too will be raptured. Such raptures may continue to occur throughout the tribulation period. (This is not a widely held view today.)
- Pretribulationism is the view that Christ will rapture the entire church before any part of the tribulation begins. This means the church will not go through the judgments prophesied in the book of Revelation (chapters 4–18).
- Posttribulationism is the view that Christ will rapture the church after the tribulation at His second coming. This means the church will go through the time of judgment prophesied in the book of Revelation, but believers will be kept safe through the judgments.

- Midtribulationism is the view that Christ will rapture the church in the middle of the tribulation period. The two witnesses of Revelation 11, who are caught up to heaven, are believed to be representative of the church.

Most Christians today are either "pretribs" or "posttribs." I believe the pretrib position—the majority evangelical view—is most consistent with the biblical testimony. For one thing, Revelation 3:10 indicates that believers will be kept from the actual hour of testing that is coming on the whole world. Further, no Old Testament passage on the tribulation mentions the church (Deuteronomy 4:29-30; Jeremiah 30:4-11; Daniel 8:24-27; 12:1-2), and no New Testament passage on the tribulation mentions the church (Matthew 13:30,39-42,48-50; 24:15-31; 1 Thessalonians 1:9-10; 5:4-9; 2 Thessalonians 2:1-11; Revelation 4–18).

Scripture does say some Christians will be alive during the tribulation period (for example, Revelation 6:9-11). But pretribs believe these people become Christians sometime after the rapture. Perhaps they will become convinced of the truth of Christianity after witnessing millions of Christians supernaturally vanish off the planet at the rapture. Or perhaps they become Christians as a result of the ministry of the 144,000 Jewish Christians introduced in Revelation 7 (who themselves apparently come to faith in Christ after the rapture). Many may also become Christians as a result of the miraculous ministry of the two witnesses of Revelation 11, prophets who apparently have the same powers as Moses and Elijah.

In any event, Scripture assures us that the church is not appointed to wrath (Romans 5:9; 1 Thessalonians 1:9-10; 5:9). This means the church cannot go through the "great day of their wrath" in the tribulation period (Revelation 6:17).

Throughout Scripture, God protects His people before judgment falls (see 2 Peter 2:5-9). Enoch was transferred to heaven before the judgment of the flood. Noah and his family were in the ark before the judgment of the flood. Lot was taken out of Sodom before judgment was poured out on Sodom and Gomorrah. The firstborn among the Hebrews in Egypt were sheltered by the blood of the Paschal Lamb before judgment fell. The spies were safely out of Jericho and Rahab was secured before judgment fell on Jericho. So too will the church be safely raptured before judgment falls in the tribulation period.

The Tribulation

Scripture reveals that the tribulation will be a definite time of great travail at the end of the age (Matthew 24:29-35). It will be of such severity that no period in history, past or future, will equal it (Matthew 24:21). It is called the time of Jacob's trouble, for it is a judgment on Messiah-rejecting Israel (Jeremiah 30:7; Daniel 12:1-4). The nations will also be judged for their sin and rejection of Christ (Isaiah 26:21; Revelation 6:15-17). The period will last seven years (Daniel 9:24,27).

Scripture is graphically clear that this period will be characterized by wrath (Zephaniah 1:15,18), judgment (Revelation 14:7), indignation (Isaiah 26:20-21), trial (Revelation 3:10), trouble (Jeremiah 30:7), destruction (Joel 1:15), darkness (Amos 5:18), desolation (Daniel 9:27), overturning (Isaiah 24:1-4), and punishment (Isaiah 24:20-21). The term *tribulation* is therefore quite appropriate. No passage in Scripture alleviates the degree of severity of this time to come.

The tribulation is the focus of Revelation 4–18, where we read about the seal judgments, the trumpet judgments, and the bowl judgments that will be poured out on humankind in steadily increasing intensity. The suffering will be immense; the death toll immeasurable.

The Antichrist

The apostle Paul warned of a "man of lawlessness," the Antichrist (2 Thessalonians 2:3,8-9). This individual will perform counterfeit signs and wonders and deceive many people during the future tribulation period (2 Thessalonians 2:9-10). The apostle John describes this anti-God individual in the book of Revelation as "the beast"

(Revelation 13:1-10). This demon-inspired individual will rise to political prominence in the tribulation period, seek to dominate the world, attempt to destroy the Jews, persecute all true believers, set himself up as God in a rebuilt Jewish temple, and set up his own kingdom (Revelation 13). He will speak arrogant and boastful words, glorifying himself (2 Thessalonians 2:4). However, he is destined for the lake of fire (Revelation 19:20).

Armageddon

Human suffering will steadily escalate during the tribulation period. First, the seal judgments will bring bloodshed, famine, death, economic upheaval, a great earthquake, and cosmic disturbances (Revelation 6). Then come the trumpet judgments, involving hail and fire mixed with blood, the sea turning to blood, water turning bitter, further cosmic disturbances, affliction by demonic scorpions, and the death of a third of humankind (Revelation 8:6–9:21). Then come the bowl judgments, involving horribly painful sores on human beings, more bodies of water turning to blood, the death of all sea creatures, people being scorched by the sun, total darkness engulfing the land, a devastating earthquake, and much more (Revelation 16). Worse comes to worst, however, when these already traumatized human beings find themselves engaged in a catastrophic series of battles called Armageddon.

The word *Armageddon* literally means "Mount of Megiddo" and refers to a location about 60 miles north of Jerusalem. This is the location of Barak's battle with the Canaanites (Judges 4) and Gideon's battle with the Midianites (Judges 7). This will be the site for the final horrific battles of humankind just prior to the second coming (Revelation 16:16).

Napoleon once commented that this site is perhaps the greatest battlefield he had ever witnessed. Of course, the battles Napoleon fought will dim in comparison to Armageddon. So horrible will Armageddon be that virtually no one would survive if Christ didn't return (Matthew 24:22).

The Second Coming

At the second coming, Jesus Christ—the King of kings and Lord of lords—will return to earth in glory at the end of the present age and set up His kingdom. The very same Jesus who ascended into heaven will come again at the second coming (Acts 1:9-11).

The second coming will involve a visible, physical, bodily return of the glorified Jesus. One key Greek word used in the New Testament to describe the second coming of Christ is *apokalupsis.* This word carries the basic meaning of "revelation," "visible disclosure," "unveiling," and "removing the cover from something that is hidden." The word is used of Christ's second coming in 1 Peter 4:13: "To the degree that you share the sufferings of Christ, keep on rejoicing, so that also at the revelation of His glory you may rejoice with exultation."

Another New Testament Greek word used of Christ's second coming is *epiphaneia,* which carries the basic meaning of "to appear" or "to shine forth." In Titus 2:13 Paul speaks of "looking for the blessed hope and the *appearing* of the glory of our great God and Savior, Christ Jesus." In 1 Timothy 6:14 Paul urges Timothy to "keep the commandment without stain or reproach until the *appearing* of our Lord Jesus Christ."

The second coming will be a universal experience in the sense that every eye will witness the event. Revelation 1:7 (NIV) says, "Look, he is coming with the clouds, and every eye will see him, even those who pierced him; and all the peoples of the earth will mourn because of him." Moreover, the second coming will bring magnificent signs in the heavens (Matthew 24:29-30). Christ will come as the King of kings and Lord of lords, and many crowns will be on His head—crowns that represent absolute sovereignty. His eyes will be like blazing fire (Revelation 19:11-16).

The Millennial Kingdom

Following Jesus' second coming, He will personally set up His kingdom on earth. This is known as the millennial kingdom. This is another one of those doctrines that Christians seemingly love to debate, and there are three theological views.

Premillennialism teaches that following the second coming, Christ will institute a kingdom of perfect peace and righteousness on earth that will last for 1000 years. After this reign of true peace, the eternal state begins (Revelation 20:1-7; see also Isaiah 65:17-25; Ezekiel 37:21-28; Zechariah 8:1-17). I subscribe to this view because it recognizes that just as the Old Testament messianic prophecies were literally fulfilled in the first coming of Christ, so the prophecies of Christ's second coming and millennial kingdom will be literally fulfilled.

Amillennialism, a spiritualized view, teaches that when Christ comes, eternity will begin with no prior literal 1000-year (millennial) reign on earth. Amillennialists generally interpret the 1000-year reign of Christ metaphorically as Christ's present (spiritual) rule from heaven.

The postmillennial view, another spiritualized view, teaches that through the church's progressive influence, the world will be "Christianized" before Christ returns. Immediately following this return, eternity will begin (without a thousand-year kingdom). Of course, a practical problem for postmillennialism is that the world seems to be getting worse instead of increasingly Christian.

A literal and plain reading of Scripture leads effortlessly to premillennialism. Here is a basic rule of thumb for interpreting the Bible: When the plain sense of Scripture makes good sense, seek no other sense. I see no reason to spiritualize Bible prophecies about the millennium. The Bible plainly teaches a literal 1000-year kingdom over which Christ will rule on the earth (Revelation 20:4,6).

Beware the Unimaginable

Do you remember what you were doing on September 11, 2001? I suspect you do. I was in Southern California with my wife when our phone rang not long after seven a.m. That wasn't a good sign because people rarely call us that early. I picked up the phone, and a friend asked, "Have you turned on your television this morning?"

"No, what's going on?" I replied.

She told me what happened, and I immediately turned on the television and watched in horror an event that ended more than 3000 lives. I later pondered the terrible grief of the spouses, the children, the relatives, and the friends of the people who died as the Twin Towers collapsed. I have been in those buildings in New York City. What a horror it must have been. The unimaginable happened.

The unimaginable can happen again—not only to the United States but also to other nations, like Israel. The next time, however, the casualties could easily exceed 3000.

The prophet Ezekiel reveals in chapters 38 and 39 that an unimaginably huge military coalition from the north will one day launch an invasion into Israel. My purpose in this book is to explore the details of Ezekiel's prophecy. So strap on your seat belt and get ready for an exciting journey through prophetic Scripture. Let's explore together what God's Word tells us about this massive end-time invasion and God's mighty deliverance.

2

The Rise of Radical Islam

Chapters 2 through 5 in this book are foundational. They deal with critically important issues that help us to better understand the nature of current world tensions in general and the Israeli-Arab conflict in particular. They also provide important data about circumstances that may be setting the stage for a future massive invasion into Israel that Ezekiel prophesied about 2600 years ago.

Chapter 2 deals with the rise of radical Islam and its threat to the nation of Israel. Chapter 3 looks at the emerging nuclear nightmare—more specifically, the attaining of nuclear weapons by Iran, the virtual epicenter of terrorist activities in the world. Chapter 4 discusses the ever-increasing worldwide addiction to black gold (oil) and how possession and control of this black gold may motivate some nations to military action. Finally, chapter 5 focuses on land battles and especially the question of to whom the holy land really belongs. Once we complete these chapters, we will be in a better position to look at the details of Ezekiel 38–39, in which Ezekiel speaks of a massive northern military coalition that will one day invade Israel.

Let's begin our study with the recognition that Islam is a monotheistic religion that arose in the seventh century AD under the leadership of Muhammad (also spelled *Muhammed* and *Mohammed*). Muhammad was allegedly the greatest of a long line of prophets that included Moses and Jesus. His primary teaching was that the one true God is Allah. Allah's revelation to Muhammad occurred over a 23-year period and is recorded in the Quran, Islam's holy book, also spelled *Koran. Quran* literally means "that which is to be read."

The word *Islam* means "submission to the will of Allah." Members of Islam are called Muslims ("those who submit"). The word *Muslim* expresses the inner attitude of those who follow Muhammad's teachings and conveys a perpetual and ongoing submission to God.[1]

> By its very form [as a verbal noun] it conveys a feeling of action and ongoingness, not of something that is static and finished, once and for all, but of an inward state which is always repeated and renewed...One who thoughtfully declares "I am a Muslim" has done much more than affirm his membership in a community...[He is saying] "I am one who commits himself to God."[2]

The Global Growth of Islam

- Islam is presently the world's second-largest religion. (Christianity is the largest.)
- More than 65 nations in the world are Islamic.
- Muslims constitute about 85 percent of the population in 32 countries.[3]
- In the past 50 years, the Muslim population in Western Europe has grown from about 250,000 to nearly 20 million.[4] (The evidence suggests that these Muslims are becoming more radical.)
- The Muslim population of Europe will double by the year 2020 and will double yet again by 2035. By that time, the majority of young people in most European cities will be Muslims.[5]
- There are more Muslims than Methodists and Baptists combined in the United Kingdom.[6]

- Though there was only one mosque in England in 1945, there are now thousands. Hundreds of the buildings currently used for mosques were originally churches—including the church that sent well-known Christian missionary William Carey to India.[7]
- More than 100 million Muslims live in India.[8]
- The number of Islamic mosques in France mushroomed from only one in 1974 to thousands today.[9]
- Muslims constitute a majority in 45 African and Asian countries.[10]
- China has 100 million Muslims.[11]
- More than 180 million Muslims live in Indonesia.[12]
- Saudi Arabia and other Muslim countries are currently donating multiple tens of millions of dollars to the furtherance of Islam in the United States.[13]

Many Muslims argue that the explosive growth of Islam around the world constitutes undeniable proof that Islam is the true religion. After all, how could the religion grow so exponentially without God's blessing?[14]

Islamic Jihad

Early in Muhammad's career, he never mentioned jihad. This was certainly the case when he was living in Mecca. Scholars have suggested that the reason for this is that during those early years he lacked a strong following and lacked any military might whatsoever. Once in Medina, however, he was able to build a strong following and a strong military. Jihad suddenly became a topic of major Quranic revelation.[15] Note the following contrasts in Muhammad's behavior in Mecca and Medina:

	Mecca	Medina
Evangelism	By preaching	By the sword
Personal behavior	Priestly	Warlike
Marriage	One wife (Khadija)	Eleven more wives in ten years
Focus of battle	Against idol worship	Against Jews and Christians
Nature of Islam	Religious movement	Political movement[16]

Muhammad's movement eventually took on the character of religious militarism. He transformed his followers into fanatical fighters by teaching them that if they died fighting Allah's cause, they would be instantly admitted to paradise. Also during this time, Muhammad's followers were given divine sanction to raid caravans en route to Mecca. The spoils were divided among Muhammad's men, with Muhammad keeping one-fifth of everything. Not unexpectedly, these caravan raids led to war with the Meccans.

Jihad soon became an emphasis in Muhammad's teaching. *Jihad* comes from the Arabic word *jahada,* which principally means "to struggle" or "to strive in the path of Allah." The term has made headlines many times in recent years, especially as related to terrorist activities around the world. It seems that whenever the United States takes a stand against terrorist Muslims, Muslims respond by declaring a jihad or holy war against the United States. Muslims use the term to refer to armed fighting and warfare in defending Islam and standing against evil.

Some Muslims, however, hold to less dangerous forms of jihad, such as a jihad of the pen, which is a written defense of Islam.[17]

Frederick Mathewson Denny notes that *holy war* doesn't fully capture the meaning of jihad, although that is certainly part of it. Denny says that Muslims distinguish between a greater jihad and a lesser jihad. A person's struggle with his own vices, the evil tendencies in his soul, and his lack of faith is considered the greater jihad. Jihad in this sense is more of a spiritual struggle. Many Muslims in the United States hold to this interpretation of jihad.

Engaging in armed struggle against the enemies of Islam is considered the lesser jihad.[18] Islam scholar Jamal Elias claims that for most Muslims today, "any war that is viewed as a defense of one's own country, home, or community is called a jihad. This understanding is very similar to what is called 'just war' in Western society."[19]

Radical Islamic fundamentalists are well-known for their use of arms and explosives in defending their version of Islam. They use jihad to terrorize perceived enemies of Islam into submission and retreat.[20]

Such Muslims seek to emulate the behavior of Muhammad (Sura 33:21), for he often led Islamic forces into battle to make Islam dominant during his time. He shed other people's blood to bolster Islam throughout the Arabian Peninsula.[21] In fact, "Muhammad's mission was to conquer the world for Allah. The goal of jihad, or holy war, is to establish Islamic authority over the whole world. Islam teaches that Allah is the only authority, and all political systems must be based on Allah's teaching."[22] Islamic history clearly reveals that jihad has been a primary tool of religious expansionism for Muhammad's religion.

This radical form of jihad is a much more serious issue today than it used to be because of the increasing number of radical Muslims and because of the growing availability of weapons of mass destruction. Radical fundamentalists constitute a relative minority of Muslims, but even a minority can be a substantial threat. As one researcher put it, "Since we are talking about 1.3 billion adherents to Islam, even a 'very small minority' can involve tens of millions of people who have the potential to cause a great deal of trouble in the world, not only for America, but for moderate Muslim governments as well."[23]

Islamic fundamentalists often cite verses from the Quran to support their view that armed conflict is permissible and even compulsory in the defense of Islam. In Sura 2:216 we read, "Fighting is prescribed for you, and ye dislike it. But it is possible that ye dislike a thing which is good for you." In Sura 47:4 we read, "Therefore, when ye meet the unbelievers [in fight], smite at their necks; At length, when ye have thoroughly subdued them, bind a bond firmly [on them]." Sura 9:5 says, "But when the forbidden months are past, then fight and slay the pagans wherever ye find them, and seize them, beleaguer them, and lie in wait for them in every stratagem [of war]."

In 1998 five Muslim caliphates (governments) representing five radical Muslim factions signed a *fatwa* (a written decision) declaring a holy war against the United States. The document they signed contains the following words:

> For over seven years the United States has been occupying the lands of Islam and the holiest of places, the Arabian Peninsula, plundering its riches, dictating to its rulers, humiliating its people, terrorizing its neighbors, and turning its bases in the Peninsula into a spearhead through which to fight the neighboring Muslim peoples...[There has been] aggression against the Iraqi people...[Their aim has been to] serve the Jews' petty state...[They express] eagerness to destroy Iraq...All these crimes and sins committed by the Americans are a clear declaration of war on Allah, his messenger, and Muslims...The ruling to kill the Americans and their allies—civilians and military—is an individual duty for every Muslim who can do it in any country in which it is possible to do it...This is in accordance with the words of Almighty Allah, "and fight the pagans altogether as they fight you altogether," and "fight them until there is no more tumult or oppression, and there prevail justice and faith in Allah."[24]

Who can doubt that the September 11, 2001, attack against the World Trade Center and Pentagon was a manifestation of this fatwa, written just three years earlier? Americans have taken jihad very seriously since that day.

Muslims certainly have a religious motivation to participate in jihad, for any Muslim who dies in service to Allah is guaranteed entrance into paradise (Hadith 9:459). According to Muslim tradition, Muhammad said, "The person who participates in [holy battles] in Allah's cause and nothing compels him to do so except belief in

Allah and His Apostles, will be recompensed by Allah either with a reward, or booty [if he survives] or will be admitted to Paradise [if he is killed in the battle as a martyr]" (Hadith 1:35).

Radical Islam: A Real and Present Danger

Radical Islam is growing on a global level. No one can afford to ignore it. Alex Alexiev, vice president for research at the Center for Security Policy, has for several decades directed numerous research projects for the U.S. Defense Department. In a recent work, Alexiev thoroughly documents that an intolerant and violent extremist creed has taken hold throughout Muslim communities in Europe. He is convinced that the fast-spreading anti-Western Islamo-fascist strain is steadily becoming the dominant face of Islam throughout Europe.[25]

Of particular relevance is Alexiev's position that "many European Muslims are increasingly willing to engage in violence against their democratic host societies." He notes that 13 percent of British Muslims approve of terrorism, and 1 percent—amounting to 16,000 Muslims—said they had "engaged in terrorist activity at home or abroad, or supported such activity." Moreover, some 25 percent of German Muslim school students openly claim they are prepared to use violence on behalf of Islam.[26]

And this is just Europe! In the Middle East, Islamic radicalism rises to a fever pitch. Anyone aware of current news headlines knows that radical Islam is flooding out of Iran. This has been thoroughly documented by Ali Ansari, who has written numerous books on the history and politics of Iran and the Middle East. In his recent volume *Confronting Iran,* Ansari forcefully suggests that "Iran is not simply a problem, it's *the* problem. It's not just a member of the Axis of Evil, but the founding member, the chief sponsor of state terrorism, or to use a more recent characterization, the central banker for terrorism."[27]

This is in keeping with a sobering report published in *U.S. News and World Report* that tells us that "Iran today is the mother of Islamic terrorism. Tehran openly provides funding, training, and weapons to the world's worst terrorists, including Hezbollah, Hamas, the

Palestinian Islamic Jihad, and the Popular Front for the Liberation of Palestine, and it has a cozy relationship with al Qaeda."[28]

One of the more nightmarish aspects of the Islamic radicalism flowing out of Iran relates to the apocalyptic nature of certain strains of Muslim theology, something that Dore Gold has thoroughly documented. Gold has served as Israel's ambassador to the United Nations (1997–1999), was a foreign policy advisor to Prime Minister Benjamin Netanyahu of Israel, and has served as a diplomatic envoy to the leaders of Egypt, Jordan, the Persian Gulf states, and the Palestinian Authority. In his recent book *The Fight for Jerusalem,* Gold speaks about this apocalyptic aspect of Islam:

> According to Islamic doctrine of recent centuries, the concept of jihad has evolved into an eschatological [end times] concept reserved for the future. Accordingly, pious Muslims are expected to proselytize their religion and gain converts worldwide, an activity known as *da`wa.* Then, at the apocalyptic end of days, mainstream Muslims envision that a great, armed jihad will result in the subjugation of the entire world to Islam. Militant Wahhabism, however, reverses the order of *da`wa* and jihad, advancing jihad to the present day as a *precursor* for spreading Islam.
>
> Hence, almost by definition, militant Islam is an apocalyptic movement preparing in the present for a final confrontation with the West and with others opposed to its agenda. It brings scenarios from the end of days to the here and now. It is therefore not surprising to find apocalyptic references in the speeches of jihadist leaders like Abu Musab al-Zarqawi, the former head of al-Qaeda in Iraq.[29]

Let's expand a bit on Gold's point. Mainstream Shiites have long believed in the eventual return of the Twelfth Imam, believed to be a direct (bloodline) descendant of Muhammad's son-in-law, Ali (whose family, it is believed, constitutes the only legitimate successors to Muhammad). The Twelfth Imam—who allegedly disappeared as a child in AD 941—will allegedly return in the future as the Mahdi ("the rightly guided One"), who will bring about a messianic-like era of global order and justice for Shiites in which Islam will be victorious. Significantly, the appearance of the Twelfth Imam can supposedly be hastened through apocalyptic chaos and violence—by unleashing an apocalyptic holy war against Christians and Jews. It is thus within man's power to bring about the end of days.[30] Interestingly, a number of Shiite leaders in Iran have gone on record saying they have witnessed physical sightings of the Twelfth Imam and claim he will reveal himself to the world soon, presumably following the imminent eruption in chaos and violence.

In this light, the current-day mission of Mahmoud Ahmadinejad—Iran's president—takes on great significance: "Our revolution's main mission is to pave the way for the reappearance of the Twelfth Imam, the Mahdi."[31] Ahmadinejad apparently informed his cabinet that just a few more years' time would bring about the appearance of the Twelfth Imam. He makes this bold claim because of his own intention to play the critical role in ousting the Jews from Israel: "For Ahmadinejad, the destruction of Israel is one of the key global developments that will trigger the appearance of the Mahdi."[32] He seeks to "wipe Israel off the map" (a phrase he borrowed from the deceased mullah, Ayatollah Khomeini).[33] Significantly, most of the government officials who used to work under Ahmadinejad were fired and replaced with Imam zealots like himself, so now his staff is in full agreement with his stated goals against Israel.[34]

Ahmadinejad is convinced that "a world without America and Zionism" is attainable, and once attained, the Twelfth Imam will return. He is sure that humanity will soon know what it is like to live in a world free of Israel and America. He has "assured that the United States and the Zionist regime of Israel will soon come to the end of their lives," according to the Islamic Republic of Iran Broadcasting's website.[35] During a military parade, Ahmadinejad had a banner proclaiming "Death to America" draped over one of Iran's long-range missiles.[36] He boldly and defiantly claims the world will soon be without the Great Satan (America) and the Little Satan (Israel), and this will give rise to the emergence of the Twelfth Imam.

Ahmadinejad believes the apocalypse will occur in his own lifetime and says Allah himself chose him to play a role in ushering in the end of days. Indeed, he claims to be one of a select group of elite men specifically chosen by the Twelfth Imam to be his representatives in the world prior to his return.

Ahmadinejad is no doubt getting much of his end-of-days theology from the messianic Hojatieh society, led by Ayatollah Mesbah Yazdi, a man he is personally close to. Interestingly, Iran's state-run television network has been airing a series of programs during 2007 that delineate the signs of the end of the world. These programs are designed to prepare Iran for the arrival of the Twelfth Imam, the Mahdi.[37]

Ahmadinejad has been very open about his extremist views. When he spoke at the United Nations, for example, he concluded his speech by invoking the soon arrival of the Islamic Messiah, the "Hidden Imam," the Twelfth Imam, or the Mahdi. He prayed, "O mighty Lord, I pray to you to hasten the emergence of your last repository, the Promised One, that perfect and pure human being, the One that will fill this world with justice and peace."[38]

Once back in Iran, in a videotaped meeting with a prominent ayatollah in Tehran, Ahmadinejad made the claim that during his speech he was surrounded by a light that caused the atmosphere to change: "For 27 or 28 minutes all the leaders did not blink; it's not an exaggeration, because I was looking. They were astonished, as if a hand held them there and made them sit. It had opened their eyes and ears for the message of the Islamic Republic."[39] Kenneth Timmerman, a U.S. expert on Iran who has for more than 20 years exposed Iran's nuclear intentions, makes this comment:

> Ahmadinejad's "vision" at the United Nations could be dismissed as pure political posturing if it weren't for a string of similar statements and actions that clearly suggest he believes he is destined to bring about the End Times—the end of the

> world—by paving the way for the return of the Shia Muslim messiah…Given the fact that the Islamic Republic of Iran continues to pursue suspect nuclear programs, having a leader with a messianic vision is no cause to rejoice.[40]

Imagine how world tensions will escalate if evidence confirms that this end-of-days Iranian president finally has gotten his hands on nuclear weapons. In his warped thinking, he may believe he can finally and definitively invoke the coming of the Islamic messiah by pushing a button.

Relevance to Ezekiel 38–39

Clearly the rise of militant Islam poses an immense and ever-increasing threat not only to the United States but also (especially) to the nation of Israel. A bit later in the book, I will document that the military hardware being used by Iranian Islamic fanatics is Russian made. I will also document the emergence of alliances between Russia, Iran, and other Muslim nations who would like to see Israel destroyed.

Such facts as these have led a number of biblical scholars to suggest that the stage may be being set for the eventual fulfillment of Ezekiel's prophecy of a northern military coalition invading Israel. Prophecy experts have also suggested that the increasing worldwide instability that results from Islamic militant terrorism may be pushing the world toward a one-world government inasmuch as a cooperation among nations may be the only ultimate means of thwarting such terrorism.[41] These are sobering days to be alive.

Before proceeding any further with this book, I want to emphasize that the information in this chapter (and, indeed, in this entire book) has nothing to do with sensationalism or date setting. My goal is twofold: to understand what biblical prophecy teaches about the end times, and to be a thoughtful and accurate observer of the times in keeping with Jesus' own instructions (Matthew 16:1-3; Luke 21:29-33). As we compare what biblical prophecy teaches with our thoughtful observations about world affairs, we can legitimately raise the possibility that the stage may be being set for the fulfillment of Bible prophecy.

If things suddenly and completely decompress in the Middle East, if present alliances between Russia and various Muslim nations dissolve, and if the threats of radical militant Muslims become things of the past, these developments would not in the least detract from my confidence in Bible prophecies like Ezekiel 38–39. The prophecies would simply not yet be fulfilled. Having said that, however, my studied opinion is that current world affairs are indeed setting the stage for the fulfillment of Ezekiel 38–39.

3

The Emerging Nuclear Nightmare

I receive daily news briefs in my office from news services all over the world. Recently, not a single day seems to pass without one or more articles having headlines relating to Iran's nuclear program. Many of these speak of Russia's assistance to the Iranians in this regard. Others speak of sanctions imposed on Iran by the United Nations. One thing is certain: Every day that passes, the nuclear threat increases.

One might wonder why I am including this chapter in a book on Ezekiel's prophecy of a future northern military coalition invading Israel. The first reason is obvious: Iran is developing nuclear weapons and has openly promised to wipe Israel off the map. The second reason is less obvious but still quite important. The United States is Israel's principal ally. If any nation bullies Israel, the United States is willing to flex its muscle. This is one reason Israel has survived so far in the face of Arab hostilities. But what happens if terrorists succeed in detonating one or more nuclear weapons on American soil? (Terrorists say they already have their eyes on seven prime target cities.) Would a substantially weakened United States be willing or able to give Israel the high level of protection it needs?

To answer this question, remember that a terrorist detonation of a single nuclear bomb on American soil would be utterly catastrophic. Consider what would happen if a 150-kiloton nuclear weapon were detonated on a typical workday in New York City.[1] Let's say the bomb goes off without warning at noontime at the foot of the Empire State Building.

One Second After Detonation

The initial blast of the nuclear weapon would generate heat in the tens of millions of degrees. Steel-reinforced concrete buildings within a radius of almost half a mile would be destroyed almost immediately. Such famous, grand buildings as the Empire State Building, Madison Square Garden, and the New York Public Library would be obliterated. The resulting debris would literally be hundreds of feet high, with concrete, steel mesh, broken furniture, glass, and human bodies mixed in a crushing, bloody pile. The approximately 75,000 people within this four-tenths of a mile circle would have no chance of survival. Those who happen to be outside at the moment would die of thermal heat and flying debris, and those in buildings would die as structures collapse.

Four Seconds After Detonation

Within four seconds, steel-reinforced concrete buildings within a radius of one mile would be destroyed or severely damaged. These would include such cultural iconic structures as Rockefeller Center and the United Nations. Most of the people in these buildings would die. Additional casualties—that is, in addition to the 75,000 who already died—would amount to 300,000, with another 100,000 suffering significant injuries and needing treatment in a hospital—but four hospitals would have been destroyed within the one-mile radius. Many of these people would have severe lung and ear injuries. None of the buildings within this radius would be usable; everything would have to be demolished and rebuilt. The scale of damage would make the debris of the collapsed Twin Towers look miniscule by comparison.

Six Seconds After Detonation

By the sixth second, the shock wave moves out to a 1.5-mile radius.

Toward the outer edge of this radius, steel-reinforced structures would be damaged, and unreinforced structures—those made of brick and wood—would be destroyed. Such iconic structures as Carnegie Hall and the Lincoln Center would suffer significant damage. People who are outside in a direct line of sight of the detonation would die—an additional 30,000 casualties. An additional 190,000 people would die in buildings due to flying debris or buildings collapsing. Just as a grenade can kill a number of people with the shrapnel that projects out from the explosion, a nuclear detonation can be like a gargantuan grenade, causing an incredible volume of flying projectiles to expand outward at a phenomenal speed. Total casualties thus far would be 595,000.

Ten Seconds After Detonation

The shock wave extends to a 2.5-mile radius in ten seconds. Far fewer buildings would be destroyed or severely damaged this far out, but another 235,000 people would die, bringing the total number of dead to 830,000. To put that number into perspective, try to envision a football stadium that holds 50,000 people. When a single 150-kiloton nuclear bomb detonates in New York City, casualties will exceed the number of people that can fill 16½ football stadiums! The carnage would be immense. Several hospitals would be destroyed, and those that remain standing would have virtually no hope of treating even a miniscule percentage of the countless more than 900,000 survivors who need treatment. The electromagnetic pulse generated by the nuclear blast would blow out all electrical devices—cell phones, computers, radios, and the like. Communication through the media would be nearly impossible for a significant time. Surviving fire fighters would be busy for days putting out fires.

And that is not the worst of it! All these numbers are based on a 150-kiloton nuclear bomb exploding. But some nuclear bombs today are far more powerful and destructive than this. No wonder the nuclear bomb is labeled an apocalyptic weapon.

Is the United States Really in Danger?

Dr. Graham Allison, director of Harvard University's Belfer Center for Science and International Affairs, said, "Is nuclear mega-terrorism inevitable? Harvard professors are known for being subtle or ambiguous, but I'll try to be clear. 'Is the worst yet to come?' My answer: 'Bet on it. Yes.'"[2]

Nuclear terrorism is not the talk of mere sensationalists or alarmists. The greatest thinkers in our land are sounding the warning bells. Indeed, our best national security experts say the risk of attack by weapons of mass destruction within the next decade may be as high as 70 percent. Senator Richard Lugar, former chair of the Senate Foreign Relations Committee, has gone on record as saying that the United States faces an existential threat from terrorists who may get their hands on weapons of mass destruction. In the next decade, we face the very real possibility of nuclear jihad.

This is the primary reason so many are concerned today about Iran. The Bush administration's 2006 foreign policy doctrine affirms, "We face no greater challenge from a single country than from Iran. We will continue to take all necessary measures to protect our national and economic security against the adverse consequences of their bad conduct."[3] As demonstrated in the previous chapter, Iran is a rogue state headed by a fanatical apocalyptically minded leader—Mahmoud Ahmadinejad—who is seeking to acquire nuclear weaponry.

Ilan Berman, vice president for policy at the American Foreign Policy Council, adjunct professor at the National Defense University in Washington, and author of *Tehran Rising,* asserts that "the single most serious threat facing the United States is nuclear proliferation." For this reason, he said the General Assembly of the United Nations passed a global treaty criminalizing nuclear terrorism in 2005.[4] I mean no disrespect to the United Nations, but such a treaty hardly gives pause to any terrorists who are planning criminal acts.

One of the United States' problems is that it has so many easy entrances across its borders that terrorists could use to smuggle a nuclear bomb in. A bomb could also be easily shipped into the United

States. Fifty thousand cargo containers enter the United States every day, but only 5 percent of them get screened.[5] A bomb could easily make its way into the country in one of the unscreened containers.

Further, the Commission to Assess the Ballistic Missile Threat to the United States believes Iran may soon be capable of constructing an intercontinental ballistic missile capable of reaching certain American cities. Experts also say Iran could launch a nuclear weapon from a commercial ship off the coast of the United States. About 75 percent of the U.S. population is within 200 miles of a coast. With so many registered merchant ships sailing off U.S. coastal waters (more than 130,000 from 195 countries), the nuclear danger is obvious.[6]

Author Kenneth Pollack believes Iran's goal of acquiring nuclear weaponry creates two other threats to the vital interests of the United States. First, if Iran acquires nuclear weapons, it may proceed on the assumption that it is no longer vulnerable to American conventional military retaliation and therefore is free to pursue aggressive anti-American policies throughout the world. Second, Iran's acquiring of nuclear weapons may encourage other nations in its region and elsewhere to likewise seek nuclear weaponry. "Because many countries fear that once Iran acquires nuclear weapons it will pursue an aggressive foreign policy, if and when Tehran crosses the nuclear threshold other Middle Eastern countries, particularly Saudi Arabia, might decide to follow suit to deter an Iranian attack, either covert or overt."[7] Multiple nations could acquire multiple nuclear warheads, increasing the threat and danger to multitudes of people worldwide.

Iran could also become a supplier to third-party terrorists, greatly increasing the chances of an attack on the United States. Jerome Corsi notes that "the prospect of a nuclear Iran is particularly frightening, not simply because of the threat that Iran itself poses to the United States and our friends in the Middle East, but also because the regime could supply terrorist groups with nuclear weapons."[8] Let us be clear that if terrorists got their hands on these weapons, they undoubtedly would use them. President Bush understandably warns that Islamic mullahs, or religious leaders, "could provide these arms to terrorists, giving them the means to match their hatred. They could attack our allies or attempt to blackmail the United States. In any of these cases, the price of indifference would be catastrophic."[9]

Some experts today are particularly sensitive about the possibility of a nuclear attack against the United States in view of Mahmoud Ahmadinejad's 2006 five-page letter to the American people, inviting them to convert to Islam. We might initially dismiss such a letter as a manifestation of Ahmadinejad's arrogance. We must keep in mind, however, that "it is a well-established Islamic tradition to offer an enemy conversion to Islam just prior to starting a war. If they refuse, according to tradition, the Muslims then are 'justified' in destroying them."[10]

The Lethal Threat Against Israel

The nuclear threat against the United States is substantial, but this book's main concern is with the nuclear threat against Israel. The threat against Israel has never been greater than it is now. As author Al Venter writes, "The country in most immediate danger would be Israel. After decades of vowing to destroy the Jewish state—albeit failing to do so with both conventional war and guerrilla tactics—the Islamic world would have the means to create a new Holocaust simply by pressing a few buttons."[11] Israel—a nation that includes about five million people and whose land is about the size of New Jersey—would likely not survive a first nuclear strike by Iran or any other rogue nation.

President Ahmadinejad has made numerous venomous statements against Israel. He spoke at a 2005 "World Without Zionism" conference at which he categorically stated to a group of 4000 people, "They [ask], 'Is it possible for us to witness a world without America and Zionism?' But you had best know that this slogan and this goal are altogether attainable, and surely can be achieved. This regime that is occupying Jerusalem must be wiped from the map."[12]

Radical Muslims: Not Easily Deterred

For quite some time, the Mutual Assured Destruction (MAD) policy has served as a deterrent for the United States and Russia not to launch their nuclear missiles at each other. If Russia had launched an attack against the United States, the United States would have retaliated by launching an attack against Russia. The fact that each superpower could virtually blow up the other served as a good deterrent.

Today, however, we are living in a different world with enemies who have an entirely different worldview. As we saw earlier, Islamic theology teaches that Muslims who lose their lives in service to Allah are guaranteed entrance into paradise (Hadith 9:459). According to Muslim tradition, Muhammad said, "The person who participates in [holy battles] in Allah's cause and nothing compels him to do so except belief in Allah and His Apostles, will be recompensed by Allah either with a reward, or booty [if he survives] or will be admitted to Paradise [if he is killed in the battle as a martyr]" (Hadith 1:35). Consequently, the MAD policy may not be as much of a deterrent for radical Muslims as it has been for Russia.

In our day, Islamic martyrdom has been glorified in Iran and other Muslim countries. Venter observes that while the MAD policy serves as a good deterrent among nations who greatly value living and personal survival, the policy fails "against a culture that glorifies death in 'Holy War'...If millions of martyrs are created in order to eradicate the state of Israel, or severely damage the United States, they might be honored for having made the supreme sacrifice."[13] Author Walid Phares offers this warning:

> The jihadists are Islamists, and one of their major doctrinal pillars is sacrificing for the other life. Suicide bombers are a chilling reminder of this ideological reality—which directly leads to one conclusion: Unlike the Soviets or even the Chinese or North Koreans, the jihadists do not fear death,

> let alone fear mass death. Fear of nuclear retaliation is not a determining factor in a jihadi state of mind.[14]

Phares also identifies clear signs that radical Muslims would indeed be willing to detonate a nuclear device. First, he notes that in 1993 such radicals exploded a massively armed truck inside the World Trade Center's underground parking garage with the hope that at least one tower might collapse, thereby killing tens of thousands. Then, in the 2001 attack against the Twin Towers, Osama bin Laden hoped for tens of thousands of casualties. Both these egregious attacks aimed at casualties of a nuclear magnitude and indicate that these terrorists—should they ever attain a nuclear weapon—would not hesitate to use it to further their radical cause.[15]

Iran's Path to Constructing a Nuclear Weapon

Iran has long claimed that its nuclear interests relate solely to generating power for its people. Iran, however, isn't fooling anyone. A growing body of formidable evidence proves that Iran's true intention is to produce nuclear weapons. Despite this well-documented evidence, Iran continues to claim innocence. President Bush's National Security Strategy, released in 2006, includes this summary: "We may face no greater challenge from a single country than from Iran. For almost 20 years, the Iranian regime hid many of its key nuclear efforts from the international community, yet the regime continues to claim that it does not seek to develop nuclear weapons."[16]

Jerome Corsi tells us that the barriers to constructing a nuclear weapon today are not intellectual (the information is readily available); rather, the barriers relate to the physical requirements needed to construct a deliverable weapon that will function reliably. "To get to this point a nation must have weapons-grade nuclear fuel, the technology to miniaturize a bomb to fit into the confines of a missile warhead, and a missile capable of covering the distance to its target. These physical requirements take time and money, even for a rogue regime such as Iran."[17]

The Iranians appear to have made steady progress in this regard and have already reached a number of important milestones in constructing a nuclear weapon, largely through assistance from Russia. For example, Iran has apparently already begun enriching uranium. President Ahmadinejad said on April 9, 2006, "I am officially announcing that Iran has joined the group of countries which have nuclear technology. At this historic moment, with the blessings of God almighty and the efforts made by our scientists, I declare here that the laboratory-scale nuclear fuel cycle has been completed and young scientists produced enriched uranium needed to the degree for nuclear power plants Sunday."[18]

Iran may already have sufficient uranium gas to make a first batch of nuclear weapons. In fact, some experts believe Iran may already possess a nuclear weapon. Frank Gaffney and his team of experts warn that "Iran is probably in a position to acquire nuclear weapons within a short period of time. (Some believe they may already have done so by purchasing them on the black market.)"[19] In keeping with this, the late Caspar Weinberger, in an interview with Joel Rosenberg, said, "I think they probably already have gone nuclear...I think they have probably equipped themselves to construct some types of nuclear weapons and...I think they could probably do quite a lot of damage right now."[20] That's a chilling statement from a man who was widely known for his foreign-policy prowess.

And, of course, once Iran actually has nuclear weapons, no one can do anything to stop them from using them. As one analyst puts it, "Once Tehran has proven its nuclear capability there is absolutely nothing that anybody—or any nation—will be able to do about it. It would be a *fait accompli*. Done!"[21] John McCain, appearing on NBC's *Meet the Press,* said that if Iran gets the bomb, "I think we could have Armageddon."[22]

Iran's Missile Development Program

Meanwhile, Iran continues to make steady progress on the development of missiles capable of delivering a nuclear warhead a great distance away. For example, Iran's Shahab-3 missiles have a maximum range of 1240 miles (the distance to Israel) and can be armed with nuclear warheads. In fact, intelligence evidence suggests that Iran intends to arm these missiles with nuclear warheads.

Iran also bought 18 BM-25 surface-to-surface missiles from North Korea. These have a maximum range of 1550 miles, so Europe will be in reach of Iran's nuclear warheads once they are developed.[23]

Related to this, Israeli Mossad chief, Ephraim Halevi, spoke to ambassadors of all 19 NATO countries at a closed session in June 2002 and informed them that Iran had invested huge sums of money to develop launch systems, mainly surface-to-surface missiles based on North Korean expertise. He noted that though the Shahab-3 missile had been tested successfully, "Iran is also involved in the research and development of even longer-range missiles, which can reach Europe and in the distant future, even the United States." He then raised the sobering question: "Who and what are the potential targets of these systems? I do not know."[24]

Some strategic thinkers believe the Shahab-3 missile is simply an interim measure for Iran while it builds the Shahab-4 missile, capable of carrying a larger payload and going farther. One expert notes that unlike its predecessor, the Shahab-4 missile is based exclusively on Russian ballistic technology and is expected to be operational within two or three years.[25] In just a matter of five or six years, Iran could possibly develop the Shahab-5 or Shahab-6 intercontinental ballistic missile, capable of reaching the United States.[26]

In addition, Iran may become an exporter of its missile technology to other weapons-hungry countries. Libya is one noted client. Western observers are concerned about the expanding WMD partnership between Tehran and Tripoli. Admiral Thomas Wilson, testifying before the Senate Armed Services Committee in 2002, warned that Iran was "beginning to proliferate missile production technologies" to a number of client states, including Libya.[27] Other equally respected personnel in the armed forces have testified to the same.

Russia's Assistance

Iran has now become the third-largest recipient of Russian arms with an estimated annual trade of $500 million. Ilan Berman tells us that in late 2000, buoyed by its expanding ties with the Kremlin, "the Iranian government announced plans for a massive, twenty-five year national military modernization program—one entailing upgrades to its air defense, naval warfare, land combat capabilities and built almost entirely around Russian technology and weaponry."[28] The modernization program includes the purchase of fighter aircraft for use by the Iranian air force, assistance in constructing military submarines, anti-aircraft missile systems, surface-to-air missile systems, radar stations, infantry fighting vehicles, naval landing craft, and patrol equipment.[29]

Perhaps the greatest concern to political leaders worldwide is that Russia has been assisting Iran in its nuclear program. Despite heavy American opposition, Russia declared in 2002 that it would finish construction of the $840 million, 1000-megawatt nuclear reactor in Bushehr. And Russia confirmed its intention of building five more reactors over the next decade—another in Bushehr and four in Ahvaz, 40 miles from Tehran—for a total of $10 billion.

Iran has always claimed that its nuclear program is for peaceful purposes—that is, to meet the energy needs of the Iranians, and that's all. "We are opposed to any proliferation of weapons of mass destruction and nuclear weapons," Ahmadinejad said in an interview in Tehran with ABC. "It's a time for logic, for rationality, and for civilization instead of thinking of finding new weapons," he said.[30]

Most observers, however, do not buy it. The Associated Press reports that "many countries, including the United States, believe that Iran is using its nuclear program as a cover to produce an atomic weapon."[31] Indeed, "Iran says the program is designed for purely peaceful, power-generation purposes, while the U.S. and its allies believe the program—which Iran hid from the international community for almost two decades before it was exposed by a regime critic—is being used as a cover to develop the know-how to build atomic bombs."[32]

Meanwhile, the Russian Atomic Energy Minister has pledged to provide Iran with critical atomic know-how—authorizing the training of about 1000 Iranian scientists and technicians in complex nuclear processes. This raises a number of concerns, not the least of which is that this Russian training may equip Iranian nuclear experts to apply their acquired knowledge to a weapons program.[33]

> US opposition to Russian construction of [the nuclear reactor at] Bushehr rests on three issues; first that weapons grade plutonium could be extracted from the reactor allowing the Iranians to construct nuclear weapons. Secondly, the US fears that the Russians and the Iranians are using Bushehr as a cover for the transfer of other sensitive technology that would normally be prohibited. Finally, the US is concerned that knowledge gained by Iranian scientists working at Bushehr could further Iran's nuclear weapons program.[34]

David Satter, a research fellow at the Hoover Institution, a senior fellow at the Hudson Institute, and a visiting scholar at Johns Hopkins University, warns that Putin's Russia has shown itself more than willing to facilitate Iran's nuclear ambitions. "It is pressing ahead—despite growing evidence that Tehran is interested in nuclear weapons, not just nuclear power—with the construction and fueling of a reactor at Bushehr that will likely help advance the Iranian arms program."[35] Satter also warns that the Iranians could secretly divert several of the massive fuel rods intended for the Bushehr reactor and, using a relatively small and undetectable centrifuge obtainable (illegally) from Pakistan, enhance the partially enriched uranium in the rods to weapons grade. "We know that the Iranians have been covertly acquiring large numbers of such devices for years."[36]

Through Russia's assistance, Iran clearly seems destined to become a dominant nation in the Middle East—far more dominant than Westerners are comfortable with. As one analyst has put it, "Iran has launched—and the Kremlin appears to have endorsed—a multifaceted strategic offensive aimed at rolling back America's recent advances, and reestablishing Iran as a dominant regional player."[37]

I am most definitely not an alarmist. I will say, however, that nuclear weapons in the hands of a nation that is world famous for its support of terrorist activities—led by Mahmoud Ahmadinejad, who uses chaos and violence to hasten the messianic appearance of the Twelfth Imam—is the stuff nightmares are made of.

Meanwhile, Deception

Until Iran actually has nuclear weapons in its hands, it will no doubt continue to deceive the rest of the world. Astute observers believe Iran is obviously playing a game of high-stakes cat and mouse with the international community over its nuclear program. One of many examples of this is that in 2003 Iran struck a deal with France, Germany, and Great Britain to suspend its uranium enrichment activities, only to renege on the agreement just eight months later.[38] According to Berman's analysis, "Tehran continues to pursue a strategy designed to delay, obfuscate, and otherwise derail international intervention until it is capable of 'going nuclear.'"[39]

A senior Israeli security official was cited in *The Jerusalem Post* as saying, "History has shown that rogue nations tend to use diplomacy as a cover while they complete their work."[40] What this means is that while Iran continues to negotiate with the West over its nuclear development program, it is undoubtedly busy bringing its nuclear weapons plans to completion. As Corsi puts it, "Iran will stay on track to develop nuclear weapons as fast as possible. Until then, sign any agreement, say anything, cheat—do whatever is necessary to throw the world off track."[41] He suggests that the entire mentality of the mullahs must be seen as cheating to buy time. "While buying time, the mullahs are willing to make whatever concessions they have to make, but they are resolved to never lose sight of their ultimate purposes—to get nuclear weapons, to defeat the United States and to wipe Israel from the face of the earth."[42]

A Preemptive U.S. Strike Against Iran?

With the threat that currently exists against both the United States and Israel, many wonder whether a preemptive military attack against Iran is appropriate. A 2006 Los Angeles Times–Bloomberg poll indicates that 57 percent of Americans are in favor of a first strike against Islamic Iran if Iran continues to pursue a course that leads to the possession of nuclear weapons.[43] This is so despite America's current disillusionment with the war in Iraq. Senator John McCain commented, "There is only one thing worse than the U.S. exercising a military option (against Iran), and that is a nuclear-armed Iran."[44]

A military attack against Iran would certainly come at a high cost.

- Iran has promised that if the United States attacks Iran, its first retaliatory strike will be against Israel.
- Iran has promised that if the United States attacks Iran, Iran will unleash 40,000 volunteer suicide bombers against U.S. interests and the interests of any U.S. allies that participate.[45] Supreme leader Ayatollah Ali Khamenei has warned that "the enemies understand well that the Iranian nation will give a comprehensive response to the aggressors and their interests worldwide."[46] The Iranian plan of retaliation, code-named Judgment Day, entails activating 50 terrorist sleeper cells allegedly pre-positioned in the United States, Canada, and Europe to use chemical and biological warfare against civilian and industrial targets.[47]
- Iran has promised that if the United States attacks Iran, the United States' problems in Iraq will escalate dramatically. The United States "should expect its current problems in Iraq to increase 10 times if it attacks Iran," said former Iranian president Akbar Hashemi Rafsanjani, who currently heads Iran's legislative arbitration body.[48]
- Iran is a major player in oil production in the Middle

East and could easily take actions that would dramatically escalate the cost of oil for Americans, thereby inflicting great damage on the U.S. economy.

- Many in the world today already believe the United States is engaged in a war against Muslims (in Iraq), and a war with Iran might seem, to some, to confirm this.
- An attack against Iran might further corrode U.S. political and diplomatic muscle in the Middle East.[49]
- Finally, the United States military is already stretched thin with the war in Iraq. To engage in concurrent military action against Iran could overtax our military.

This last point has been a topic of discussion among Iranian leaders. Indeed, Mahmoud Ahmadinejad seems to think that because the U.S. military is overtaxed, an attack against Iran will not happen. When asked whether U.S. military action against Iran was probable, he said, "I think, there are wise people in America who would not let this happen. They are incapable. The pressure is more psychological."[50] In an interview, Ahmadinejad made this comment:

> The era of threatening other countries with bombings and missiles has passed...especially those who think they can pressure Iran by using the language of threat, are mistaken...I doubt there is such will in America (to attack Iran)...but anyway under any circumstances, we will defend our rights...as an independent nation we can protect our integrity. Naturally, when a nation becomes under attack it will use appropriate measures to respond...and like any other nation we have various ways to respond...Iran's foreign policy is based on peace and friendship. Iran will not attack any country but if attacked we would defend ourselves with full power.[51]

Khamenei would seem to agree with Ahmadinejad. "We believe that no one will make such an irrational and erroneous move and will not jeopardize his nation's interests," Khamenei told Iranian air force commanders.[52] Likewise, Iranian foreign minister Manouchehr Mottaki said that "we do not see America in a position to impose another crisis on its tax-payers...by starting another war in the Middle East."[53]

Still, if the United States does launch a strike, Iranian officials claim they are ready with a response. Mottaki claimed Iran is ready for anything the United States does to stop its nuclear program and warned that Iran was keeping "all options on the table." He said, "We are ready for any possible option taken by America."[54] "Naturally a military action will have a military response," chief nuclear negotiator Ali Larijani said when asked if Iran would strike back if attacked by the United States. "Our response will be appropriate."[55]

A Preemptive Strike by Israel?

Another viable scenario is that Israel might launch a preemptive strike against Iran. Israel's governmental leaders have often affirmed that for Iran to come into possession of nuclear weapons is "intolerable."

Experts have noted the difficulty of such a strike. Iran's nuclear technology infrastructure is spread over 300 or more different sites. Obviously, the more sites there are, the more difficult it is to successfully destroy Iran's overall nuclear capabilities.[56] Many of these sites are strategically located within populated urban areas, thereby risking significant civilian casualties in any kind of attack. (World publicity regarding such casualties would be horrendous, no doubt giving rise to heightened levels of anti-Semitism around of the world.)

Still, leaders in Israel have sworn that never again will the Jews be passive in the face of her enemies. Jewish leaders believe that one reason for the Holocaust was the passivity of the European Jews against Hitler's thugs. Certainly Israel has indicated in her past that she is willing to act when it is necessary. For example, Israel's air force launched a first-strike air assault on June 5, 1967, during which the entire Egyptian air force on the ground was destroyed at the start of the Six-Day War. An attack against one or more of Iran's nuclear sites, while more difficult, is entirely feasible. "Israel will watch for the moment of no return, the time when Iran has everything necessary on its own to make a deliverable nuclear weapon. Just after Israeli intelligence is convinced that Iran has reached that point, Israel will feel compelled to strike."[57]

I hesitate to ponder the consequences of an Israeli attack against Iran. Iran's president already has a fanatical hatred for Israel. How would that hatred manifest itself following an Israeli attack? Indeed, Iranian leaders have already claimed that if Israel attacks its nuclear installations, Iran will retaliate with its own missiles, which are already pointed at strategic sites in Israel.[58] More than that, an Israeli attack might give radical Muslims in multiple Middle Eastern countries all the justification they need for launching an all-out attack against Israel.

A Real and Present Danger

All the evidence suggests that Iran is on a collision course with the United States and Israel. The world may soon witness a nuclear showdown. Will anything be done to prevent it?

Doing nothing is certainly not an option. As many analysts have long noted, Hitler revealed in *Mein Kampf* his intention to wipe out the Jews of Germany, but many failed to take him seriously.[59] Israeli president Shimon Peres describes Ahmadinejad as a "Persian version of Hitler." Ahmadinejad must be taken seriously in his statements calling for Israel's destruction and his attempts to acquire the capability to do so. John Bolton, former United States ambassador to the United Nations, informed an international symposium that "historians often look back after huge tragedies have occurred and say, 'How is it that responsible policy-makers at the time didn't see this coming?' "[60]

Of course, 2600 years ago the prophet Ezekiel foresaw a massive invasion into Israel, not just by Iran but by a coalition of Muslim nations led by Russia. The events we are witnessing today may be setting the stage for this eventual invasion.

4

The Addiction to Black Gold (Oil)

The world runs on oil. Americans consume approximately 21 million barrels of oil per day—a quarter of the world's total consumption.

Our cars, trucks, buses, trains, ships, and jets require oil. Without oil, transportation shuts down. No one can get anywhere of any substantial distance. No food—indeed, no products of any kind—can be transported anywhere, at least not fast. Eighteen-wheel tractor-trailers become a thing of the past. Life becomes much more difficult without oil. Indeed, if we were to run out of oil, we could easily find ourselves reverting back to the transportation options of the nineteenth century.

Bulldozers and various kinds of construction equipment require oil. Without oil, our efforts to build new houses and buildings are greatly impeded.

Tractors and other kinds of equipment that are a necessity on today's large farms require oil. Industrial machinery requires oil. If the machines won't run, the production of multiple thousands of products comes to a standstill. Moreover, machine operators lose their jobs. The economy soon collapses.

The United States military runs on oil. Without oil, our military jeeps, trucks, tanks, planes, and ships won't run. If our military shuts down, we can't protect ourselves. We become vulnerable. That is bad news because there are many who hate Americans today.

We need to make sure we have oil.

This may seem a rather dramatic way to begin a chapter, but the hard reality is that we have an oil crisis facing us, and this oil crisis has implications regarding not only the survival of the United States but also the United States' relationship to Russia and Middle East nations, as well as the relationship of these nations to Israel. By the time you finish this chapter, you will understand how oil fits into the overall Middle East dilemma and how it may possibly relate to the Ezekiel invasion.

Do We Have Enough Oil?

Our best data tell us that nations around the world (especially the United States, China, and India) are collectively using oil faster than we are finding it. Moreover, the oil that exists is getting much harder to find. Because it is getting harder to find, we have to spend more money to find it. That makes acquiring oil a much more expensive proposition.[1] Warren Brown's *Washington Post* article "We're Running Out of Oil" informs us that "oil is running out, and it is running out as global demand for available energy resources is growing rapidly. That means per barrel prices and pump prices are going up and will stay up."[2]

In 1985, the United States imported less than 30 percent of its oil. Just five years later, in 1990, the United States was importing almost 50 percent of its needed oil. If the current rate of growth continues, by 2015 America will be importing up to 75 percent of its oil.[3] We have a steadily increasing appetite for increasingly expensive (and finite) resources. Economically, this spells danger.

> The margin between oil supply and demand today is razor thin. At present, we are basically pumping out crude oil at about the same rate we're consuming it—1,000 barrels a second. The level of spare capacity (known as the world's

> safety blanket) is only about two million barrels a day. This means that the world's oil supply chains are operating at an unbelievable 97.5 percent capacity. This leaves almost no margin for error for such things as natural disasters, accidents, terrorist attacks, geopolitical stress, or whatever else could disrupt the fragile supply chain.[4]

The million-dollar question relates to precisely when the "oil peak" will be upon us. The oil peak is the point at which we have used up half of the available oil reserves in the earth. If the world's total supply of oil is three trillion barrels (an optimistic estimate), peaking would occur when we've produced about 1.5 trillion barrels.[5] No one is sure when the peak will come, but it will come, whether five years from now or thirty.[6] This means we will reach a peak in the supply of cheap oil, after which we will have a dwindling supply of increasingly expensive oil.[7]

Some experts believe we reached the oil peak in 2004. The Association for the Study of Peak Oil and Gas (ASPO), a European network of scientists, projects the peak in 2007. Independent experts Matthew Simmons, Colin Campbell, and Kenneth Deffeyes have each projected the peak will occur between now and 2010. The French oil company TotalFinaElf believes the year will be 2010. The official position of the U.S. Geological Survey says the peak will occur between 2011 and 2015. A number of major oil companies project dates sometime after 2015.[8] The U.S. Energy Department is optimistically (some might say foolishly) holding out for 2037.[9]

Dr. Gal Luft, executive director of the Institute for the Analysis of Global Security, and Anne Korin, codirector of the institute, note that "even the major U.S. oil companies have begun to acknowledge that the growth in world demand is expected easily to exceed available world supplies for the foreseeable future."[10] David O'Reilly, the chairman and CEO of Chevron Corporation, tells us that the days of easy oil are over, for many of the world's oil and gas fields are "maturing." O'Reilly says that "new energy discoveries are mainly occurring in places where resources are difficult to extract—physically, technically, economically, and politically."[11]

Mike Bowlin, chairman and CEO of ARCO, says, "We have embarked on the beginning of the last days of the age of oil."[12] Dr. Colin Campbell, who wrote a report entitled "The World Oil Supply 1930–2050," agrees:

> The major oil companies are merging, downsizing and outsourcing, and not investing in new refineries because they know full well that production is set to decline and that exploration opportunities are getting less and less. We have depleted most of our high-quality resources; the supply obtainable from low-quality deposits is largely limited by the supply of fuel; and the supply of fuel itself is bound by these constraints.[13]

Stephen Leeb, a respected investment analyst who consistently finishes among the leaders in the annual stock-picking contests of the *Wall Street Journal* and *Forbes,* wrote a book entitled *The Coming Economic Collapse* in which he made this warning:

> The world's demand for oil is growing faster than oil production can increase. Some petroleum geologists...now believe that worldwide oil production may be close to its permanent long-term peak and will soon start to decline. Even if the peak is farther away than they think, demand for oil, especially from large developing nations such as India and China, is rising faster than production. If this trend continues—and we fully expect it will—the result will be an inevitable clash between supply and demand that will send oil prices soaring to unprecedented levels.[14]

Experts are increasingly warning that the gap between oil demand and supply, once considerable, has steadily narrowed to the point that today it is almost negligible. An oil shortfall could cause a global recession and make the typical American lifestyle unaffordable, even in two-income families.[15] Leeb put it this way:

> No one is one hundred percent certain how much oil is left in the ground, how expensive it will be to extract, or how high demand for oil will grow long-term. While the world will never completely run out of oil, oil will become increasingly difficult and expensive to extract, to the point where diminishing returns make further production increases unaffordable, and worldwide production begins to decline.[16]

Saudi Arabia to the Rescue?

One might be tempted to think that oil-rich Saudi Arabia will come to the rescue. Based on the best data we have, however, this is wishful thinking. Analysts Edward Morse and James Richard tell us why:

> Global demand for oil has been increasing by between 1.5 and 2 mbd [million barrels a day] *each year,* a rate of growth with alarming long-term consequences. The U.S. Department of Energy and the International Energy Agency both project that global oil demand could grow from the current 77 mbd to 120 mbd in 20 years, driven by the United States and emerging markets of South and East Asia. The agencies assume that most of the supply required to meet this demand must come from OPEC, whose production is expected to jump from 28 mbd in 1998 to 60 mbd in 2020. Virtually all of this increase would come from the Middle East, especially Saudi Arabia.[17]

The problem, Morse and Richard tell us, is that such expectations for Saudi Arabia's growth does not seem to fit the facts. Indeed, "Saudi Arabia has been unable for 20 years to increase its production capacity. Nor is its position unique: Few OPEC countries in 2002 have more production capacity than they did in 1990 or 1980."[18] In order for the world to obtain the increasing level of oil it needs, the very countries that have been utterly unable to raise their production capacity for more than 20 years must more than double their oil production over the next 20 years.[19] To borrow a metaphor, dark clouds are gathering on the horizon.

To make matters worse, some experts are now claiming that the Saudis and other OPEC members may be guilty of inflated reporting. In other words, they may not have as much oil as they've been claiming all along.[20]

Still further, David Goodstein of the California Institute of Technology tells us that for the most part, we're not finding new sources of oil in the world. "Better to believe in the tooth fairy than in future supply of new sources of oil. Most of the planet has been explored extensively, and even if some new fields are found, they won't delay the peak by more than a few years."[21] Jane Bryant Quinn, in her *Newsweek* article "The Price of Our Addiction," likewise affirms that "we're running out of the capacity to produce surpluses of oil. Demand for crude is expected to rise much faster than new supplies...Most producer nations can't find enough new oil, or drill out more from their reserves, to replace what we're using up. Production from most of the large, older fields is in irreversible decline."[22] Analyst Richard Vodra agrees, adding that "no huge fields have been discovered since the North Sea in the 1970s, and the world's annual production has exceeded annual discoveries for more than 25 years."[23]

Dark Days Ahead

Difficult days are ahead. Princeton professor, geologist, and oil maverick Kenneth S. Deffeyes says that once supply begins to dwindle, the years to follow will see shortages that at best will cause "global recession, possibly worse than the 1930s Great Depression." At times, Deffeyes sounds outright apocalyptic in his warnings, suggesting that all this could lead to "war, famine, pestilence and death."[24]

A growing body of energy experts and academics fear that

Deffeyes' arguments may have merit. Physicist David Goodstein, in his book *Out of Gas,* muses that "we can, all too easily, envision a dying civilization, the landscape littered with the rusting hulks of SUVs."[25] James Schlesinger, the country's first secretary of energy, is less dramatic but nevertheless forceful in his conclusion that "a growing consensus accepts that the peak is not that far off." He added, "The inability readily to expand the supply of oil, given rising demand, will in the future impose a severe economic shock."[26]

"The world has never faced a problem like this," according to a report prepared for the U.S. Department of Energy's National Technology Laboratory. Although oil companies have searched intensively for new oil finds, "results have been disappointing," says the report, and the resulting "oil peaking will be abrupt and revolutionary."[27]

Houston investment banker Matthew Simmons agrees with this assessment and claims in his 2005 book *Twilight in the Desert* that the Saudi Arabians are lying about the size of their reserves and that they are really running on empty.[28] If he is correct, as many fear he may be, the fallout from the oil shortage will come sooner rather than later.

Make no mistake about it: We will experience a fallout. A depletion of oil will affect our lives right where we live. Adam Porter, in his *New Internationalist* article "Running on Empty," writes, "Oil is the main ingredient in petrochemicals, and petrochemicals are everywhere. They make plastics and polyester: the clothes we wear, the carpets we walk on, frames for our computers, seats to sit on, bottles to drink from and band-aids to salve our wounds. What will replace them—who will be able to afford them—as the price of oil starts to rise?"[29]

Experts tell us that oil shortages will affect every emerging and traditional industry. After all, oil powers industrial machinery and lubricates all the engines in the world. Further, without oil to lubricate train engines and truck engines and jet engines, how will materials be transported?[30] Adam Porter is spot on in his assessment that a significant increase in oil prices, due to a significant shortage, "will fundamentally change transport in general. Every single internal combustion engine, every single turbo engine, every single turbine will find its running costs dramatically increased. You want to replace them? With what?"[31]

One shudders to even ponder how a significant oil shortage will affect both the American and world economies. The formula is not complicated: Damage to industry due to a shortage of oil plus damage to transportation due to a shortage of oil equals a plummeting economy.

No wonder Matt Crenson suggests that "major oil-consuming countries will experience crippling inflation, unemployment and economic instability."[32]

Nations Increasingly Vying for Control

Inevitably, the ongoing depletion of world oil leaves nations vying for control of the world's oil fields. As Joel Bainerman put it, "The subsequent decline in availability of fossil fuels could plunge the world into global conflicts as nations struggle to capture their piece of a shrinking pie."[33]

> We're all jockeying for control of oilfields, in a vast game that runs the risk of turning mean. China and Japan are running warships near disputed oil and natural-gas deposits in the East China Sea. China is doing deals in Sudan, Venezuela, and Iran. Russia looks less friendly as we continue to invest in the oil countries around the Caspian Sea—Azerbaijan, Kazakhstan, Turkmenistan.[34]

All this has particular relevance to the United States, the world's single remaining superpower. One analyst has noted that "oil must remain at the center of US foreign policy because any superpower that wants to remain a superpower will do whatever is necessary to ensure this goal."[35] The problem is that most of the oil-rich countries of the world don't like the United States. "The bad news is that much of the world's oil reserves are in the custody of unstable and sometimes hostile regimes."[36] No wonder some observers warn that in the near future, "we'll be paying in both treasure and blood, as we fight and parley to keep ever-tighter supplies of world oil flowing our way."[37]

Iran and Black Gold

Iran has recently become a major player in the global oil market, with some 90 billion barrels of proven oil reserves, and claiming it has 30 billion more.[38] The majority of Iran's crude oil reserves are located in the southwestern Khuzestan region near the Iraqi border and the Persian Gulf. Iran at present has 32 producing oil fields—25 onshore, 7 offshore.[39]

With the world's steadily increasing demand for oil, Iran is making a fortune with its oil income. Ali Ansari, author of *Confronting Iran,* tells us that "Iran possesses the second-largest reserves of oil in the world, larger than those of Iraq and second only to those of Saudi Arabia."[40] He believes Iran's position in the oil market will strengthen over time, given the present and ever-growing importance of the Persian Gulf in the world oil market.

Jerome Corsi estimates that Iran's gross revenue from oil is about $150 million per day. He tells us that oil export revenues constitute some 80 percent of Iran's total export earnings, 40 to 50 percent of its government budget, and 10 to 20 percent of its gross domestic product.[41]

Iran has understandably been called a regional energy superpower in its own right. "Home to 10 percent or more of the world's oil, it is the second largest exporter in the Organization of Petroleum Exporting Countries (OPEC), producing an average of 3.9 million barrels of oil per day."[42] Few significant new discoveries of oil have been made in the rest of the world, but new discoveries of oil reservoirs in southern Iran have significantly boosted the country's projected oil reserves. Some analysts suggest that "these discoveries, coupled with the rising price of crude oil, have done more than simply give Tehran a growing foothold in the world energy market; they have positioned the Iranian regime as a major strategic asset for energy-hungry states."[43]

In addition to its oil reserves, Iran also possesses gas reserves. "More important than oil is Iran's position as the country with the second largest natural gas reserves in the world"[44]—estimated at some 940 trillion cubic feet, second only to Russia.[45] Approximately 62 percent of Iran's natural gas reserves have not been developed, so Iran has huge potential for future gas development.[46] This means that Iran is economically secure for the future.

While the United States in particular and the rest of the world in general is using more oil than ever, and while the available oil is getting harder and more expensive to find, Iran—one of our greatest enemies—has turned out to be a major oil player with enormous resources and influence in the Middle East. This is not a healthy political or economic state of affairs.

This is especially lamentable in view of the fact that every year that passes, the United States becomes more dependent on foreign oil to meet its needs. "Having burned through more than half of America's oil reserves," Leeb says, "we have become increasingly dependent on foreign oil imports to keep up with demand."[47] As a result of this sad state of affairs, the United States economy has grown increasingly vulnerable to external political and economic factors.

Aware of this, President Bush has sought to move the United States away from dependence on Middle Eastern oil. In his 2006 State of the Union address, he affirmed that "America is addicted to oil, which is often imported from unstable parts of the world." He therefore urged that it was time for the United States to "move beyond a petroleum-based economy and make our dependence on Middle Eastern oil a thing of the past." His goal is "to replace more than 75 percent of our oil imports from the Middle East by 2025." Of course, a lot can happen between now and 2025.

Despite President Bush's good intentions, past presidents have likewise sought energy independence but failed to achieve their goals. This does not bode well for the future. In 1973, during the Arab oil embargo, President Richard Nixon urged, "In the last third of this century, our independence will depend on maintaining and achieving self-sufficiency in energy." He made reference to Project Independence

1980, with the goal of ensuring "that by the end of this decade, Americans will not have to rely on any source of energy beyond our own."[48] Under President Gerald Ford's leadership, the date was pushed back to 1985 when he signed the Energy Policy and Conservation Act.

President Jimmy Carter in 1977 declared that energy independence was an issue of such vital national interest that it was the "moral equivalent of war." Later that year he signed a law that brought into being the U.S. Department of Energy to manage America's ongoing energy crisis. In his July 1979 nationally televised speech, after the doubling of oil prices due to the Iranian oil crisis, President Carter flatly asserted, "Beginning this moment, this nation will never use more foreign oil than we did in 1977—never." He came up with a new plan designed to achieve energy independence by 1990.[49]

The year after, in 1991, President George H.W. Bush announced an energy strategy engineered to reduce "our dependence on foreign oil." The year after that, in 1992, President Bill Clinton proposed a tax on crude oil designed to discourage dependence on foreign oil. The year after that, in 1993, he launched a partnership with auto makers engineered to produce a car at least three times more fuel-efficient than existing cars.

No one can deny that efforts have been made by past administrations. But despite all such efforts, the United States today is more dependent on foreign oil than ever before.[50] Certainly there is good reason to be skeptical about the current administration's plan.

Without being alarmist or sensationalistic, a crisis seems inevitable. Many authorities blindly continue to claim that today's soaring energy prices are temporary, that the supply of oil is limitless, and that supply will outpace demand into the distant future. This, however, is an outright contradiction of the facts. "The trends in place for the last thirty years show declining returns from oil exploration, peaking or declining oil production everywhere but in a few OPEC nations, and increasing demand for energy, especially among the world's largest developing nations."[51]

The Growing Threat of Blackmail

What I have described above is a recipe for extortion. The very countries who possess the natural resources to help the United States with its immense consumption of oil are precisely those countries who have the most intense hatred of Americans. These nations may eventually play the oil card against the United States. Americans must come to realize that oil can function as part and parcel of the radical Islamic arsenal of weapons. Because the Islamic mullahs recognize they are sitting on one of the massive pools of available oil in the world, they believe they have power and leverage. One analyst suggests that "the prestige of having a corner on a commodity as important to the world economy as oil is only equaled in the eyes of the mullahs with the prestige they imagine they will have once they possess nuclear weapons. The prospect of possessing two weapons so powerful—oil *plus* nuclear weapons—is a terrorist's dream."[52]

Meanwhile, without a doubt, Iran is currently using some of its oil profits to fund terrorist activities around the world. Its oil revenues are financing its version of Islamo-fascism and underwriting Tehran's support of the world's most dangerous Islamist movements—including the Lebanese terrorist group Hezbollah.[53] Thomas Kraemer, of the Strategic Studies Institute of the U.S. Army War College, laments that "America is buying billions of dollars of oil from nations that are sponsors of, or allied with, radical Islamists who foment hatred against the United States. The dollars we provide such nations contribute materially to the terrorist threats facing America."[54]

The United States thus finds itself in the untenable position of spending great amounts of money to fight terrorism while at the same time spending great amounts of money to purchase oil that ends up funding terrorism.[55] Kraemer concludes that "in the War on Terror, the United States is financing both sides. While spending billions of dollars on U.S. military efforts in the war, we are sending billions more to nations such as Saudi Arabia, Iran, and the Sudan, where the cash is used to finance training centers for terrorists, pay bounties to the families of suicide bombers, and fund the purchase of weapons and explosives."[56] The ultimate result is that Americans are subsidizing acts of war against themselves. Iran is undoubtedly using American oil dollars to develop nuclear weapons that they could one day use against us.

Some Westerners believe Iran may try to play the oil card as a deterrent to the United States trying to thwart its nuclear program. As Mark Hitchcock puts it, Iran continuously threatens the United States with "harm and pain" if we initiate military attacks on her nuclear facilities. "While part of this 'harm and pain' could be terrorist attacks against foreign U.S. interests or even on U.S. soil, one has to believe that oil figures into Iran's plan."[57] Iran could easily cut production or disrupt the flow of oil through the Strait of Hormuz, and things could go bad pretty quickly. Kraemer laments, "America is hamstrung because any forceful action on our part against nations like Iran and Saudi Arabia could result in the disruption of oil supplies that the world economy completely depends on."[58]

I close this chapter by considering the collective force of what we are witnessing on the world scene today:

- We are facing an imminent oil crisis that could not only weaken the United States and damage the world economy but also generate an increasing level of world tensions as nations seek to protect their "piece of the pie" of available oil reserves.
- Iran has become a major player in the global oil market.
- Iran continues its hot pursuit of nuclear weapons with Russia's assistance.
- Alliances are emerging or have emerged between Russia, Iran, and other Muslim nations—the precise nations Ezekiel identifies as being part of the northern military coalition that will one day invade Israel.
- Many of these Muslim nations—especially Iran—are spewing increasingly vitriolic threats against Israel. They seek to wipe Israel off the map.

- Mahmoud Ahmadinejad, the president of Iran, promises that this will happen in the near future.

All of this is truly sobering in view of Ezekiel's prediction of a massive end-times invasion into Israel by enemies from the north. It is especially sobering in view of the fact that this military coalition will invade in order to "capture spoil and to seize plunder" (Ezekiel 38:12). A recent and unexpected major oil discovery in Israel may be among the motivating factors for the future Ezekiel invasion.

5

Land Battles: To Whom Does the Holy Land Really Belong?

The city of Jerusalem has appropriately been called the Holy City. The city is famous worldwide for being the scene of Jesus' arrest, trial, crucifixion, and resurrection.

Jerusalem rests in the Judean hills at about 2640 feet above sea level. In Jesus' time, the city was probably home to about a quarter of a million people.

In the Jewish thinking of biblical times, no city could possibly compare with Jerusalem. People from neighboring towns and villages traveled to Jerusalem for the three major Jewish festivals, as well as to pay the annual temple tax. Jerusalem was the geographical heart of the Jewish religion. Jesus Himself made a number of visits to Jerusalem (for example, Luke 2:22-51; John 4:45; 7:10; 10:22).

King David captured the city in the tenth century BC. During the reign of his son Solomon, Jerusalem became the center of religious life with a magnificent temple. As Jesus prophesied would happen, Jerusalem was utterly destroyed in AD 70 by Titus and his Roman warriors (Matthew 24:2).

How ironic that Jerusalem literally means "city of peace." There is anything but peace in Jerusalem now. In fact, external threats threaten peace throughout Israel. Mahmoud Ahmadinejad, the president of

Iran, has been very open in saying he wants to push Israel into the sea and annihilate the Jews.

This chapter will examine the Jewish and Arab claims to this land. This is one issue that lies at the very heart of the present conflict in the Middle East and is directly related to the coming invasion into Israel by the northern military coalition prophesied in Ezekiel 38–39.

God's Promises to the Jewish Patriarchs

Abraham's name literally means "father of a multitude." He lived around 2000 BC, originating from the city of Ur, in Mesopotamia, on the River Euphrates. He was apparently a very wealthy and powerful man.

God called Abraham to leave Ur and go to a new land—the land of Canaan, which God was giving to Abraham and his descendants (Genesis 11:31). Abraham left with his wife, Sarah, and his nephew Lot. Upon arriving in Canaan, his first act was to construct an altar and worship God. This was typical of Abraham; God was of first importance to him.

God made a pivotal covenant with Abraham around 2100 BC. In this covenant, God promised Abraham a son and that his descendants would be as numerous as the stars in the sky (Genesis 12:1-3; 13:14-17). The promise might have seemed unbelievable to Abraham because his wife was childless (Genesis 11:30). Yet Abraham did not doubt God; he knew God would faithfully give what He had promised. God reaffirmed the covenant in Genesis 15, perhaps to emphasize to Abraham that even in his advanced age, the promise would come to pass. God also promised Abraham that he would be personally blessed, that his name would become great, that those who bless him would be blessed and those who curse him would be cursed, and that all the families of the earth would be blessed through his posterity.

At one point, an impatient Sarah suggested producing an heir through her Egyptian handmaiden, Hagar. Ishmael was thus born to Abraham through Hagar when he was 86 years old. But Ishmael was not the child of promise. In God's perfect timing, God's promise to Abraham and Sarah of bearing a son was fulfilled when they were very old (Abraham was 100 years old, and Sarah was 90), far beyond normal childbearing age (Genesis 17:17; 21:5). They named their son Isaac. As promised, the entire Jewish nation eventually developed from his line. *Isaac* means "laughter" and is fitting because it points to the joy derived from this child of promise. Recall that when Abraham and Sarah heard they would have a son in their old age, they laughed (see Genesis 17:17-19; 18:9-15).

Isaac would carry on the covenant first given to his father, Abraham. The New Testament calls him a child of promise (Galatians 4:22-23), and he was a man of good character. He trusted in God (Genesis 22:6,9), practiced regular prayer (Genesis 26:25), and sought peace (Genesis 26:20-22).

In a famous episode in the Bible, Abraham's faith was stretched when God commanded him to sacrifice his beloved son of promise, Isaac. Abraham obeyed without hesitation, believing God would provide a substitute lamb for the burnt offering (Genesis 22:8). God, of course, intervened before Abraham actually sacrificed Isaac, but the episode demonstrated Abraham's tremendous faith in God. In God's providence, Isaac indeed was the son of promise.

God made specific land promises to Abraham. We read in Genesis 15:18-21 (NIV), "On that day the LORD made a covenant with Abram and said, 'To your descendants I give this land, from the river of Egypt to the great river, the Euphrates—the land of the Kenites, Kenizzites, Kadmonites, Hittites, Perizzites, Rephaites, Amorites, Canaanites, Girgashites and Jebusites.'"

The land promises made to Abraham were then passed down through Isaac's line. In Genesis 26:3-4 (NIV) we read the Lord's words to Isaac: "Stay in this land for a while, and I will be with you and will bless you. For to you and your descendants I will give all these lands and will confirm the oath I swore to your father Abraham. I will make your descendants as numerous as the stars in the sky and will give them all these lands, and through your offspring all nations on earth will be blessed."

The land promises then passed from Isaac to Jacob (not to Esau). The Lord said to Jacob, "I am the LORD, the God of your father Abraham and the God of Isaac. I will give you and your descendants the land on which you are lying. Your descendants will be like the dust of the earth, and you will spread out to the west and to the east, to the north and to the south. All peoples on earth will be blessed through you and your offspring" (Genesis 28:13-14 NIV).

Randall Price has written a concise, helpful book entitled *Fast Facts on the Middle East Conflict.* In it he summarizes the significance of these land promises to the Jewish patriarchs:

> The Bible states that the covenant was re-established not with Ishmael, but only with Isaac and his descendants (see Genesis 17:18-21). This means that the Abrahamic Covenant and the land promise contained within it (Genesis 15:18-21) is exclusive to the Jewish people as the sole descendants of Isaac. This promise, in turn, was selectively passed on to Isaac's son Jacob (who was renamed "Israel") rather than his son Esau (Genesis 28:13-15; 35:12).[1]

This distinct family line, through which God's covenant promises were to be fulfilled, is affirmed later in the Bible. For example, in Psalm 105:8-11 (NIV) we read, "He remembers his covenant forever, the word he commanded, for a thousand generations, the covenant he made with Abraham, the oath he swore to Isaac. He confirmed it to Jacob as a decree, to Israel as an everlasting covenant: 'To you I will give the land of Canaan as the portion you will inherit.' "

Clearly, then, the land promises made by God and recorded in the Bible are for the descendants of Abraham, Isaac, and Jacob—the Jews. The Bible leaves no question about God's intended recipients of the land.

The Muslim View

Muslims, however, have a different view. They claim that the original Bible was the Word of God (apparently still in good shape during the time of Muhammad in the seventh century), but it quickly became corrupted by Jews and Christians.[2] The Bible of today has been mingled with many "untruths." These untruths relate particularly to areas where the Bible disagrees with the Quran. World religion scholar Stephen Neill observes that "it is well known that at many points the Quran does not agree with the Jewish and Christian Scriptures. Therefore, from the Muslim point of view, it follows of necessity that the Scriptures must have been corrupted."[3] Muslim apologist Ajijola asserts this position:

> The first five books of the Old Testament do not constitute the original Torah, but parts of the Torah have been mingled up with other narratives written by human beings and the original guidance of the Lord is lost in that quagmire. Similarly the four Gospels of Christ are not the original Gospels as they came from the prophet Jesus...The original and the fictitious, the divine and human are so intermingled that the grain cannot be separated from the chaff. The fact is that the original Word of God is preserved neither with the Jews nor with the Christians.[4]

Muslims believe, then, that what used to be the Word of God in the Bible has been so adulterated by human hands that it is now hardly distinguishable from the word of man. Some verses may contain a glimmer of the truth, but these are few and far between in "the jungles of interpolations and contradictions with which the Bible is dense."[5]

More to the point, Muslims claim the Jews inserted many things into the Old Testament that served to personally benefit them. Muslim apologist Maurice Bucaille, for example, claims that "a revelation is mingled in all these writings, but all we possess today is what men have seen fit to leave us. These men manipulated the texts to please themselves, according to the circumstances they were in and the necessities they had to meet."[6]

Muslims claim that they are the true and rightful heirs to the promises made to Abraham through Ishmael (who, they claim, gave rise to the Arab nations) and that the Jews, for personal gain, concocted a story that Isaac became Abraham's heir of the Palestinian land promises. In this Jewish version, Ishmael and his descendants became outcasts and thus have no right to the land.[7] The original Old Testament, we are told, did not have this concocted story. Palestine, by divine right, thus belongs to the Muslims and not to the Jews.

The Folly of Muslim Reasoning

Arguing that the Bible became corrupted during or after Muhammad's time is unreasonable. By Muhammad's time, hundreds of thousands of copies of the Bible were dispersed over a large part of the world. To successfully corrupt the Bible, all these copies would have to be meticulously gathered (assuming people around the world would be willing to surrender them, an impossible scenario) and changed.

Another scenario is that hundreds of thousands of Bible-owning people from around the world met together and colluded to make the changes. But most of these people were true believers, so would they have been likely to tamper with a book upon which they were basing their eternal salvation? Would such collusion even be physically possible?

Moreover, hundreds of years before Muhammad was even born, the Bible had already been translated into a number of languages. Would Muslims have us believe these various translations were identically altered all over the world so they would have a uniform corruption? Of course, this would have been impossible.

Further, could both Jews and Christians have been involved in corrupting the Bible, as Muslims claim? Jews and Christians of that time were hostile to one another, and if either party tried to alter the biblical text, the other party would have cried "foul" and exposed the misdeed by producing the accurate manuscripts.[8] Further, many dissenting Christian sects existed during this time. An alteration of the biblical text by any one of these sects would have brought immediate condemnation by the others.

Still further, if the Jews had corrupted their Scriptures, wouldn't they have changed all the horrible things we read about them in the Torah—such as their total unfaithfulness during the wilderness sojourn and their participation in idolatry?[9] Likewise, if Christians corrupted the New Testament, wouldn't they have removed unflattering episodes about Christians, like Peter denying Christ three times and the disciples scattering like a bunch of faithless cowards when Christ was arrested?

The early Jews had meticulous rules to ensure that the scribes accurately copied the text of the Hebrew Scriptures. This text was then handed down to the Massoretes.

> The Massoretes, in turn, numbered the verses, words, and letters of every book. They calculated the middle word and the middle letter of each. They enumerated verses which contained all the letters of the alphabet, or a certain number of them; and so on. These trivialities, as we might rightly consider them, had yet the effect of securing minute attention to the precise transmission of the text; and they are but an excessive manifestation of a respect for the sacred Scriptures which in itself deserves nothing but praise. The Massoretes were indeed anxious that not one jot or tittle—not one smallest letter nor one tiny part of a letter—of the Law should pass away or be lost.[10]

Muslims claim that the Arabs are descendants of Abraham through Ishmael, but the evidence seems to be otherwise. Indeed, Randall Price provides substantive evidence that this is not the case. In his discussion, Price cites Semitic specialist S.D. Goiten, who affirms that "there is nothing in the Bible to indicate that Ishmael was the forefather of the Arabs, nor was this a belief of the ancient Arabs."[11] The Quran is in error in making the Ishmael-Arab connection in the first place.

Israel's Divine Right to the Land

When Israel finally took possession of the land of milk and honey, it was in direct fulfillment of God's promise to the nation.

> So the LORD gave Israel all the land he had sworn to give their forefathers, and they took possession of it and settled there. The LORD gave them rest on every side, just as he had sworn to their forefathers. Not one of their enemies withstood them; the LORD handed all their enemies over to them. Not one of all the LORD's good promises to the house of Israel failed; every one was fulfilled (Joshua 21:43-45 NIV).

Proponents of replacement theology argue that because God gave the Israelites the land in Joshua 21:43-45, God's obligation regarding the land promises to Israel are completely fulfilled, and no future promises are yet to be fulfilled. After all, the text tells us that "not one of all the LORD's good promises to the house of Israel failed; every one was fulfilled." Such individuals thus believe the modern state of Israel has no legitimate biblical basis. They claim it is not a fulfillment of biblical prophecy. All of God's land promises to Israel were fulfilled in the past.

It is not the purpose of this book to provide a polemic against replacement theology, for this has ably been done elsewhere. However, several pertinent responses are appropriate.

First, Joshua 21:43-45 is absolutely true regarding God fulfilling His part in giving the Israelites the promised land. Israel, however, failed to take full possession of what was promised to the nation by God, and they failed to dispossess all the Canaanites. The land was there for the taking. God had faithfully done for Israel what He promised. Israel, by contrast, was not completely faithful. As prophecy expert John F. Walvoord put it, "The Lord had not failed to keep His promise even though Israel had failed by faith to conquer all the land."[12]

The idea that no further land promises remain to be fulfilled for Israel is false because many prophecies written after the time of Joshua speak of Israel possessing the land in the future (Isaiah 60:18,21; Jeremiah 23:6; 24:5-6; 30:18; 31:31-34; 32:37-40; 33:6-9; Ezekiel 28:25-26; 34:11-12; 36:24-26; 37; 39:28; Hosea 3:4-5; Joel 2:18-29; Micah 2:12; 4:6-7; Amos 9:14-15; Zephaniah 3:19-20; Zechariah 8:7-8; 13:8-9). In fact, every Old Testament prophet except Jonah speaks of a permanent return to the land of Israel by the Jews. Theologian Donald Campbell makes this observation:

> Some theologians have insisted that the statement in Joshua 21:43 means that the land promise of the Abrahamic Covenant was fulfilled then. But this cannot be true because later the Bible gives additional predictions about Israel possessing the land *after* the time of Joshua (e.g., Amos 9:14-15). Joshua 21:43, therefore, refers to the extent of the land as outlined in Numbers 34 and not to the ultimate extent as it will be in the messianic [millennial] kingdom (Gen. 15:18-21). Also, though Israel possessed the land at this time, it was later dispossessed, whereas the Abrahamic Covenant promised Israel that she would possess the land *forever* (Gen. 17:8).[13]

Old Testament scholar Walter Kaiser, well-known and respected for his many writings on the Old Testament, makes a similar affirmation:

> Repeatedly, the prophets of the Old Testament had depicted an Israelite remnant returning to the land (e.g., Isa. 10:20-30) and becoming prominent among the nations (Mic. 4:1) in the end day. In fact, Zechariah 10:8-12 is still repeating this same promise in 518 B.C., well after the days when many in Israel had returned from their last and final exile, the Babylonian Exile.[14]

The Bible portrays Israel as having a national future in which she dwells in the land promised her by God. Contrary to the wishful hopes of replacement theologians, no New Testament verse negates God's land promises to Israel.

Eventually, Israel will finally and wonderfully come to recognize Jesus as the divine Messiah and come into full possession of the promised land. The fullness of this possession will be in the future millennial kingdom. At present, however, Israel's regathering to the land is only partial and Israel is yet in unbelief. This partial regathering in unbelief is setting the stage for Israel to eventually go through the tribulation period—the "time of Jacob's trouble" (Jeremiah 30:7 NKJV)—during which time a remnant of Israel will be saved (see Romans 9–11).

Thomas Ice reminds us of the importance of distinguishing verses that speak of Israel's partial gathering to the land before the tribulation and those that speak of Israel's full possession of the land after the tribulation:

> To properly understand the end-time homecoming or regathering of the Jews to their promised land, we need to keep in mind that the Bible predicts that Israel will experience two worldwide, end-time regatherings to the promised land. The first regathering will be partial, gradual, and in unbelief, while the second regathering will be full, instantaneous, and when Israel enters into belief in Jesus as their personal and national Messiah.
>
> Dozens of biblical passages predict this global event. It is a common mistake, however, to lump all of these passages into one fulfillment time frame, especially in relation to the current state of Israel. Modern Israel is prophetically significant and is fulfilling Bible prophecy. But when we read God's Word, we need to be careful to distinguish which verses are being fulfilled in our day and which await future fulfillment.
>
> In short, there will be two end-time regatherings: one before the tribulation and one after the tribulation. The first worldwide regathering will be a return in unbelief, in preparation for the judgment of the tribulation. The second worldwide regathering will be a return in faith at the end of the tribulation, in preparation for the blessing of the millennium, or thousand-year reign of Christ.[15]

Tim LaHaye also speaks of this:

> We may expect two regatherings. The one we are seeing in our day under the direction of world Zionism—this occurs

> in unbelief. It is a partial regathering which will, as we shall see, give Jews opportunity to rebuild their temple. But it will not be a permanent regathering, for the coming world dictator will desecrate their temple and drive them out of the Holy Land. The second and final regathering, accomplished by Christ Himself, will be universal in that all believing Israelites will be included. And they will never again leave the Land of Promise (Ezekiel 36:24-38; 11:17-20).[16]

At the end of the tribulation, when Israel finally recognizes Jesus as her divine Messiah, the covenant stipulations regarding full possession of the promised land will finally have been met.

> Israel will fulfill the conditional terms of the covenant because in the Last Days, every Israelite will know the Lord (Jeremiah 31:34), for God will have given them a new heart and a new spirit and put His Spirit within them and caused them to walk in His ways (see Ezekiel 36:25-28). According to the prophets, it will be at this time (the Last Days) that the territorial aspects of the Abrahamic Covenant (such as possession of the full extent of the promised boundaries and the universal blessing of all mankind) will find fulfillment (Isaiah 2:2-4; Hosea 3:4-5; cf. Ezekiel 37:24-28; Zechariah 8:7-8,11-13).[17]

1948—A Regathering in Unbelief

When the present-day state of Israel was born in 1948 as a self-governing nation, it represented the beginnings of an actual fulfillment of specific Bible prophecies about an international regathering of the Jews in unbelief before the judgment of the tribulation. This regathering was to take place after centuries of exile in various nations around the world. It is interesting to ponder that if Ezekiel 36 and 37 are literally being fulfilled in regard to the regathering of the Jews to Israel, then it is likely that Ezekiel 38 and 39, which predict the invasion of

Russia and various Muslim nations into Israel, will also be literally fulfilled in the future.

In Ezekiel 36:10 (NIV) God promised, "I will multiply the number of people upon you, even the whole house of Israel. The towns will be inhabited and the ruins rebuilt." God promised, "I will take you out of the nations; I will gather you from all the countries and bring you back into your own land" (36:24). Israel would again be prosperous, for God "will increase the fruit of the trees and the crops of the field, so that you will no longer suffer disgrace among the nations because of famine" (36:30).

The vision of dry bones in Ezekiel 37 portrays the Lord miraculously bringing the bones back together into a skeleton, wrapping the skeleton in muscles and tendons and flesh, and breathing life into the body. This chapter in Ezekiel is undoubtedly speaking about Israel, for we read, "Son of man, these bones are the whole house of Israel" (verse 11 NIV). This chapter portrays Israel as becoming a living, breathing nation, brought back from the dead. To be sure, this is portrayed as a gradual process, but the passage will absolutely be fulfilled.

The year 1948 was a turning point. In AD 70, Titus and his Roman warriors trampled on and destroyed Jerusalem, definitively ending Israel's existence as a political entity (see Luke 21:20). Since then, the Jews have been dispersed worldwide for many centuries. In 1940, no one could have guessed that within a decade Israel would be a nation again. And yet it happened. Israel achieved statehood in 1948, and the Jews have been returning to their homeland ever since.

> Consider the numbers. When Israel declared her independence on May 14, 1948, the country's population stood at only 806,000. Yet by the end of 2005, nearly 7 million people lived in Israel, 5.6 million of whom were Jewish. Thousands more arrive every year. In 2005 alone, some 19,000 Jews immigrated to Israel. In fact, today more Jews live in the greater Tel Aviv area than in New York City, as many Jews live in Israel as in the United States, and it will not be long before more Jews live in Israel than Jews who do not.[18]

Ezekiel predicted it 2600 years ago! And Christian writers living in the sixteenth and seventeenth centuries were already writing about Jews coming back to the land, centuries before 1948! They wrote in this manner because they believed God's prophecies in Ezekiel would literally come to pass.

I have no interest or motive in setting dates for specific fulfillments of biblical prophecies, but the divine program of restoring Israel does appear to be in progress. These are some of the key elements in recent history:

- 1881–1900: About 30,000 Jews who had been persecuted in Russia moved to Palestine.
- 1897: The First Zionist Congress convened in Basel, Switzerland, and adopted Zionism as a program.
- 1904–1914: 32,000 more Jews who had been persecuted in Russia moved to Palestine.
- 1924–1932: 78,000 Polish Jews moved to Palestine.
- 1933–1939: 230,000 Jews who had been persecuted in Germany and central Europe moved to Palestine.
- 1940–1948: 95,000 Jews who had been persecuted in central Europe moved to Palestine. Meanwhile, more than six million Jews were murdered by Adolph Hitler and Nazi Germany.
- 1948: The new state of Israel was born.
- 1967: Israel captured Jerusalem and the West Bank during the Six Day War, which was precipitated by an Arab invasion.[19]

Such facts seem to indicate that since the late nineteenth century, God has been in the process of bringing gradual fulfillment to what He promised in Scripture. Israel at this time still remains in unbelief. But according to Joel 2:28-29, a spiritual awakening will someday occur in Israel.

The Prophetic Necessity of the Regathering

A regathering of Jews in Israel is necessary for key biblical prophecies about the tribulation to make sense. For example, the returning of the Jews to the land in unbelief prior to the tribulation period is clearly implied in the peace covenant to be signed between the Antichrist and the leaders of Israel during the tribulation period. This relates to the 70 weeks of Daniel.

The backdrop is that in Daniel 9, God provided a prophetic timetable for the nation of Israel. The prophetic clock began ticking when the command went out to restore and rebuild Jerusalem following its destruction by Babylon (Daniel 9:25). According to this verse, Israel's timetable was divided into 70 groups of seven years, totaling 490 years.

The first 69 groups of seven years—or 483 years—counted the years "from the issuing of the decree to restore and rebuild Jerusalem until the Anointed One, the ruler, comes" (Daniel 9:25 NIV). The Anointed One, of course, is Jesus Christ. *Anointed One* means "Messiah." The day that Jesus rode into Jerusalem to proclaim Himself Israel's Messiah was exactly 483 years to the day after the command to restore and rebuild Jerusalem had been given.

At that point God's prophetic clock stopped. Daniel describes a gap between these 483 years and the final seven years of Israel's prophetic timetable. Several events take place during this gap, according to Daniel 9:26: (1) The Messiah is killed, (2) the city of Jerusalem and its temple are destroyed (which occurred in AD 70), and (3) the Jews encounter difficulty and hardship from that time forward.

The final "week" of seven years begins for Israel when the Antichrist confirms a covenant for seven years (Daniel 9:27). When the Antichrist and the leaders of Israel sign this peace pact the tribulation period begins. That signature marks the beginning of the seven-year countdown to the second coming of Christ, which follows the tribulation period. However, such a treaty would make absolutely no sense if the Jews had not returned to their land and Israel were not a viable political entity. The point is, then, that Israel must be regathered to the land in unbelief before the beginning of the tribulation period. This is what makes the year 1948 so significant.

Israel Remains at Great Risk

From the time the Jews returned to their homeland in 1948, they have been at great risk from the Arab/Muslim nations that surround them. Israel might not exist today if it hadn't developed a very powerful military and the United States were not a committed ally.

Walid Phares, author of *Future Jihad,* comments that "as the Jewish state became a reality and prospered, Islamists viewed the entire existence of Israel as an aggression. The initial settlement was illegitimate to start with; Jews had no right to 'return' or come back to an Islamic land." Muslim resentment toward the Jews is based on "the principle of a non-Muslim state reemerging on a Muslim land. Following the logic of the Fatah and of jihad, any territory that was at some time 'opened' by a legitimate Islamic authority cannot revert to a non-Islamic authority."[20] Clearly, then, Islamic resentment toward the Jews in Israel is in the first place doctrinal, not geopolitical.

This is why Iran's ever-increasing hostilities against Israel are of such grave concern today. Since 2000, Iran has assumed the leading role in the Palestinian insurgency against Israel. Iran funnels both arms and money to terrorists active in the West Bank and the Gaza Strip. By 2003, Iran was offering some $50,000 to the families of Palestinian suicide bombers.

Iran's growing military capabilities also cause grave concern. Ilan Berman, author of *Tehran Rising,* tells us that "over the past several years, Israeli military planners have viewed Iran's burgeoning strategic arsenal with mounting alarm. According to top Israeli intelligence officials, Iran's nuclear program now constitutes the single greatest 'threat to the existence of Israel' since the Jewish state's founding in 1948."[21]

Berman's point is legitimate. However, our purpose is to focus attention on what the ancient prophet Ezekiel said about the *true* upcoming single greatest threat to the existence of Israel—a threat that will come not just from the hands of Iran. Rather, it will involve a massive northern military coalition made up of Iran and other Muslim nations, headed by the Russians. This invading force will be so large, so formidable, that Israel will have virtually no hope of its own defense. But God will intervene. Ezekiel is clear about that. We begin our formal study of Ezekiel 38–39 in the next chapter.

Part Two

THE EZEKIEL INVASION

6

Interpreting Ezekiel 38–39

Anyone who has studied the book of Ezekiel knows that Ezekiel 38 and 39 are the two most debated chapters in the book. Questions abound! For example: Do chapters 38 and 39 seem out of place in the context of the other chapters in Ezekiel's book? Should these chapters be taken literally, or are they metaphorical? If we are to take them literally, did the battle of Gog and Magog take place in the past, or is it yet future? If it is yet future, at what point on the prophetic timeline does the invasion take place—before the tribulation, during the tribulation, after the tribulation, at the beginning of the millennial kingdom, or at the end of the millennial kingdom? Who are the nations that comprise the invading northern military coalition? Is Russia one of the nations involved? Does Ezekiel describe the weapons literally (spears and swords and the like), or do these ancient weapons metaphorically refer to modern weapons? The debate seems endless.

In view of these questions, we will begin our discussion of the Ezekiel invasion by briefly addressing a few broad interpretative options and then lay out some specific interpretive principles. This will help guide our thinking for all that follows.

Interpretive Option 1: These Chapters Were Inserted Much Later by a Different Author

Some liberal interpreters—those who do not have a very high view of the inspiration of the Bible—claim that chapters 38 and 39 were inserted into Ezekiel much later by a different author, perhaps by a disciple of Ezekiel or an editor. Perhaps the chapters were inserted, we are told, with good intentions—to give a discouraged Israel hope that God would defend Israel from her enemies (like Babylon) and that Israel would eventually be victorious. But the inserted chapters really do not belong there.

These interpreters arrive at this conclusion because they think the material in Ezekiel 38–39 is out of place. After all, Ezekiel 33–37 speak of the restoration of Israel to the land, ending with a promise that God's sanctuary will be set in the midst of Israel (Ezekiel 37:26-28). A discussion of God's sanctuary continues in chapters 40–48. Chapters 38–39, however, speak of the battle of Gog and Magog. These chapters supposedly interrupt the flow of thought.[1]

These interpreters generally suggest that we cannot take these "inserted" chapters literally. However, their reasons for avoiding a literal interpretation of the passage are weak at best.

1. Interpreters suggest that the nations mentioned in this coalition against Israel are not contiguous to Israel or one another, so they would be unlikely to act together. But this claim fails to recognize that the nations that make up this coalition are predominantly Muslim nations, and that in itself is more than enough reason for them to act together—especially given current Islamic hatred for Israel. As one scholar put it, "The astonishing rise of pandemic Islamic fundamentalism, with its anti-Semitism and a hatred of the restored Land of Israel as central tenets, has already linked remote countries in coordinated action, as the Muslim invasions and attempted

invasions of Israel in 1948, 1956, 1967, 1973, 1982, and 2000 to the present, demonstrate."[2]

2. Liberal commentators also claim that Israel's limited resources would not be sufficient to entice an enemy to attack (see Ezekiel 38:12-13). Such a claim today seems groundless, for recent developments indicate that Israel may have substantial untapped oil reserves. Moreover, substantial mineral wealth remains to be found in the Mediterranean Sea.

3. Finally, the number of corpses to be buried (casualties of war) during the seven-month period stipulated in Ezekiel 39:12 would be too large. This may be a legitimate objection if one is thinking in terms of individual burials, but mass burials using earth moving equipment create a realistic scenario.[3]

What about the claim that the chapters seem out of place? Properly interpreted, the chapters do not seem out of place.

Chapters 36–37 speak of God bringing the Jews back to their homeland. This happens well before the future tribulation period.

Chapters 38–39 speak of an invasion into this new, regathered state of Israel by an end-times northern military coalition that takes place either before, during, or sometime after the future tribulation period. (I'll give you my take on when it happens later in the book.)

Chapters 40–48 speak of Israel in the future millennial kingdom, which follows the tribulation period. God's sanctuary (or temple) is set in the millennium.

All in all, then, the liberals' arguments that these chapters feel out of place, were inserted by a later author, and should not be taken literally have no merit. We have no good reason *not* to interpret these chapters literally. As scholar Charles Feinberg put it, "It is either the grammatical, literal, historical interpretation or we are adrift on an uncharted sea with every man the norm for himself. There is not a syllable at the beginning of this chapter to alert us to explain the passage in any other than the literal method."[4]

Interpretive Option 2: Ezekiel 38–39 Is Metaphorical

Other interpreters reject a literal interpretation of Ezekiel 38–39 by arguing that these chapters are metaphorical. They believe these chapters have little or no connection to historical events. Rather, these chapters describe, in a general way, the struggle between good and evil. Gog is representative of spiritual powers that are hostile to God. Ezekiel mentions specific nations as an apocalyptic device to represent various enemies of God's people. "The fulfillment of this strange prophecy can never be literal. In general it seems to refer to the last and desperate attempts of a dying heathenism to overturn the true religion of Yahweh."[5]

Those who hold to replacement theology would certainly fall into this category. This misguided form of theology subscribes to the idea that "the Church has replaced Israel entirely in God's plan, and, accordingly, future prophecies about Israel are fulfilled in some sense in the Church. In this case [Ezekiel 38–39], at least implicitly, the prophecy can be seen *figuratively* in the same sense that the New Testament views the conflict between the kingdom of God and the kingdom of Satan."[6]

One reason this view is untenable is that the church and Israel are distinct in the New Testament. For example, we are instructed in 1 Corinthians 10:32 (NIV), "Do not cause anyone to stumble, whether Jews, Greeks [Gentiles] or the church of God." Moreover, Israel and the church are distinct throughout the book of Acts, which uses the word *Israel* 20 times and the word *church* 19 times.

Also, the metaphorical hermeneutic of replacement theology does not account for the fact that the scriptural prophecies that have already been fulfilled (such as the Old Testament messianic prophecies that refer to the first coming of Jesus Christ) have been fulfilled quite literally. From the book of Genesis to the book of Malachi, the

Old Testament abounds with anticipations of the coming Messiah. Numerous Old Testament predictions of His birth, life, ministry, death, resurrection, and glory (for example, Isaiah 7:14; Micah 5:2; Zechariah 12:10) are literally fulfilled in the New Testament. *The Popular Encyclopedia of Bible Prophecy* notes that "prophecies that have been fulfilled *completely* have been fulfilled *literally,* and that gives us confidence to expect that those prophetic utterances that are not yet fulfilled (or completely fulfilled) will also end up being fulfilled literally."[7] Mark Hitchcock likewise affirms that "the fulfillment of past prophecies establishes an unbroken pattern of literal fulfillment. All of the biblical prophecies that have already been fulfilled were fulfilled literally. With this kind of precedent established, we can expect that the future, unfulfilled prophecies will also be literally fulfilled."[8] This certainly applies to Ezekiel 38–39.

Interpretive Option 3: The Prophecy Was Fulfilled in Ezekiel's Day

A third view is that Ezekiel's prophecy was fulfilled during the time of Ezekiel or perhaps shortly after his time. The nations and events were contemporary with the prophet himself. The Gog prophecy may refer to the ruthless Scythians, far to the north of Israel. Others suggest that the Gog prophecy refers to the Babylonians, while still others relate the prophecy to Alexander the Great.[9]

This view is plagued with weaknesses. It fails to acknowledge Ezekiel's time clues in the very text of the prophecy. Ezekiel was clear that the things he predicted would be fulfilled "in the latter years" (Ezekiel 38:8) and "in the last days" (38:16). As I will demonstrate later in the book, Ezekiel uses these terms to point to the end times.

This view also fails to recognize that the invasion occurs after Israel has been regathered from all around the earth (Israel's inhabitants "have been gathered from many nations"—Ezekiel 38:8) to a land that had been a wasteland. These facts alone would disqualify the prophecy from relating to Ezekiel's own time. We are not talking about the Jews emerging out of, say, Babylon following the Babylonian exile. We are talking about the Jews emerging out of many nations and being gathered to their homeland—something that has been occurring steadily since 1948.

Further, even a cursory examination of biblical history shows that no invasion into Israel has matched Ezekiel 38–39. Nor has an invasion into Israel involved the specific nations mentioned in the passage. Since it hasn't been fulfilled yet, its fulfillment must yet be future.

Interpretive Option 4: Ezekiel's Prophecy Will Be Fulfilled in the Future

The most viable approach to Ezekiel 38–39 is to take the passage quite literally, recognizing that the prophecy will be fulfilled in the future. Several arguments support this approach:

1. As noted above, no invasion into Israel has matched the scale of what Ezekiel 38–39 describes. Nor has an invasion into Israel involved the specific nations mentioned in the passage. It hasn't been fulfilled yet, so its fulfillment must yet be future.

2. Ezekiel was clear that the things of which he spoke would be fulfilled "in the latter years" (Ezekiel 38:8) and "in the last days" (38:16). Such phrases point to the end times.

3. The unique alignment of nations described in Ezekiel 38–39 has never occurred in the past, but it *is* occurring now. I will describe key alliances in detail later in the book, but even now one can observe alliances between Russia, Iran, and other Muslim nations, all of whom would like to see Israel obliterated.

4. Related to this, an alliance between many of the nations mentioned in Ezekiel 38–39 may not necessarily have made good sense in Ezekiel's day because some are not located near each other, but it makes great sense in our day because the nations that make up the coalition are predominantly Muslim. That alone is more than enough reason for them to unify in attacking Israel—especially given current Islamic hatred for Israel.

5. Ezekiel's invasion occurs after Israel is regathered from all over the earth—"gathered from many nations" (Ezekiel 38:8,12)—to

a land that had been a wasteland. Certainly the Jews had been in bondage before. For example, they were held in bondage in Egypt. They went into captivity in Assyria and Babylon. But in each of these cases, they were freed from a single nation, not many nations around the world. The only regathering of Jews from many nations around the world in Israel's history is that which is occurring today.

6. Ezekiel 36–37, which prophesies the rebirth of Israel, appears to be being fulfilled before our very eyes as Jews return to their homeland from all over the world. Chapters 36–37 are apparently being fulfilled literally, so we can reasonably assume that chapters 38–39 will likewise be fulfilled literally. This is in keeping with the well-established precedent of biblical prophecies throughout the Old Testament being fulfilled literally.

7. Ezekiel 38:11 (KJV) informs us that during the time of the future invasion, Israel will be a "land of unwalled villages" and will be "at rest" and "dwell safely, all of them dwelling without walls, and having neither bars nor gates." This certainly could not be said of the Israel that existed during Ezekiel's day. This can only be fulfilled in the future (more on this later in the book).

8. Finally, without a literal approach, we are left in a sea of relativism regarding what prophetic passages teach.

> Undoubtedly one of the major problems in understanding prophecy is determining whether it should be understood in its natural, or literal meaning. Unless prophetic statements are taken in their normal sense, it is almost impossible to determine their meaning with any consistency. If one denies that a prophecy is to be taken in its normal sense, the door is opened to dozens of unauthorized interpretations. The nonliteral interpretation of prophecy has been a major source of confusion and contradiction.[10]

Biblical Principles for Literal Interpretation

Having established that a literal approach is the best approach for interpreting Ezekiel 38–39, let's consider some basic interpretive principles to be used throughout the rest of this book. The best interpreters accept these standard hermeneutical principles.

When the Plain Sense Makes Good Sense, Seek No Other Sense

A plain reading of Genesis indicates that when God created Adam in His own rational image, He gave Adam the gift of intelligible speech. This enabled him to communicate objectively with his Creator and with other human beings through sharable linguistic symbols—words (Genesis 1:26; 11:1,7). Scripture shows that God sovereignly chose to use human language as a medium of revelational communication, often through the "Thus saith the Lord" pronouncements of the prophets (Isaiah 7:7; 10:24; 22:15; 28:16; 30:15; 49:22; 51:22; 52:4 KJV).

If God created language in order to communicate with human beings and to enable human beings to communicate with each other, He would undoubtedly use language and expect man to use it in its normal and plain sense. This view of language is a prerequisite to understanding not only God's spoken word but His written Word (Scripture) as well. As one expositor put it, "Literal interpretation assumes that God wants people to understand His revelation, so He based it on the normal rules of human communication."[11]

So when the plain, literal sense of Scripture makes good sense, seek no other sense. For example, when God says in His Word that He loves us so much that He sent His Son to die for us (Romans 5:8), let's accept that literally and give thanks to God for it. When God says in His Word that His gift of salvation comes only by faith in Christ (Acts 16:31), let's accept that literally and respond accordingly. Likewise, when God says in His Word that those who reject this gift will spend eternity in hell (Matthew 25:41), we need to accept that literally, without trying to spin biblical Christianity into a "kinder and gentler," culturally acceptable religion. When God says an invasion will be launched into Israel by a massive northern military coalition

(Ezekiel 38–39), let's accept that and then determine what we can learn from Scripture about it.

Submit All "Preunderstandings" to Scripture

Theological "preunderstandings"—doctrinal opinions we have previously formed—should not bias our interpretation of Scripture. The International Council on Biblical Inerrancy addresses this issue: "We affirm that any preunderstandings which the interpreter brings to Scripture should be in harmony with scriptural teaching and subject to correction by it. We deny that Scripture should be required to fit alien preunderstandings, inconsistent with itself."[12] The point of this affirmation is to avoid interpreting Scripture through an alien grid or filter that obscures or negates its true message. It acknowledges that a person's preunderstanding will affect his or her understanding of a text. To avoid misinterpreting Scripture, students must be careful to examine their presuppositions in the light of Scripture.

We must frankly admit that all interpreters are influenced to some degree by personal, theological, denominational, and political prejudices. None of us approaches Scripture with a completely blank state. For this reason, preunderstandings must be in harmony with Scripture and subject to correction by it. Only those preunderstandings that are compatible with Scripture are legitimate.

Graham Stanton, a professor of New Testament studies at the University of London's King's College, suggests that "the interpreter must allow his own presuppositions and his own pre-understandings to be modified or even completely reshaped by the text itself. Unless this is allowed to happen, the interpreter will be unable to avoid projecting his own ideas on to the text." He notes that "the text may well shatter the interpreter's existing pre-understanding and lead him to an unexpectedly new vantage point from which he continues his scrutiny of the text."[13]

This principle is a warning to biblical interpreters in all of the prophetic camps—pretribulationists, midtribulationists, posttribulationists, premillennialists, amillennialists, postmillennialists, preterists, and all the rest. As a pretribulationist who believes the rapture of the church will take place before the future tribulation period, I must constantly test my theological belief on this matter against Scripture. Should I ever become convinced that the Bible does not teach this, I must change my view. Having engaged in decades of study on the issue, however, I firmly believe this to be the correct biblical view. I also encourage those who disagree with pretribulationism to consistently test their theological models against Scripture.

Pay Close Attention to the Context

Each statement in Scripture must be taken in its proper context. Every word in the Bible is part of a sentence, every sentence is part of a paragraph, every paragraph is part of a book, and every book is part of the whole of Scripture. As Bible scholar Bernard Ramm has noted, "The entire Holy Scripture is the context and guide for understanding the particular passages of Scripture."[14] The interpretation of a specific passage must not contradict the total teaching of Scripture on a point. Individual verses do not exist as isolated fragments, but as parts of a whole. The exposition of these verses, therefore, must explain their relation both to the whole and to each other. Scripture interprets Scripture. As J.I. Packer put it so well, "If we would understand the parts, our wisest course is to get to know the whole."[15]

Certainly this principle applies to biblical prophecy. As we interpret individual verses of Bible prophecy, we should compare them with other verses of Bible prophecy. After all, "prophecies weave their way from some of the earliest chapters in Genesis to the very end of Revelation. Thus, the interpreter of prophecy should compare Scripture with Scripture in order to ascertain the entire teaching on prophetic subjects."[16] By following this method, the interpreter will gain an accurate picture of what God is going to do in the future and perhaps how and why He is going to do it.

Make a Correct Genre Judgment

The Bible contains a variety of literary genres, each of which has certain peculiar characteristics we must recognize in order to interpret the text properly. Biblical genres include history (Acts), the dramatic epic (Job), poetry (Psalms), wise sayings (Proverbs), and apocalyptic writings (Revelation). An incorrect genre judgment will lead us far astray in interpreting Scripture. A parable, for example, should not be treated as history, nor should poetry (which contain many symbols) be treated as straightforward narrative. A case in point would be how the psalms refer to God as a rock (Psalm 18:2; 19:14). This should be understood not literally but as a symbol of God's sturdiness: God is our rock-solid foundation. The psalms often use such metaphors.

The wise interpreter allows his knowledge of genres to guide his approach to each individual biblical text. This helps him accurately determine what the biblical author was intending to communicate to the reader.

I must emphasize that even though the Bible contains a variety of literary genres and many figures of speech, the biblical authors most often employed literal statements to convey their ideas. When they express their ideas literally, the Bible student must explain them literally. A literal interpretation of Scripture gives to each word in the text the same basic meaning it would have in normal, ordinary, customary usage whether employed in writing, speaking, or thinking. Without such a method, communication between God and man would be impossible.

Charles Feinberg's quote is worth revisiting: "There is not a syllable at the beginning of this chapter to alert us to explain the passage in any other than the literal method."[17] The context of Ezekiel 38–39 gives no indication that we should interpret it symbolically.

Consult History and Culture

The interpreter of Scripture must try to step out of his Western mind-set and into an ancient Jewish mind-set, paying special attention to such things as Jewish marriage rites, burial rites, family practices, farm practices, business practices, the monetary system, methods of warfare, slavery, the treatment of captives, the use of covenants, and religious practices. Armed with such detailed historical information, interpreting the Bible correctly becomes a much easier task because we better understand the world of the biblical writers. So, for example, a thorough historical understanding of the Jewish belief in the land promises made to Abraham, Isaac, and Jacob (Genesis 15:18-21; 26:3-4; 28:13-14) helps us better appreciate why Jews believe the land of Israel is their land and why they won't leave it even if threatened or attacked by a massive northern military coalition.

Recognize Figures of Speech

It is critical to emphasize that a literal approach to interpreting Scripture allows for metaphors and figures of speech. The Bible does include figures of speech, but what is a figure of speech and what is taken literally should be based on the biblical text itself—such as when Jesus used obviously figurative parables to express spiritual truth. In other words, we should watch for textual clues to point out metaphors and figures of speech, and when we come across such a figure of speech, we must use our hermeneutical skills to ascertain the literal truth behind the metaphor. As John Walvoord notes, figures of speech "are 'word pictures' that present literal truths in a picturesque way."[18]

Figures of speech or symbols should be interpreted in the broader context of all of Scripture. For example, I remember professor J. Dwight Pentecost, at Dallas Theological Seminary, teaching that if he had six months to study the book of Revelation, he would spend the first three months studying the Old Testament because most of the symbols in the book of Revelation are found in the Old Testament. Our basic policy should be to "look within the Bible for the interpretation of figurative language. Symbols and figures of speech need to be interpreted in light of (1) the immediate context, (2) the larger context, and (3) the historical-cultural context."[19]

Thomas Ice notes how figures of speech can communicate a clear meaning:

> Early in Christ's ministry, John the Baptist said of Jesus as He approached him: "Behold, the Lamb of God who takes away the sin of the world" (John 1:29). John used a symbol to designate Jesus "the Lamb of God." Yet, just because a symbol was used does not mean that Jesus did not literally die, as a sacrificial lamb, for man's sin. We all know that He did. John's use of a symbolic reference to Christ complemented the point that Jesus came to "take away the sin of the world" through His actual, sacrificial death...
>
> In a similar way, the Bible uses the term "beast" throughout Daniel and Revelation as a symbol for the person that is often known as the Antichrist. Apparently the symbol of the beast was chosen by God to designate the beastly or animal nature of the Antichrist. This does not mean that the beast is just the personification of evil in the world. No, even though a symbol is used to describe this still future human being, it means that the Antichrist will display ungodly character *as a real historical person.* This prophecy will be fulfilled *literally,* just as was Christ's death, as the Lamb of God.[20]

Distinguish Between a Literal Approach and "Newspaper Exegesis"

Arnold Fruchtenbaum, in his book *The Footsteps of the Messiah,* commented that "current events must never be the means of interpreting the Scriptures, but the Scriptures must interpret current events."[21] Fruchtenbaum is correct. At the same time, we must distinguish between a literal approach in interpreting biblical prophecies and what has come to be called "newspaper exegesis."

When I state that certain events transpiring in our world today—such as the political alliances emerging between Russia, Iran, and other Muslim nations—seem to be setting the stage for the fulfillment of end-time prophecies described in Ezekiel 38–39, I am not taking sensational headlines from the newspaper and forcing them into Ezekiel's prophecies as the definitive fulfillment of these prophecies. Rather, I have first studied the Scriptures to find out what God has revealed about the future, and then—trying to accurately discern the times, something Christ clearly wants us to do (Matthew 16:1-3; Luke 21:29-33)—I measure current events against what the Bible reveals in order to thoughtfully consider whether a legitimate correlation exists. If we conclude it does, we can rejoice in God's sovereign control of human history while at the same resisting the temptation to set dates, recognizing that this is something God forbids (Acts 1:7). All the while, we avoid sensationalism, recognizing that Christ calls His followers to live soberly and alertly as they await His coming (Mark 13:32-37).

Though I personally believe that what is taking place today is setting the stage for the fulfillment of prophecies relating to the end-times northern military coalition that will eventually invade Israel, I will continue to believe what Scripture says about this end-time invasion even if current-day events turn out to not be related to the fulfillment of these prophecies. In other words, even if all current-day alliances between Russia, Iran, and other Muslim nations dissolve and these Muslim nations decide to back off in their threat against Israel, and even if tensions in the Middle East substantially decompress, I will still believe in what Ezekiel 38–39 says about this eventual invasion. I will simply adjust my attitude in recognition that the timing of this invasion has a "not yet" status. But I am convinced it will one day happen! A plain reading of Ezekiel's prophecy leaves us no other interpretive choice.

7

Identifying the Nations of Ezekiel 38

God is absolutely sovereign over human affairs. Psalm 50:1 (NIV) makes reference to God as the Mighty One who "speaks and summons the earth from the rising of the sun to the place where it sets." Psalm 66:7 (NIV) affirms that "He rules forever by his power." We are assured in Psalm 93:1 (NIV) that "the Lord reigns" and "is armed with strength." God asserts, "My purpose will stand, and I will do all that I please" (Isaiah 46:10 NIV). God assures us, "Surely, as I have planned, so it will be, and as I have purposed, so it will stand" (Isaiah 14:24 NIV). Proverbs 16:9 (NIV) tells us, "In his heart a man plans his course, but the Lord determines his steps." Proverbs 19:21 (NIV) says, "Many are the plans in a man's heart, but it is the Lord's purpose that prevails."

So we should not be surprised that Scripture also portrays God as sovereign over the nations of the earth. Ezekiel 38–39 clearly shows that God is absolutely sovereign over the nations that participate in the end-times invasion of Israel. God says to these future invaders, "I will turn you about and put hooks into your jaws, and I will bring you out" (Ezekiel 38:4). God also says, "You will be summoned" (38:8), and "I shall bring you against my land" (38:16). Such words indicate that God is sovereignly orchestrating the events that are unfolding on earth.

And yet, as numerous biblical expositors have observed, these nations are not absolved of their crimes against Israel, for they themselves have chosen to attack.[1] Ezekiel 38:10 tells us that they will "devise an evil plan" and will resolve to "go up against the land" of Israel. For this, they will be judged and destroyed (Ezekiel 39).

The Big Picture

We noted earlier that some 2600 years ago, the ancient prophet Ezekiel prophesied that the Jews will be regathered from many nations to the land of Israel in the end times (Ezekiel 36–37). He then prophesied that sometime later, a massive northern assault force will conduct an all-out invasion of Israel. Russia will head up this coalition of Muslim nations, which includes modern Iran, Sudan, Turkey, and Libya. Their goal will be to utterly obliterate the Jews. The sheer size of this assault force will leave Israel with virtually no chance of defending itself. God, however, will intervene and supernaturally destroy the invaders (38–39).

Amazingly, Ezekiel prophesied that these specific nations would ally themselves together for this invasion into Israel. These nations have never allied together for any kind of invasion, and yet, more than 2600 years ago, Ezekiel said they would eventually come together.

More than a few students of the Bible have recognized that the very nations prophesied to join this alliance in the end times are, in fact, already coming together in our own day. (I'll document this later.) The fact that this alliance is emerging after Israel became a nation again in 1948—with Jews continuing to stream into their homeland ever since, so that today there are more Jews in Israel than anywhere else on earth—is highly significant. The stage may be being set for this prophesied future invasion into Israel.

Of course, circumstances could always change, in which case the invasion could still be a long way off. Nevertheless, seeking to obey Jesus' injunction to accurately discern the times (Matthew 16:1-3; Luke 21:29-33), we can't help but wonder if what we witness happening today is preparing the way for the eventual invasion of this northern alliance into Israel.

One of the debated issues regarding the interpretation of Ezekiel 38–39 is the identity of the nations that make up the invading force. Our primary concern is this: What modern nations are equivalent to the ancient territories of Rosh, Magog, Meshech, Tubal, Persia, Cush, Gomer, and Beth-togarmah? Can we come to a consensus about the proper identity of these nations? Though the debate continues, I believe we can be virtually certain about the identity of some of these nations and reasonably sure about some of the others. Take a look at the evidence and see if you agree with me.

Some Preliminary Considerations

Consider Ezekiel 38:1-6:

> And the word of the LORD came to me saying, "Son of man, set your face toward **Gog** of the land of **Magog**, the prince of **Rosh**, **Meshech** and **Tubal**, and prophesy against him and say, 'Thus says the Lord GOD, "Behold, I am against you, O **Gog**, prince of **Rosh**, **Meshech** and **Tubal**. I will turn you about and put hooks into your jaws, and I will bring you out, and all your army, horses and horsemen, all of them splendidly attired, a great company with buckler and shield, all of them wielding swords; **Persia**, **Ethiopia** and **Put** with them, all of them with shield and helmet; **Gomer** with all its troops; **Beth-togarmah** from the remote parts of the north with all its troops—many peoples with you (Ezekiel 38:1-6).

Notice the terms in bold. All these nations are found in the table of the nations in Genesis 10:2-7 except for Rosh, and this requires some explanation. I will discuss the controversy over whether this term is a proper noun (referring to a nation) or an adjective (translated "chief prince") later in the chapter. For now, note that the term *Rosh* may indeed be found in the table of nations in Genesis 10:2-7. *Rosh* may derive from the term *Tiras* in Genesis 10:2. Scholar Clyde E. Billington notes the Acadian practice of dropping the initial T, especially if followed by an R-sound, and explains, "It appears that the name Tiras was shortened under the influence of the Acadian language into something that sounded like 'Rosh' or 'Ros.'"[2] Certainly it would be logical to find some form of the word *Rosh* in Genesis 10 because all the other nations in Ezekiel 38:1-6 are found there.

Though the names of these nations were common in ancient times, they are no longer in use today. However, through historical and geographical studies, we can ascertain with a reasonable degree of certainty what their modern counterparts are. I will demonstrate in this chapter that these modern counterparts constitute a confederation of Israel's greatest enemies, who would like to see Israel pushed into the sea.

The Identity of Gog

The word *Gog* is a reference not to an invading nation but rather to the individual who leads this invasion. How do we know he is an individual? We know this because Gog is referred to as the "prince of Rosh, Meshech and Tubal" (Ezekiel 38:2). He is the leader of these nations. He's the one in charge. These nations follow his lead in moving against Israel. The name *Gog* appears 11 times in Ezekiel 38–39, thereby indicating that he plays a significant role in this end-times invasion.

The term *Gog* may or may not be a proper noun (like George or Tom). An altogether different Gog appears in 1 Chronicles 5:4, where we read that among the sons of Joel were "Shemaiah his son, Gog his son, Shimei his son," and others. This verse at least indicates that the term can be used as a proper name. However, the term does not seem to be intended as a proper name in Ezekiel 38–39. Numerous prophecy experts have suggested that the term may refer to a king-like role—such as pharaoh, caesar, czar, or president.[3] The term literally means "high," "supreme," "a height," or "a high mountain."[4] Apparently, then, this czarlike military leader will be a man of great stature who commands tremendous respect.

Gog is not another name for the Antichrist. Trying to make this identification leads to prophetic chaos. The Antichrist heads up a revived Roman Empire (Daniel 2; 7), but Gog heads up an invasion force made up of Russia and a number of Muslim nations (Ezekiel 38:1-6). Moreover, Gog's invasion into Israel constitutes a direct challenge to the Antichrist's covenant with Israel (Daniel 9:27). Further, Gog's moment in the limelight is short-lived (it's all over when God destroys the invading force—Ezekiel 39), whereas the Antichrist is in power during much of the tribulation.

The Identity of Magog

Magog, mentioned in the table of nations in Genesis 10:2, probably constitutes the geographical area in the southern portion of the former Soviet Union. Many scholars take *Magog* to generally refer to an area near the Black Sea or the Caspian Sea.[5] The *Expositor's Bible Commentary* suggests that *Magog* refers to "the land of the Scythians, a mountainous region around the Black and Caspian seas. This position is generally accepted."[6] Thomas Constable likewise comments, "The land of Magog probably refers to the former domain of the Scythians, who lived in the mountains around the Black and Caspian seas (modern southern Russia)."[7]

Prophecy expert Mark Hitchcock gets more specific and suggests that what used to be Magog in ancient times is today occupied by the former southern Soviet republics of Kazakhstan, Kyrgyzstan, Uzbekistan, Turkmenistan, Tajikistan, and possibly even northern parts of modern Afghanistan.[8] Significantly, Muslims dominate these nations and provide more than enough religious motivation to move against Israel.

This identification of Magog with the former domain of the Scythians is based not on speculation but rather on historical sources. For example, the ancient historian Flavius Josephus, in his 20-volume *The Antiquities of the Jews,* documents what happened to the descendents of Noah following their attempt to build the Tower of Babel (Genesis 11). He says "they were dispersed abroad, on account of their languages, and went out by colonies everywhere." He notes that "each colony took possession of that land which they light upon and unto which God led them." Then he comments that "Magog founded those that from him were named Magogites, but who are by the Greeks called Scythians."[9] Bible scholar Charles Feinberg notes that early Church Father Jerome "stated that the Jews of his day held that Magog was a general designation for the numerous Scythian tribes."[10] Indeed, Jerome commented that *Magog* denotes "Scythian nations, fierce and innumerable, who live beyond the Caucasus and the Lake Maeotis, and near the Caspian Sea."[11]

The Scythian tribes, known for their savage and destructive warfare, spanned a wide geographical area from central Asia to the southern territory of modern Russia.[12] (One only need look at a map to see how wide this territory spans.) Scholar Edwin Yamauchi suggests that the Scythians were divided into two groups, a narrow and broad grouping: "In the narrow sense, the Scythians were the tribes who lived in the area which [ancient historian] Herodotus designated as Scythia (i.e., the territory north of the Black Sea)...In the broad sense the word Scythian can designate some of the many other tribes in the vast steppes of Russia, stretching from the Ukraine in the west to the region of Siberia in the east."[13]

Try to picture all this in your mind's eye. The Black Sea and Caspian Sea are essentially parallel to each other, with the Black Sea to the west and the Caspian Sea to the east. The Ukraine is on the northern side of the Black Sea. Russia borders the northeast side of the Black Sea and the northwest side of the Caspian Sea. Bordering on the eastern side of the Caspian Sea are Kazakhstan and Turkmenistan. Just a bit further east, we come to Uzbekistan. Continuing east, we come to Kyrgyzstan and Tajikistan. Dropping south from this area, we come to Afghanistan. These are some of the modern-day geographical areas that long ago were inhabited by the ancient Magogites. And, as noted previously, these are predominantly Muslim territories.

The Identity of Rosh

Tremendous debate exists regarding the proper meaning of the term *Rosh* in Ezekiel 38:2 and 39:1. This common Hebrew word literally means "head," "top," "summit," or "chief." The problem for Bible interpreters is that in Ezekiel 38–39, the term could be either a proper noun or an adjective. Many English translations take the term as an adjective and translate the word as "chief." An example is the New International Version, which reads, "Son of man, set your face against Gog, of the land of Magog, the chief prince of Meshech and Tubal." After significant study, I believe that Hebrew scholars C.F. Keil and Wilhelm Gesenius are correct in taking the term as a proper noun in Ezekiel, referring to a geographical place. The New American Standard Bible, taking the term as a proper noun, reads, "Son of man, set your face toward Gog of the land of Magog, the prince of Rosh, Meshech and Tubal."

The evidence suggests that the errant translation of Rosh as an adjective ("chief prince") can be traced to the Latin Vulgate, translated by Jerome. Hebrew scholar James Price explains:

> The origin of the translation "chief prince of Meshech and Tubal" is traced to the Latin Vulgate. The early translators of the English Bible were quite dependent on the Latin Version for help in translating difficult passages. They evidently followed Jerome in Ezek 38:2, 3; 39:1...Evidently by the second century A.D. the knowledge of the ancient land of Rosh had diminished. And because the Hebrew word Rosh was in such common use as "head" or "chief," Aquila [a Jewish translator] was influenced to interpret Rosh as an adjective ["chief prince"], contrary to the LXX [Septuagint] and normal grammatical conventions. Jerome followed the precedent set by Aquila, and so diminished the knowledge of ancient Rosh even further by removing the name from the Latin Bible.
>
> By the sixteenth century A.D. ancient Rosh was completely unknown in the West, so the early English translators of the Bible were influenced by the Latin Vulgate to violate normal Hebrew grammar in their translation of Ezekiel 38–39. Once the precedent was set in English, it was perpetuated

> in all subsequent English Versions until this century when some modern versions have taken exception. This ancient erroneous precedent should not be perpetuated.[14]

Scholar Clyde Billington offers a similar comment: "Jerome's incorrect translation of Rosh as an adjective has been followed by many of today's popular translations of the Bible. It is clear that this translation originated with the Jewish translator Aquila [and] was adopted by Jerome in the Vulgate."[15] Billington explains Jerome's faulty reasoning process in translating the way he did:

> Jerome himself admits that he did not base his decision on grammatical considerations! Jerome seems to have realized that Hebrew grammar supported the translation of "*prince of Rosh,* Meshech, and Tubal" and that it did not support his own translation of "*chief prince* of Moshoch and Thubal." However, Jerome rejected translating Rosh as a proper noun because, "we could not find the name of this race [i.e. the Rosh people] mentioned either in Genesis or any other place in the Scriptures, or in Josephus." It was this non-grammatical argument that convinced Jerome to adopt Aquila's rendering of Rosh as an adjective ["chief"] in Ezekiel 38–39.[16]

Exegetically, the evidence supports taking Rosh as a proper noun (that is, as a geographical area). G.A. Cook, a Hebrew scholar, affirms that this is "the most natural way of rendering the Hebrew."[17] Thomas Ice concludes that "normal Hebrew and Arabic grammar supports *Rosh* as a noun...Actually, Hebrew grammar demands that *Rosh* be taken as a noun. No example of Hebrew grammar has ever been cited that would support taking *Rosh* as an adjective."[18] Likewise, Randall Price concludes that "on linguistic and historical grounds, the case for taking Rosh as a proper noun rather than a noun-adjective is substantial and persuasive."[19] Billington concludes that the features of Hebrew grammar "dictate that Rosh be translated as a proper noun and not as an adjective...the grammatical arguments for the translation of 'Rosh' as a proper noun in Ezekiel 38–39 are conclusive and not really open for serious debate."[20]

If we are correct in taking the term as a geographical place, the question becomes, where is this geographical place? This too has been an issue of substantial debate. Below I will offer evidence supporting why I believe the term is best taken as referring to modern Russia. I want to begin, however, by noting that some scholars today absolutely deny any connection with Russia.

- D.R.W. Wood, in the *New Bible Dictionary,* says that "the popular identification of Rosh with Russia...has nothing to commend it from the standpoint of hermeneutics."[21]
- Daniel Block, in his commentary on Ezekiel, says that "the popular identification of Rosh with Russia is impossibly anachronistic and based on a faulty etymology, the assonantal similarities between Russia and Rosh being purely accidental."[22]
- Edwin Yamauchi, in his book *Foes from the Northern Frontier*, likewise argues that Rosh "can have nothing to do with modern 'Russia,'" and that such a view "would be a gross anachronism."[23]
- John Bright said that Ezekiel 38–39 contains "a prophecy which some (quite wrongly!) believe will be fulfilled by present-day Soviet Russia."[24]

Some critics of the idea that Rosh is Russia build a straw man argument and argue that simply because an ancient Hebrew word sounds similar to a modern English word must mean that Rosh is Russia is ridiculous. Frankly, if the view that Rosh is Russia were based solely on the similarity of sound between the two, I would agree. As will become clear below, however, we have much deeper and more substantive reasons for taking the term as referring to Russia.

1. First, as noted previously, highly respected Hebrew scholars

have taken the term as referring to Russia. This should not be taken lightly. Wilhelm Gesenius, for example, said in 1846 that "without much doubt Rosh designates the Russians, who are described by the Byzantine writers of the 10th century, under the name of the Ros, as inhabiting the northern parts of Taurus; and also by Ibn-Fosslan, an Arabic writer of the same period, under the name Rus, as dwelling upon the river Volga."[25] Billington notes that "Gesenius in the original Latin version of his lexicon titled *Thesaurus Linguae Hebraeae et Chaldaeae Veteris Testamenti* has nearly a page of notes dealing with the word Rosh and with the Rosh people mentioned in Ezekiel 38–39. This page of notes on Rosh does not appear in any of the English versions of Gesenius' Lexicon."[26] Those who wish to see Gesenius' substantive reasons for his conclusions on Rosh should consult Billington's translation of these notes in his article "The Rosh People in History and Prophecy," published in the *Michigan Theological Journal*.[27]

2. Another Old Testament scholar of note is C.F. Keil, who argues that "the Byzantine and Arabic writers frequently mention a people called Ros and Rus, dwelling in the country of Taurus, and reckoned among the Scythian tribes, so that there is no reason to question the existence of a people known by the name Rosh." He concluded that "the name of the Russians is connected with this Rus."[28] Building on the work of Gesenius, Keil, and other reliable sources, Thomas Ice concludes that "there is considerable historical evidence that a place known as Rosh was very familiar in the ancient world. While the word appears in a multitude of various languages, which have a variety of forms and spellings [Rus, Ros, and Rox], it is clear that the same people are in view."[29]

3. Related to this, the Septuagint (LXX), the Greek translation of the Hebrew Old Testament that predates the time of Christ, translates *Rosh* as *Ros*. Scholar Jon Ruthven notes that "the translation of the LXX is not much more than three centuries removed from Ezekiel."[30] We should also note that there is evidence of a people named *Rosh* or *Rashu* in the ninth through seventh centuries BC in Assyrian sources that predate the book of Ezekiel.[31] So quite early, we find evidence of

a Ros people that some of the most respected Hebrew scholars say is geographically located in Russia. These Rosh people, "who migrated to the Caucasus Mountains in Southern Russia, are one of the genetic sources of the modern Russians of today."[32]

4. "Rosh appears as a place name in Egyptian inscriptions as *Rash* as early as 2600 BC, and one inscription from 1500 BC refers to a land called *Reshu* that was located to the north of Egypt. As a toponym (place name), *Rosh* (or its equivalent) is found over 20 times in other ancient documents."[33] Indeed, the term *Rosh* "is found three times in the Septuagint (LXX), ten times in Sargon's inscriptions, once in Assurbanipal's cylinder, once in Sennacherib's annals, and five times in Ugaritic tablets."[34]

5. Placing Rosh in present-day Russia has long been a tradition in the Christian church. Indeed, "as early as 438 AD, Byzantine Christians placed Gog, Magog, Meshech, Tubal and Ros peoples to the north of Greece in the area that is today Russia."[35]

6. Finally, in Ezekiel 39:2 Rosh is said to be "from the remotest parts of the north." The term *north* is to be understood in relation to Israel. Russia is directly north of Israel. In his book *The Nations in Prophecy,* John Walvoord notes that "if one takes any map of the world and draws a line north of the land of Israel he will inevitably come to the nation Russia. As soon as the line is drawn to the far north beyond Asia Minor and the Black Sea it is in Russia and continues to be in Russia for many hundreds of miles all the way to the Arctic Circle." Walvoord emphatically states that "one cannot escape Russia if he goes north of the Holy Land. On the basis of geography alone, it seems quite clear that the only nation which could possibly be referred to as coming from the far north would be the nation Russia."[36] This important contextual clue in Ezekiel 39 points to modern Russia being the geographical area Ezekiel refers to.

The Identity of Meshech and Tubal

In his popular *Scofield Study Bible,* C.I. Scofield interpreted Meshech and Tubal (Ezekiel 38:2) to be Moscow and Tobolsk, based primarily on the similarity of the pronunciation of the terms. In fact, he indicated that "all agree" on this identification. A more recent scholar, Jon Mark Ruthven, provides historical evidence supporting the possible identification of Meshech with Moscow.[37]

Meshech and Tubal were the sixth and fifth sons of Japheth, the son of Noah (Genesis 10:2). *Meshech* and *Tubal*—often mentioned together in Scripture—seem to refer to the geographical territory to the south of the Black and Caspian seas, which is modern Turkey, though there may be some overlap with some neighboring countries. Many reliable sources bear this identification out:

- Mark Hitchcock writes, "Meshech and Tubal are identified in ancient history with the Mushki and Tabal of the Assyrians, and the Moschi and Tibareni of the Greeks who inhabited territory that is in the modern nation of Turkey."[38]
- The *Expositor's Bible Commentary* tells us, "The biblical and extrabiblical data, though sparse, would imply that Meshech and Tubal refer to geographical areas or countries in eastern modern Turkey, southwest of Russia and northwest of Iran."[39]
- Professor Thomas Constable likewise tells us that "Meshech and Tubal occur together in Scripture (27:13; 32:26; Gen. 10:2; 1 Chron. 1:5) and apparently refer to regions of Anatolia (modern western Turkey), the areas that became known as Phrygia and Cappadocia."[40]
- Scholar Edwin Yamauchi comments, "Since the late nineteenth century Assyrian texts...locate Mushku (Meshech) and Tabal (Tubal) in central and eastern Anatolia respectively."[41]
- *The International Standard Bible Encyclopedia* says this about Tubal and Meshech: "Obvious is their identity with the Tabali and Muski of the Assyrian monuments, where the latter is mentioned as early as Tiglath-pileser I,

and the former under Shalmaneser II; both are described as powerful military states."[42] These territories are in modern Turkey.

- *The New Unger's Bible Dictionary* confirms that Tubal and Meshech were "the Tabali and Mushki of the Assyrian monuments." The dictionary also informs us that "the Moschoi and Tibarenoi are referred to by Herodotus as living in the mountains SE of the Black Sea (3.94; 7.78)."[43] This too points us to modern Turkey.
- The *Wycliffe Bible Encyclopedia* likewise confirms that Meshech is the same as "the Mushki of the Assyrian inscriptions, first mentioned by Tiglath-pileser I (c. 1100 BC) and then by Shalmaneser III (859–824 BC)." We are told that "in Herodotus' time they moved to the mountains to the SE of the Black Sea" (thereby placing them in the territory that today is Turkey). Further, Tubal "is the Tabali of the Assyrian inscriptions."[44]
- The *New Bible Dictionary* agrees: "The close association of the name with Tubal renders likely their identification with the people often named together as Tabâl and Musku or Mušku in the Assyrian inscriptions and Tibarenoi and Moschoi in Herodotus."[45]

Modern scholarship seems to have established, with a fairly high degree of certainty, that *Meshech* and *Tubal* refer to the geographical area now occupied by modern Turkey.

The Identity of Persia

Of all the nations mentioned in Ezekiel 38–39, Persia is perhaps the easiest to identify. An ancient map of Persia shows that this same territory is occupied by modern Iran. In fact, Persia became modern Iran in 1935. Then, during the Iranian Revolution in 1979, the name changed to the Islamic Republic of Iran. This identification is practically uncontested.

A number of prophecy experts have noted that just as multiple prophecies about ancient Persia have been literally fulfilled, so the prophecy in Ezekiel 38–39 about Persia's modern counterpart (Iran) will also be literally fulfilled. In other words, Iran will, in fact, be part of the northern military coalition that invades Israel in the end times. I will talk a great deal about Iran in this book.

The Identity of Cush

The end-times northern military coalition against Israel will also include Ethiopia (NASB) or Cush (NIV) (Ezekiel 38:5). These terms refer to the geographical territory just south of Egypt on the Nile River—modern-day Sudan.

Sudan is a hard-line Islamic nation and a kindred spirit with Iran in its venomous hatred of Israel. In fact, these nations are already close allies, so a mutual stand against Israel would not be surprising. This nation is infamous for its ties to terrorism and for harboring Osama bin Laden from 1991 to 1996.

The Identity of Put

Ancient Put is a North African ally that joins up with the end-times northern military coalition against Israel. The *Brown-Driver-Briggs Hebrew Lexicon* tells us that Put, a land to the west of Egypt, is modern-day Libya. The Septuagint, the Greek translation of the Hebrew Old Testament from about 165 BC, translated *Put* as *Libya*.

But ancient Libya is larger than the Libya that exists today, so the boundaries of Put in Ezekiel 38–39 may extend beyond modern Libya.[46] Joel Rosenberg suggests that Put may include "the modern-day countries of Algeria and Tunisia, though it may not have extended as far as Morocco."[47] In any event, today's Libya is an Islamic nation ruled by Muammar al-Gadhafi and known for its hatred of Israel, so it is a natural fit with the other nations in this coalition.

The Identity of Gomer

Identifying Gomer is difficult. No clear consensus exists among Bible scholars. The best guess among scholars is that it refers either to modern-day Turkey or modern-day Germany.

In support of the Turkey hypothesis, the ancient historian Josephus said Gomer founded those whom the Greeks called the Galatians. The Galatians of New Testament times lived in the region of central Turkey.[48] This forms a direct connection between ancient Gomer and modern Turkey.

Moreover, many claim Gomer may be a reference to the ancient Cimmerians or Kimmerioi. *Nelson's New Illustrated Bible Dictionary,* for example, states that "they were probably the Cimmerians of classical history."[49] The *New Bible Dictionary* likewise affirms that they "are probably to be identified with the ancient Gimirrai (Cimmerians)."[50] *The Wycliffe Bible Encyclopedia* confirms, "Gomer represents the people termed Gimirra by the Assyrians and Cimmerians by the Greeks."[51] History reveals that from around 700 BC, the Cimmerians occupied modern Turkey.

In support of the Germany hypothesis, the Jewish Talmud claims *Gomer* refers to Germani, or the Germans.[52] Arnold Fruchtenbaum says Gomer is "located in present-day Germany. This too was the rabbinic view. The Midrash calls Gomer *Germania,* and that is also the way the Talmud refers to Gomer."[53]

Which view is correct? We can't be sure. The Josephus reference as well as the historical data we possess on the Cimmerians leads me to believe that *Gomer* probably refers to part of the geographical territory around modern Turkey, an Islamic territory.

The Identity of Beth-togarmah

In Hebrew, *Beth* means "house." *Beth-togarmah* is a Hebrew term that literally means "the house of Togarmah." Ezekiel 38:6 refers to "Beth-togarmah from the remote parts of the north." Beth-togarmah must be located to the north of Israel.

Some prophecy experts believe Beth-togarmah is yet another reference to modern-day Turkey: "Going back to Ezekiel's time, we discover that there was a city in Cappodocia (modern Turkey) known as Tegarma, Tagarma, Til-garimmu, and Takarama. This fits Ezekiel's identification exactly because Turkey is far north of Israel."[54] If this identification is correct, this means that a number of the locations cited in Ezekiel 38–39 refer to modern-day Turkey. Apparently, Turkey plays a significant role in the coalition that will invade Israel.

Beth-togarmah may refer to Turkey *and* some neighboring geographical territories. For example, the ancient historian Josephus identified the people of Togarmah as Phrygians. Phrygia was located in Asia Minor, in the geographical territory we now know as Turkey. Wilhelm Gesenius confirms that around 700 BC, some of the inhabitants of Phrygia crossed over to a different territory in order to found Armenia. Beth-togarmah thus apparently could refer to Turkey, Armenia, and perhaps other Turkic-speaking peoples who spread into other countries across central Asia.[55]

The Northern Coalition

What nations, then, make up the northern military coalition that will one day launch a massive invasion into Israel? Based on our best information, I believe the coalition will be led by Russia and will include Iran, Sudan, Turkey, Libya, Kazakhstan, Kyrgyzstan, Uzbekistan, Turkmenistan, Tajikistan, Armenia, and possibly northern Afghanistan. This massive invading coalition will seem unstoppable. But as I will demonstrate later in the book, God Himself will destroy the invaders. This will be a defeat for the record books!

What About Iraq?

Why doesn't Ezekiel include the Islamic country of Iraq in this invading Islamic coalition? Certainly today's Iraq would love to see Israel annihilated.

Several answers are possible. First, Iraq may well be a part of this invading coalition. In addition to the specific nations Ezekiel 38 mentions, we find the phrase "many peoples with you" (Ezekiel 38:6,9,15; see also 38:22). Could Iraq be a part of this "many peoples"? We cannot say for sure, but this phrase opens the door to that possibility.

Another possible scenario is that Iraq will not be a part of this Islamic invading coalition because a rebuilt Babylon (capital of Iraq) will be the headquarters of the Antichrist during the tribulation period (Revelation 17–18). Scripture reveals that the Antichrist will sign a seven-year peace pact with Israel (Daniel 9:27), and this will signal the beginning of the tribulation period. If the Ezekiel invasion takes place in the first half of the tribulation, Iraq could not possibly be a part of the invading force simply because Iraq, with its capital in Babylon, will be controlled by the Antichrist, who signed the peace pact with Israel.[56] J. Dwight Pentecost suggests the possibility that when God destroys the invading coalition, the Antichrist may try to take credit for it.

Does America figure in to the Ezekiel 38–39 prophecies? We turn our attention to this controversial issue in the next chapter.

8

Is America Involved?

Is America mentioned in Bible prophecy?

Through the years I have read several books and articles that have examined various theories about whether America is mentioned in biblical prophecy. Many have been speculative and farfetched. Others take a more reasoned approach.

This chapter's primary concern is whether America plays any role in the unfolding of the events in Ezekiel 38–39. No one can be absolutely dogmatic on this issue, but I will present several possible scenarios that I believe are compatible with end-times prophecies throughout the Bible.

The Rise and Fall of Great Civilizations

We begin with the sobering reality that many great nations have risen and fallen throughout human history. Each nation had no expectation of its impending demise. Indeed, people who lived within these nations believed they could never fall. But the harsh reality of documented history is that great nations do fall—hard.

The Babylonians never thought Babylon would fall, but its demise came in less than a century. The Persians never thought the Persian Empire would end, but it finally capitulated after about two centuries. The Greeks thought Greece would last forever, but it waned in less than three centuries. No one thought the mighty Roman Empire would ever decline, but it too fell after holding out for nine centuries.[1]

Today, Americans believe the United States is too strong to ever fall. But will United States citizens claim immunity from what history has proven over and over again—that great nations do fall? Is the United States invincible? We all tend to think we are special—that we will succeed where others have failed. But that is a dangerous mentality. As one researcher put it, "Anthropology tells us that many of the fallen civilizations in history also thought they were superior to their neighbors and forebears. Few of their citizens could have imagined their society would suddenly collapse."[2]

To be sure, I would never want to see the United States decline. I love this country. But the United States could suffer a decline—morally, economically, militarily, or in global influence.

Studies have shown that no civilization is invulnerable. One study, published in *Scientific American,* researched 60 ancient and modern civilizations to discover the lifespan of the average civilization. The study found that the average lifespan of a civilization is 421 years. Surprisingly, modern civilizations do not last as long as ancient ones. Indeed, among the 28 most recent civilizations, the average lifespan has only been 305 years.[3]

Two books—*Collapse,* by Jared Diamond, and *The Collapse of Complex Societies,* by Joseph Tainter—document how past civilizations have fallen because the leaders of these civilizations did not adequately prepare for a shortage of resources.[4] The reason may run deeper than this, however. Stephen Leeb writes, "Lack of foresight and an almost childlike decision not to worry about the future seem to be human characteristics that are timeless. Ultimately, these psychological weaknesses may be more responsible for why civilizations have failed than resource shortages alone."[5]

Many twentieth-century Americans had a mind-set of worry-free invincibility—at least until 9/11! That day was a wake-up call for many of us. No one in America expected that such a catastrophic attack could succeed on American soil. Meanwhile, at the time of this writing, the U.S. military is stretched thin in the war in Iraq. Military leaders are extending the stay of duty for American soldiers because of a shortage of replacements. This does not bode well for the future.

At the same time, some of America's political leaders have become increasingly concerned that much of the world's oil supply is controlled by Muslim countries (as we have seen in this book). Even worse, they are concerned about the possibility of Iran obtaining nuclear weapons. Maybe some of us finally have been shocked into a clearer vision—one that recognizes that the United States is not invulnerable and invincible.

Possible Prophetic Scenarios for America

America is not directly mentioned in Bible prophecy. That is a fact! And that leaves us with two possible prophetic scenarios for America.

1. America is only indirectly mentioned in Bible prophecy.
2. America is not mentioned in Bible prophecy at all.

Let's consider both of these scenarios.

America Is Only Indirectly Mentioned in Bible Prophecy

No verses in the Bible mention America by name, but several theories suggest indirect references to America in Bible prophecy. Here is a brief sampling of some of these theories:[6]

1. One of the "nations." This theory says that several general prophetic references to "the nations" in the tribulation may apply to the United States. These passages might include Isaiah 66:18-20; Haggai 2:6-7; and Zechariah 12:2-3. Such general passages, however, do not tell us anything specific about the role of the United States in the end times.[7]

2. Cooperation with Europe. Another theory is that even though the United States is not specifically mentioned in biblical prophecy, perhaps the United States will, in the end times, be in general cooperation with

Europe—the revived Roman Empire headed by a powerful leader (the Antichrist). Many U.S. citizens have come from Europe, so some say the United States could naturally become an ally of this Roman power in the end times.

3. The Babylon of Revelation 17–18. Some interpreters have seen parallels between Babylon the Great in the book of Revelation and the United States (or, more specifically, New York City). "The reason this symbol is the most widely accepted symbol of the United States is because the shoe seems to fit."[8] After all, both Babylon and the United States are dominant, both are immoral, both are excessively rich, and both think they are invulnerable. However, serious Bible interpreters do not give credence to this theory. Such a view involves more eisegesis (reading a meaning into the text of Scripture) than exegesis (drawing the meaning out of the text of Scripture).

4. The land "divided by rivers" (Isaiah 18:1-7 NIV). Some interpreters claim that the United States is the fulfillment of Isaiah 18:1-7 because it is divided by the Mississippi River. The passage also makes reference to the nation being feared because of its military conquests, something believed to fit how many people around the world view the United States.[9] The obvious problem with this view is that the nation is explicitly identified in Isaiah 18:1-2 as ancient Cush, or modern Sudan.

5. The Land of Tarshish (Ezekiel 38:13). According to Ezekiel 38:13, when the great northern military coalition invades Israel, a small group of nations will lamely protest the invasion: "Sheba and Dedan and the merchants of Tarshish with all its villages will say to you, 'Have you come to capture spoil? Have you assembled your company to seize plunder, to carry away silver and gold, to take away cattle and goods, to capture great spoil?' "

Without going into too much detail, a good number of Bible expositors believe the Tarshish of ancient times may be a reference to Spain. Hebrew scholar Wilhelm Gesenius as well as *The New Brown-Driver-Briggs Hebrew Lexicon of the Old Testament* take this view.[10] Others say Tarshish may refer to Great Britain.[11] Still others say Tarshish might represent all the Western nations of the end times (which would at least include the United States). Making a definitive conclusion on the matter is difficult.

An interesting discussion has arisen over the phrase, "Tarshish *with all its villages.*" Thomas Ice is one of many who believe the phrase "refers to the colonies of Western Europe and the nations that have subsequently arisen from them. This would include North America and the United States."[12] What are the arguments for this interpretation?

> First, merchants of Tarshish refer to the Phoenician maritime and trading community located in Spain during the general time of King Solomon, 3,000 years ago. Second, the merchants of Tarshish, during the last 500 years, developed into the modern mercantile nations of Western Europe like Spain, Holland, and Britain. Third, the phrase "with all its villages" or the variant rendering "with all the young lions" [in the KJV] would be a reference to its trans-Atlantic colonies, which would include America. Thus, it is reasoned, because America is the most dominant of these Western nations, this must be a reference to America.[13]

If this interpretation is correct, then according to Ezekiel 38:13, the United States would be among the nations lodging a protest against this massive invasion into Israel. But the protest is not backed with action.

Many today believe this passage refers to the United States, but I just don't find enough scriptural evidence to support the view. Therefore I cannot subscribe to it.

America Is Not Mentioned in Bible Prophecy at All

My assessment is that America is not mentioned in Bible prophecy at all. Using proper hermeneutics and sound exegesis, I cannot find America in any of the verses so often suggested by prophecy buffs. If I am correct in this belief, the key question becomes, why isn't America mentioned in Bible prophecy? I'll offer five points to consider.

1. The Bible doesn't mention most nations in the world. Still, the United States is the world's single remaining superpower and also happens to be Israel's principal ally. One therefore might naturally expect at least a passing mention of this country.

2. America may not play a significant role in the unfolding of God's end-time plans. Again, however, the United States is the world's single remaining superpower and also happens to be Israel's principal ally (financially supporting Israel with vast sums of money), so we might naturally expect at least some reference. So again, why no reference?

3. America may eventually implode due to ever-escalating moral and spiritual degeneration. Lots of statistics show the trouble this country is in morally and spiritually. At present, four out of five adults—some 83 percent—say they are concerned about the moral condition of the United States. One statistical study measured ten moral behaviors of U.S. citizens, and the findings are not encouraging:

> Of the ten moral behaviors evaluated, a majority of Americans believed that each of three activities were "morally acceptable." Those included gambling (61%), co-habitation (60%), and sexual fantasies (59%). Nearly half of the adult population felt that two other behaviors were morally acceptable: having an abortion (45%) and having a sexual relationship with someone of the opposite sex other than their spouse (42%). About one-third of the population gave the stamp of approval to pornography (38%), profanity (36%), drunkenness (35%) and homosexual sex (30%).[14]

If the moral fiber of this country continues to erode, the demise of this country is only a matter of time.

4. Perhaps the United States will be destroyed or at least greatly weakened by nuclear weapons and so will play no significant role in the end times. Earlier in the book, I documented the nuclear threat against the United States. The United States could certainly be attacked with nuclear weapons at some point in the future. Harvard

professor Graham Allison has written a book titled *Nuclear Terrorism* in which he affirms that a nuclear attack on U.S. soil within the next ten years is "more likely than not." To say that the entire United States could be destroyed would be a stretch, but if one major city—such as New York City—were destroyed, the effect on the U.S. economy would be absolutely devastating.

Jerome Corsi, in his book *Atomic Iran,* says that Iran's nuclear program as well as its missile production program should be of great concern to Americans: "Already on the drawing boards is the Shahab-5 [missile] with sufficient range to reach the continental United States. By the time the Shahab-6 is developed, there will be no place on earth the mad mullahs could not strike with a nuclear weapon on a day and at a time of their choosing."[15] No wonder almost half of all Americans say they worry about the possibility of a nuclear terrorist attack. Moreover, some 17 percent of Americans believe the end of the world will come in their lifetime.[16]

5. Perhaps the United States will become incapacitated due to an EMP attack. One scary but realistic scenario involves a foreign power—such as Iran—launching an electromagnetic pulse (EMP) attack against the United States. This is not a sensationalistic speculation of prophecy fanatics. It is a potential, realistic scenario documented in a report issued in 2004 by a blue-ribbon commission created by Congress—"Commission to Assess the Threat to the United States from Electromagnetic Pulse Attack." Based on this report, U.S. Representative Jim Saxton lamented that the "technology is now here" to bring America's way of life to an end.[17]

Frank Gaffney is a highly regarded national security expert who held senior positions in the Reagan Department of Defense and on the staffs of leading Democratic and Republican senators. He presently heads up the Washington-based Center for Security Policy. His recent (2006) book is entitled *War Footing.* In it, U.S. Representative Curt Weldon and U.S. Representative Roscoe Bartlett join him in coauthoring an eye-opening chapter on the realistic possibility of an EMP attack.

In this chapter, Gaffney and friends note that "the commission found that a single nuclear weapon, delivered by a ballistic missile to an altitude of a few hundred miles over the United States, would be 'capable of causing catastrophe for the nation.' "[18] Such a missile could easily be launched off of a freighter off the coast of the United States. The commission explained that the higher the altitude of the weapon's detonation, the larger the affected geographic area would be. At a height of 300 miles, the entire continental United States would be exposed, along with parts of Canada and Mexico.

> The blast, through a variety of physical mechanisms, generates an electromagnetic pulse from the detonation point through the atmosphere to the Earth's visible surface, all the way out to the horizon. Thus, a single nuclear weapon could produce an EMP attack that damages or destroys electronic systems across the entire continental United States.[19]

The commission warned that such a weapon's electromagnetic pulse would be likely to severely damage electrical power systems, electronics, and information systems—all of which Americans depend on. Electronic control, the infrastructures for handling electric power, sensors and protective systems of all kinds, computers, cell phones, telecommunications, cars, boats, airplanes, trains, fuel and energy, banking and finance, emergency services, and even food and water supplies would be at high risk.[20]

In one test, the United States detonated a 1.5-megaton weapon at an altitude of 248 miles over Johnston Island in the Pacific. "Eight hundred miles away in Hawaii, street-lights went out within seconds... Fuses failed on Oahu, telephone service was disrupted on Kauai, and the power system went down on Hawaii itself. What caused it was the high-powered electromagnetic pulse set off by the nuclear explosion, which hit Hawaii like a lightning bolt."[21]

The consequences of an EMP attack would be especially harmful to American society today, since the infrastructure of our society—civilian and military—virtually runs on electricity and electronic components. The commission estimated that "it could take 'months to years' to fully restore critical infrastructures after an EMP attack."[22] One expert warned that an electromagnetic pulse attack "could make the United States go dark, silent, and cold for months."[23]

Starvation and disease could ultimately result following an EMP attack. Dr. Lowell Wood (of the Lawrence Livermore Laboratory, and member of the EMP Threat Commission) warned in testimony before the U.S. Congress that an EMP attack could reduce to a pre–Industrial Age the United States' transportation options and ability to provide vital food and water to the general population.[24] A report published by United Press International makes this warning:

> Imagine the only people you could communicate with are those within your visual range or within the sound of your voice. Imagine the only way you could travel was to walk or ride a bike. Imagine no electricity, working telephones or computers; no fuel for cars or airplanes, no running elevators, no heat or light for houses and buildings, no running water and after a few days, no food. Imagine that you had to live under these conditions for weeks, months or even years...An electromagnetic pulse attack could inflict this catastrophic scenario across the entire United States.[25]

The question is, do the Russians and Iranians and other nations know how to launch such an EMP attack against America? Without a doubt they do. U.S. intelligence reveals that at least ten countries are presently working on EMP weapons.

Russia itself invoked the specter of an EMP attack against the United States when Vladimir Lukin, chairman of the Duma International Affairs Committee, notified American legislators that Russia was not helpless in the face of U.S.-led interventions. He commented that if Russia had the desire to hurt the United States in retaliation for NATO's bombing of Yugoslavia, they could easily launch a ballistic missile from a submarine and detonate a single nuclear warhead at high altitude over the United States. The resulting electromagnetic pulse would "massively disrupt U.S. communications and computer systems, shutting down everything."[26]

U.S. intelligence has discovered that Iran has performed tests on its Shahab-3 medium-range ballistic missile in a manner consistent with an EMP attack scenario. And amazingly, many of our military systems may be as vulnerable as our civilian technologies.[27] Indeed, Kenneth Timmerman tells us that pulses could "disable virtually all advanced weapons systems as if they were the surge from a lightning bolt striking your home and frying your computer."[28] The hard reality is that the U.S. Department of Defense does not have the funds necessary to shield equipment from electromagnetic pulses.

As if this weren't bad enough, Timmerman documents that, at present, smaller nonnuclear versions of EMP technology—known as high-powered microwave (HPM) and radio-frequency (RF) weapons—are now proliferating around the world. "They readily are available to potential terrorists, either directly from Russia, which long led the world in developing these technologies, or in more rudimentary forms from off-the-shelf components."[29] A recent small-scale test of a low-level RF pulse "ended up totally disrupting the global positioning system (GPS) being used to land commercial aircraft in Albany, New York, for a couple of weeks."[30] High-level weapons are immeasurably more damaging.

6. Perhaps the United States will suffer substantial economic weakening due to its gross overdependence on oil. I spoke of this earlier in the book. A progressive lessening in the oil supply will progressively weaken the economy of our oil-driven society. Princeton professor and geologist Kenneth S. Deffeyes says that once supply begins to dwindle, the years to follow will see shortages that at best will cause "global recession, possibly worse than the 1930s Great Depression." He warns that all this could lead to "war, famine, pestilence and death."[31]

Stephen Leeb, author of *The Coming Economic Collapse,* warns that just because a nation has been around for two or three hundred years does not mean it will last forever. He suggests that our next major crisis will likely be a shortfall in energy production, and this could severely injure the country.[32] He raises the possibility that competition for oil could escalate to war—even nuclear war:

> Energy is essential to wealth. Just as the United States will feel compelled to defend its access to oil, other nations, who feel they have an equal right to enjoy a share of the world's wealth, may fight to secure some of the remaining oil deposits. With nuclear weapons becoming more widespread, the possibility of nuclear war grows greater, and with it the most dramatic, large-scale collapse of civilization the world has ever witnessed.[33]

I recognize that this may sound alarmist. That is not my intention. We should keep in mind, however, that a conclusion is as sound as its premise. If the premise of an argument is sound, the conclusion of an argument is sound. The best evidence we have proves that U.S. civilization virtually runs on oil. The evidence also proves that global oil resources are depleting and will continue to do so. An oil energy crisis will certainly not hit us with the suddenness of Hurricane Katrina, but if the leaders of our country do not prepare for such a crisis, we will in the end pay for such shortsightedness. "Without cheap energy, our civilization would be unable to sustain itself much above the nineteenth-century level...Few people today have the knowledge or the skills to grow food, make clothes, manufacture items, repair tools, or build houses the way their great-great-grandparents did."[34]

7. Finally, the rapture may catastrophically affect the United States. This is the position of Mark Hitchcock:

> At the rapture, America will lose somewhere between 25 and 65 million citizens: Christians and their small children. The impact of such a disappearance will be nothing short of cataclysmic. Not only would our country lose a minimum of 10 percent of her population, but she would also lose the very best, the "salt and light" of this great land (see Matthew 5:13-14).[35]

The rapture could hurt the United States more than most other nations. More Christians per square mile live in the United States than anywhere else on earth. Following the moment of the rapture, many workers will no longer show up for work, many bills and mortgages will go unpaid, many college tuition bills and loans will go unpaid, many business leaders will no longer show up to lead their companies, many law enforcement personnel will no longer be here to keep the peace, and the stock market will likely crash because of the panic over millions of people suddenly vanishing.[36] This and much more will result following the rapture.

These scenarios demonstrate how the United States could become too weak to be a significant player in Bible prophecy. Of course, a substantially weakened United States would not be in a position to flex military muscle on Israel's behalf when the Ezekiel invasion occurs. These are sobering things to ponder.

God Controls Nations

Regardless of what happens to the United States, one fact is absolutely certain from the perspective of Scripture: God is absolutely sovereign over human affairs. God rules the universe, controls all things, and is Lord over all (see Ephesians 1). Nothing can happen in this universe that is beyond His control. All forms of existence are within the scope of His absolute dominion. Psalm 50:1 (NIV) makes reference to God as the Mighty One who "speaks and summons the earth from the rising of the sun to the place where it sets." Psalm 66:7 (NIV) affirms that "He rules forever by his power." Psalm 93:1 assures us that "the LORD reigns" and "is armed with strength." God asserts, "My purpose will stand, and I will do all that I please" (Isaiah 46:10 NIV). God assures us, "Surely, as I have planned, so it will be, and as I have purposed, so it will stand" (Isaiah 14:24 NIV).

God is also absolutely sovereign over the affairs of individual nations in the world. In the book of Job we read, "He makes the nations great, then destroys them; He enlarges the nations, then leads them away" (Job 12:23). We are told that "from one man he created all the nations throughout the whole earth. He decided beforehand which should rise and fall, and he determined their boundaries" (Acts 17:26 NLT). Daniel 2:20-21 tells us that "it is He who changes the times and the epochs; He removes kings and establishes kings."

In view of such facts, no Christian should be fearful of what is taking place in the world. Our God reigns!

9

The Final Jihad: The Coalition Invades (Ezekiel 38:1-16)

Our knowledge about the future invasion of a northern military coalition into Israel comes from the prophet Ezekiel. We begin our study in this chapter with a few brief historical insights on prophets in general and Ezekiel in particular. This will help prepare us for all that follows in this chapter.

The Hebrew word for a prophet, *nabi*, refers to people who were taken over by the power of God and who spoke God's words to the people. Often they directed their words at specific situations or problems. At other times (as in Ezekiel 38–39), they foretold the future. They often prefaced their words with, "Thus saith the Lord," thereby indicating that their words were not their own but God's.

God directly called these prophets into service, some even before birth (Jeremiah 1:5; Luke 1:13-16). They came from all walks of life, from farmers (Amos 7:14) to princes (Genesis 23:6). Whatever their background, the prophets were messengers of the Lord (Isaiah 44:26) who served God and shepherded God's people (Amos 3:7; Zechariah 11:4,7; Jeremiah 17:16).

Some prophets carried out their work before Israel's captivity. Because of Israel's sin and complacency, these prophets warned that a time of judgment was coming. God would not permit the sins of

His people to continue (see, for example, Amos 9:1-10). Though the prophets called the people to repentance, however, the people progressively became hardened in their sin, and judgment therefore inevitably came.

During the Israelites' captivity, the people started to perceive the clear message that God had them there on purpose—because of their sins!* Some of the people became despondent because they realized they had brought this on themselves. The prophets responded with soothing words of comfort and promised them that God still had a plan for their future and would one day deliver them from their suffering (see Isaiah 6:13; 28:5; 29:5; 31:5).

Prophets received messages from God in various ways, including visions, dreams, and even hearing God's voice. Likewise, prophets used various means to deliver their messages, including a simple proclamation of the message in a sanctuary, speaking face-to-face with an individual, and acting out a message (see Jeremiah 19). Isaiah even went barefoot and naked for three years to demonstrate his people's shame (Isaiah 20:2-3). Regardless of the means the prophets used to deliver the message, the people were expected to hear and obey.

The book of Ezekiel was written by the prophet Ezekiel, the son of Buzi, between 593 and 570 BC, and his messages were for the Jews in exile. God had called him into service as a prophet when he was about 30 years old. At the time, he was training to be a priest. Like all the other Jews, however, he soon found himself living in exile in Babylon, and this captivity would last 70 years.

Ezekiel's name literally means "God is strong" or "strengthened by God." To carry on his work of confronting the people regarding their sins and bringing comfort to them while in exile, Ezekiel surely needed God's strength.

---

* In the book of Deuteronomy, God through Moses promised great blessings if the nation lived in obedience to the covenant. God also warned that if the nation disobeyed His commands, it would experience the punishments listed in the covenant—including exile from the land (Deuteronomy 28:15-68). Old Testament history is replete with illustrations of Israel's unfaithfulness to the covenant. The two significant periods of exile for the Jewish people were the fall of Israel to the Assyrians in 722 BC and the collapse of Judah to the Babylonians in 597–581 BC. As God promised, disobedience brought exile to God's own people.

As a prophet, Ezekiel was unique. He often dramatized God's message by using signs, symbols, and parables. (For example, he said the dispersed Jews are like dry bones in the sun in Ezekiel 37.) By using such techniques, Ezekiel graphically communicated that God's judgment falls as a result of human sin. This is the message he proclaimed during the first part of his ministry.

In 597 BC, when Nebuchadnezzar (the uncontested ruler of the world at that time) carried Ezekiel and other Jews into exile in Babylon, Ezekiel started to speak a new message—words of hope and comfort, teaching that God would regather His people from the ends of the earth (bringing all those bones back together again and resurrecting Israel from the dead—Ezekiel 37) and that a new temple would one day be built (chapter 40). He tried to give the people something to look forward to. At the same time, however, Ezekiel spoke of a horrendous invasion into Israel that would take place in the end times, an invasion that God Almighty would deliver them from (chapters 38–39). We turn our attention to this invasion in this chapter.

Throughout this prophecy, Ezekiel is referred to as the "son of man." Why is Ezekiel identified in this way? I think Thomas Ice is correct in suggesting that the term "underscores his humanity in relation to God. In other words, God is the One who is the Revealer while Ezekiel, as a human, is the recipient of the Divine message that he is to pass on to other human beings. Thus, Ezekiel is passing on to us the infallible prophecy of these two chapters, which will surely come to pass."[1]

Ezekiel Prophesies an Invasion

In Ezekiel 38:1-16 we read details of Ezekiel's sobering prophecy of the future invasion into Israel by a powerful northern military coalition led by Russia. Though lengthy, let's set the context of our study by reading all the way through it. (If parts seem unclear to you, don't worry. I'll make all this clear throughout the rest of the chapter.)

> And the word of the LORD came to me saying, "Son of man,

set your face toward Gog of the land of Magog, the prince of Rosh, Meshech and Tubal, and prophesy against him and say, 'Thus says the Lord GOD, "Behold, I am against you, O Gog, prince of Rosh, Meshech and Tubal. I will turn you about and put hooks into your jaws, and I will bring you out, and all your army, horses and horsemen, all of them splendidly attired, a great company with buckler and shield, all of them wielding swords; Persia, Ethiopia and Put with them, all of them with shield and helmet; Gomer with all its troops; Beth-togarmah from the remote parts of the north with all its troops—many peoples with you.

" ' "Be prepared, and prepare yourself, you and all your companies that are assembled about you, and be a guard for them. After many days you will be summoned; in the latter years you will come into the land that is restored from the sword, whose inhabitants have been gathered from many nations to the mountains of Israel which had been a continual waste; but its people were brought out from the nations, and they are living securely, all of them. You will go up, you will come like a storm; you will be like a cloud covering the land, you and all your troops, and many peoples with you."

" 'Thus says the Lord GOD, "It will come about on that day, that thoughts will come into your mind and you will devise an evil plan, and you will say, 'I will go up against the land of unwalled villages. I will go against those who are at rest, that live securely, all of them living without walls and having no bars or gates, to capture spoil and to seize plunder, to turn your hand against the waste places which are now inhabited, and against the people who are gathered from the nations, who have acquired cattle and goods, who live at the center of the world.' Sheba and Dedan and the merchants of Tarshish with all its villages will say to you, 'Have you come to capture spoil? Have you assembled your company to seize plunder, to carry away silver and gold, to take away cattle and goods, to capture great spoil?' " '

> "Therefore prophesy, son of man, and say to Gog, 'Thus says the Lord GOD, "On that day when My people Israel are living securely, will you not know it? You will come from your place out of the remote parts of the north, you and many peoples with you, all of them riding on horses, a great assembly and a mighty army; and you will come up against My people Israel like a cloud to cover the land. It shall come about in the last days that I will bring you against My land, so that the nations may know Me when I am sanctified through you before their eyes, O Gog." ' "

In these verses, we read Ezekiel's words about the future invasion. In Ezekiel 39 (which I'll discuss in another chapter), we learn that even though this massive military force is too much for Israel to handle, God Almighty Himself will destroy the invading force. So at the outset, we see that one of Ezekiel's primary purposes in these chapters is to provide comfort to Israel. Ezekiel 37 speaks of Israel's regathering to the land from many nations (something happening in our day), and then in chapters 38 and 39 Ezekiel prophesies that even though there will be an invasion into their land, God will thwart this invasion. Israel can rest assured that their regathering into the land will be final and secure. This message was particularly meaningful to Ezekiel's audience because they had already suffered catastrophic invasion at the hands of the Babylonians. Ezekiel's words thus constitute a prophetic guarantee regarding Israel's future. This was good news for Israel.

An Overview of the Invasion

The big picture of this invasion looks like this: Russia will apparently lead Iran, Sudan, Turkey, Libya, Kazakhstan, Kyrgyzstan, Uzbekistan, Turkmenistan, Tajikistan, Armenia, and possibly northern Afghanistan, Algeria, and Tunisia in a massive invasion of Israel. Israel will seem like easy prey.

The invaders' goals will include to acquire more territory (Ezekiel

38:8), to amass increased wealth (38:12-13), and to destroy the people of Israel (38:16). We can easily understand why the Muslim nations would join in the destruction of Israel. (They are quite vocal in their hatred of Israel.)

God, however, has His steady eye on human affairs and utterly thwarts this invasion. He destroys the northern armies using a variety of means, including confusion among the armies so that they fire on each other, plagues, and physical disturbances such as floods, hail, and volcanic eruption (Ezekiel 38:18-22; 39:2-6). The disposal of the dead enemy bodies will take seven months (39:12), and clearing the debris and weaponry will take seven years (39:9-10). (I'll discuss alternative interpretations of the timing of this invasion—and its aftermath—in a later chapter.)

Details on the Invaders

I addressed this topic in chapter 7. Because we are now investigating the details of Ezekiel 38:1-16, we will briefly review our findings from that chapter.

- The word *Gog* refers to the powerful leader of the invading coalition. He is referred to as the "prince of Rosh, Meshech and Tubal" (Ezekiel 38:2).
- *Magog* refers to the southern portion of the former Soviet Union—probably including the former southern Soviet republics of Kazakhstan, Kyrgyzstan, Uzbekistan, Turkmenistan, Tajikistan, and possibly even northern parts of modern Afghanistan.
- *Rosh*—a much-debated term—likely refers to modern Russia, to the uttermost north of Israel.
- *Meshech* and *Tubal* refer to the territory to the south of the Black and Caspian seas, which is modern Turkey.
- *Persia* refers to modern Iran. Persia became Iran in 1935 and the Islamic Republic of Iran in 1979.

- *Ethiopia* refers to the geographical territory to the south of Egypt on the Nile River—what is today known as Sudan.
- *Put,* a land to the west of Egypt, is modern-day Libya. The term may also include the modern-day countries of Algeria and Tunisia.
- *Gomer* apparently refers to part of modern Turkey.
- *Beth-togarmah* also apparently refers to modern-day Turkey, though it may also include Azerbaijan and Armenia.

These are the countries that will make up the northern military coalition that will one day invade Israel.

Why Do They Invade?

One might naturally wonder why these nations would attack Israel in this way. Several reasons are possible:

1. God is in sovereign control of human history, and He Himself has decreed this invasion. God tells the invaders, "I will turn you about and put hooks into your jaws, and I will bring you out, and all your army" (Ezekiel 38:4). One Bible expositor notes that "Gog is portrayed as a huge animal, perhaps a crocodile, that will be controlled by hooks."[2] God also tells them, "I will turn you around and drag you along. I will bring you from the far north and send you against the mountains of Israel" (39:2 NIV). Clearly, this invasion is ultimately an outworking of the sovereign plan of God for Israel.

If God sovereignly decreed this invasion, are we to assume that these invaders have no personal responsibility in the matter? By no means! Scripture reveals that the invaders themselves "devise an evil plan" (Ezekiel 38:10). Indeed, the enemy will say, "I will go up against the land" of Israel (38:11). And for this, God judges and destroys the entire coalition. We may not fully understand the relationship between divine sovereignty and human freedom, but our passage is clear that both come into play in the Ezekiel invasion.

Thomas Ice suggests a possible "hook in the jaw" that God might use to cause Russia to move against Israel:

> I could see the Muslims coming to the Russians and telling them that America has set a precedent for an outside power coming into the Middle East to right a perceived wrong. (America has done it again in recent years by going into Afghanistan and Iraq.) On that basis, Russia should help out her Muslim friends by leading them in an overwhelming invasion of Israel in order to solve the Middle East conflict in favor of the Islamic nations. Will this be the "hook in the jaw" of Gog? Only time will tell. But something is up in the Middle East and Russia appears to have her fingerprints all over things. We know that the Bible predicts just such an alignment and invasion to take place "in the latter years."[3]

2. A religious motivation for the invasion—one that is especially important to the Islamic allies of Russia who bitterly hate Israel—is the utter and complete destruction of Israel. The massive invading coalition will come against "those who are at rest" in Israel (Ezekiel 38:11), "against the people who are gathered from the nations" and restored to Israel (38:12), "against My people Israel like a cloud to cover the land" (38:16). These armies will be motivated by a satanic hatred for the Jewish people. Muslims are unified in their desire to see Israel wiped off the map. (See chapter 2, "The Rise of Radical Islam.")

3. Russia and the other nations in the coalition may try to cash in on the tremendous wealth of Israel (see Ezekiel 38:11-12). Ezekiel states that the invaders want Israel's "silver and gold" and "cattle and goods" and "great spoil" (38:13). Arnold Fruchtenbaum suggests that these are general Old Testament references to the spoils of war.[4] This "great spoil" might actually take a number of very enticing forms. To begin, quite a number of wealthy people live in Israel—more than

6600 millionaires with total assets exceeding $24 billion.[5] Moreover, the mineral resources of the Dead Sea—including 45 billion tons of sodium, chlorine, sulfur, potassium, calcium, magnesium, and bromide—are worth virtually trillions of dollars.[6] Whoever controls the land of Israel can look forward to an incalculably large economic boost.

Gas and oil reserves have recently been discovered in Israel. The three to five trillion cubic feet of proven gas reserves beneath Israel's soil could be worth up to $6 billion. Moreover, an Israeli oil company has recently made the largest oil find in the history of the country. One news agency in Israel reports, "Israel may have struck gold—black gold, that is. A deposit close to a billion barrels may have been discovered at a site east of Kfar Saba, according to the fuel exploration company Givot Olam. The company announced...that latest estimates of the Meged-4 oil well have exceeded original predictions, and that it contains an extremely valuable deposit of oil...The value of the oil at today's prices is approximately $46 billion."[7] The gas and oil beneath Israel's soil are surely an enticement to Russia and her Muslim allies.

4. Another possible motivation for the invasion is that it may well give Russia greater control over the Middle East—economically, militarily, and politically.

5. Finally, this invasion will constitute a direct challenge to the authority of the Antichrist. Many pretribs believe Israel will be living in peace and security as a direct result of signing a peace pact with the head of the revived Roman Empire (the Antichrist—see Daniel 9:27). To attack Israel would constitute a brazen challenge against this world leader.

Ancient Weapons of Warfare and Transportation?

One of the highly debated aspects of this future invasion relates to the fact that the invading force is described as having "horses and horsemen, all of them splendidly attired, a great company with buckler and shield, all of them wielding swords" (Ezekiel 38:4) and "all of them with shield and helmet" (verse 5). This seems to be a description of ancient warfare. The question is, why are ancient weapons mentioned if this is a prophecy of a yet-future invasion into Israel?

We can understand this passage in two general ways. First, it is always possible (albeit strange) that this passage might be literally fulfilled, with armies riding horses and carrying swords. Second, Ezekiel may have used terms familiar to his own day in order to describe modern techno-warfare he could not have possibly understood. Let's consider both options.

A Literal Interpretation

It is always possible (though it would be strange) that this passage might be literally fulfilled, with armies riding horses and carrying swords. Do any conceivable scenarios make sense with this type of invasion? I'm initially inclined to say no, but a few scenarios are possible.

1. This largely Muslim invasion into Israel might purposely mimic the prophet Muhammad, who—as the "prophet of the sword"—led an invading force of more than 10,000 men on horseback into Mecca in order to overtake the holy city and bring it into submission. Allah in the Quran virtually commands the faithful to deal with infidels (Sura 2:216; 9:5; 47:4). So perhaps a Muslim invasion into Israel will seek to fulfill this injunction from Allah in the style and glory of Muhammad. This would be in keeping with the desire of Muslims worldwide to emulate the behavior of Muhammad (Sura 33:21), which is the primary reason for the existence of Muslim tradition—the *Hadith* (which contains massive records of Muhammad's behavior under various circumstances).

2. Perhaps a more likely scenario is that Israel—a nuclear power—becomes aware of an impending invasion from the Russians and Muslim nations through its intelligence agency—the Mossad, one of the best in the world. Israel might therefore detonate one or more nuclear weapons in the atmosphere of these countries, thereby causing an electromagnetic pulse (EMP) that completely fries all electronic

components in these countries including computers, phones, radios, all kinds of communication devices, transportation systems, guidance systems, radar, and the like. Recall that earlier in the book I provided concise details regarding the affects of an EMP attack.

If Israel should become aware of an impending invasion from multiple nations, might not Israel launch a preemptive EMP attack against these nations? And if the military hardware of these nations becomes disrupted (as American-made military hardware would be), a retaliatory attack might use non-electric transportation, such as horses. If nothing electronic works—and these various means of transportation will continue not to work for months and maybe even a year or more—then a military invasion on horseback suddenly becomes much more realistic.

3. Some interpreters have suggested that if ancient weapons are used in this invasion, perhaps some kind of disarmament treaty has previously been signed and enforced among the nations. Some claim that primitive weapons, such as those Ezekiel describes, would be easy to manufacture and use, thereby making possible a surprise attack.[8] (This option seems highly unlikely to me.)

4. Other interpreters suggest that the first three and a half years of the tribulation period may be so catastrophic, so destructive in certain parts of the world, that a reversion to ancient weaponry becomes a necessity. *The Bible Knowledge Commentary,* produced by the faculty of Dallas Theological Seminary, suggests that "with the other worldwide catastrophes evident during the first three and one-half years of Daniel's 70th Week (Matt. 24:6-8; Rev. 6), a reversion to more primitive methods of warfare might become possible."[9]

A Metaphorical Interpretation

Another interpretive option before us is that *swords* and *horses* are simply metaphorical terms Ezekiel uses to describe a modern invasion using transportation and weapons for which he had no words. Ezekiel may have been simply speaking in the language of his day to describe an otherwise indescribable invasion.

As John F. Walvoord put it, "The Bible describes the use of primitive weapons—horses and horsemen clothed in full armor. Some believe these were the best words available to the prophet to describe modern technological warfare depending largely on tanks and armor."[10]

Mark Hitchcock likewise suggests that "biblical prophets could easily be speaking of warfare in the distant future using descriptions of weaponry and tactics that would be familiar to them and their original audience."[11] He also says, "Ezekiel, inspired by the Holy Spirit, spoke in language that the people of that day could understand. If he had spoken of planes, missiles, tanks, and rifles, this text would have been nonsensical to everyone until the twentieth century."[12] Scholar Charles Feinberg thus asks, "*How else* could an ancient writer have described warfare? He knew nothing of planes and guns."[13]

Regardless of which approach is used in interpreting the transportation and weapons Ezekiel describes—literal or metaphorical—Russia *will* lead a northern military coalition against Israel in the end times. So large will the invading force be that it will seem utterly unstoppable.

A Lame Diplomatic Protest

When the northern military coalition invades Israel, a group of nations lodges a lame protest against the invasion. As we read in Ezekiel 38:13, "Sheba and Dedan and the merchants of Tarshish with all its villages will say to you, 'Have you come to capture spoil? Have you assembled your company to seize plunder, to carry away silver and gold, to take away cattle and goods, to capture great spoil?' "

Sheba and *Dedan* apparently refer to the geographical territory that today is Saudi Arabia. As Arnold Fruchtenbaum puts it, "Sheba and Dedan are countries in northern Arabia, which shows that at least some of the Arab states will not favor the Russian presence in the Middle East."[14] Tarshish is harder to locate—perhaps it is England, Spain, or all the nations of Western Europe. Whoever Tarshish is, it will join with Saudi Arabia in lodging a weak protest against this invasion into Israel. All words and no action!

No Hope for Israel

Israel will seem to have virtually no hope of surviving this massive invasion. She will be surrounded by hostile nations—Russia and Turkey to the north, Iran to the east, Libya to the west, and Sudan to the south. The end will appear to be very near. How can tiny Israel repel the combined forces of this massive, spread-out enemy? The answer is in the next chapter.

10

The Defeat of the Invading Forces (Ezekiel 38:17–39:8)

Israel will stand alone when the massive northern military coalition attacks. As we saw in the previous chapter, some nations—"Sheba, Dedan, the merchants of Tarshish" (apparently Saudi Arabia and some Western nations)—will diplomatically ask, "Have you come to plunder Israel?" But all they give is words with no action. Israel stands utterly alone.

The odds of Israel's survival, from a human perspective, will be nil. Israel will be vastly and overwhelmingly outnumbered. If this were a mere human battle, the outcome would be easy to predict. However, though Israel will appear weak and alone in the face of this Goliath intruder, God is strong!

Scripture portrays God as all-powerful (Jeremiah 32:17). He has the power to do all that He desires and wills. Some 56 times Scripture declares that God is almighty (for example, Revelation 19:6). God is abundant in strength (Psalm 147:5) and has incomparably great power (2 Chronicles 20:6; Ephesians 1:19-21). No one can hold back His hand (Daniel 4:35). No one can reverse Him (Isaiah 43:13), and no one can thwart Him (Isaiah 14:27). Nothing is impossible with Him (Matthew 19:26; Mark 10:27; Luke 1:37), and nothing is too difficult for Him (Genesis 18:14; Jeremiah 32:17,27). The Almighty reigns (Revelation 19:6).

Scripture reveals that this all-powerful God will utterly thwart the invasion of the northern military coalition. God is always watchful—"He who keeps Israel will neither slumber nor sleep" (Psalm 121:4)—and He will be Israel's defender. The invaders may think their success is guaranteed, but God sees all, and Israel's attackers stand no chance of success. God had earlier promised His people that "no weapon that is formed against you will prosper" (Isaiah 54:17). In the Old Testament, God often fulfills this promise by battling against Israel's enemies (see, for example, Exodus 15:3; Psalm 24:8). Scripture even describes God in military terms—the "Lord of Hosts" (2 Samuel 6:2,18).

Ezekiel 38:18-19 describes God's attitude with highly revealing words: *fury, anger, zeal,* and *wrath.* These words express the sheer and almost unrestrained intensity of God's display of vengeance against those who attack His people. These invaders will come face-to-face with the blazing wrath and jealousy of the Almighty.

The Defeat Described

Ezekiel 38:17–39:8 describes the defeat of the northern military coalition. As you read these verses, pay special attention to the words I have highlighted in bold:

> Thus says the Lord God, "Are you the one of whom I spoke in former days through My servants the prophets of Israel, who prophesied in those days for many years that I would bring you against them? It will come about on that day, when Gog comes against the land of Israel," declares the Lord God, "that **My fury will mount up in My anger. In My zeal and in My blazing wrath I declare that on that day there will surely be a great earthquake in the land of Israel**. The fish of the sea, the birds of the heavens, the beasts of the field, all the creeping things that creep on the earth, and all

the men who are on the face of the earth will shake at My presence; the mountains also will be thrown down, the steep pathways will collapse and every wall will fall to the ground. I will call for a sword against him on all My mountains," declares the Lord GOD. "**Every man's sword will be against his brother. With pestilence and with blood I will enter into judgment with him; and I will rain on him and on his troops, and on the many peoples who are with him, a torrential rain, with hailstones, fire and brimstone**. I will magnify Myself, sanctify Myself, and make Myself known in the sight of many nations; and they will know that I am the LORD.

"And you, son of man, prophesy against Gog and say, 'Thus says the Lord GOD, "Behold, I am against you, O Gog, prince of Rosh, Meshech and Tubal; and I will turn you around, drive you on, take you up from the remotest parts of the north and bring you against the mountains of Israel. **I will strike your bow from your left hand and dash down your arrows from your right hand. You will fall on the mountains of Israel, you and all your troops and the peoples who are with you; I will give you as food to every kind of predatory bird and beast of the field. You will fall on the open field; for it is I who have spoken," declares the Lord GOD. "And I will send fire upon Magog and those who inhabit the coastlands in safety**; and they will know that I am the LORD.

" ' "My holy name I will make known in the midst of My people Israel; and I will not let My holy name be profaned anymore. And the nations will know that I am the LORD, the Holy One in Israel. Behold, it is coming and it shall be done," declares the Lord GOD. "That is the day of which I have spoken." ' "

Is there any doubt in your mind, after reading these verses, that the God of the Bible is a God of judgment? Most people today seem to prefer to focus almost exclusively on the love of God. And certainly God is a God of love. But He is also a holy and righteous Judge! This has always been true of Him. J.I. Packer, in his modern classic *Knowing God,* forcefully reminds us of this sobering, oft-forgotten truth:

> The reality of divine judgment, as a fact, is set forth on page after page of Bible history. God judged Adam and Eve, expelling them from the Garden and pronouncing curses on their future earthly life (Gen. 3). God judged the corrupt world of Noah's day, sending a flood to destroy mankind (Gen. 6–8). God judged Sodom and Gomorrah, engulfing them in a volcanic catastrophe (Gen. 18–19). God judged Israel's Egyptian taskmasters, just as He foretold He would (see Gen. 15:14), unleashing against them the terrors of the ten plagues (Ex. 7–12). God judged those who worshipped the golden calf, using the Levites as His executioners (Ex. 32:26-35). God judged Nadab and Abihu for offering Him strange fire (Lev. 10:1ff.), as later He judged Korah, Dathan, and Abiram, who were swallowed up in an earth tremor. God judged Achan for sacrilegious thieving; he and his family were wiped out (Josh. 7). God judged Israel for unfaithfulness to Him after their entry into Canaan, causing them to fall under the dominion of other nations (Judg. 2:11ff., 3:5ff., 4:1ff.).[1]

I have often heard people express the idea that the Old Testament seems to characterize God as a judge, and the New Testament characterizes Him as loving. God is a God of love, but He continues to be a God of judgment even in the New Testament. Indeed, in the New Testament we find that judgment falls on the Jews for rejecting Jesus Christ (Matthew 21:43), on Ananias and Sapphira for lying to God (Acts 5), on Herod for his self-exalting pride (Acts 12:21), and on Christians in Corinth who were afflicted with serious illness and even death in response to their irreverence in connection with the Lord's Supper (1 Corinthians 11:29-32; see also 1 John 5:16). Christians will one day stand before the judgment seat of Christ (1 Corinthians 3:12-15;

15; 2 Corinthians 5:10). Unbelievers, by contrast, will be judged at the Great White Throne judgment (Revelation 20:11-15).

So let us be clear that God is a God of judgment, and He will sovereignly exercise judgment against the northern military coalition when it invades Israel. The judgment will be thorough, effective, and utterly lethal. The Islamic invading force will be annihilated.

God's Means of Destroying the Coalition

According to Ezekiel's prophecy, God will use four primary means to destroy this massive invading force. As a result of this fourfold judgment, lifeless enemy bodies will be scattered about as far as the eye can see.

A Massive Earthquake (Ezekiel 38:19-20)

Phase one of God's execution of enemy forces will involve a massive earthquake. Elsewhere, prophetic Scripture informs us that the tribulation period will see an increase in the number and the intensity of earthquakes (see Matthew 24:7). The devastating earthquake described by Ezekiel—in which "the mountains...will be thrown down, the steep pathways will collapse and every wall will fall to the ground"—will kill many troops, disrupt transportation, and throw the multinational forces into utter chaos. This earthquake will be so intense that all the creatures on the earth will feel its effect: "The fish of the sea, the birds of the heavens, the beasts of the field, all the creeping things that creep on the earth, and all the men who are on the face of the earth will shake at My presence" (Ezekiel 38:20).

Infighting Among the Invading Troops (Ezekiel 38:21)

In phase two of God's execution of enemy forces, He will sovereignly induce the armies of the invading nations to turn on each other and kill each other. They will suffer massive outbreaks of "friendly fire." This may be at least partially due to the confusion and chaos that results following the massive earthquake. As John F. Walvoord puts it,

"In the pandemonium, communication between the invading armies will break down and they will begin attacking each other. Every man's sword will be against his brother (Ezek. 38:21). Fear and panic will sweep through the forces so each army will shoot indiscriminately at the others."[2] The armies of the various nations will speak different languages, including Russian, Farsi, Arabic, and Turkic, so communication will be difficult at best, adding to the confusion.[3] The troops seemingly opt for the modus operandi "Shoot first, ask questions later."

Another possibility is that the Russians and Muslim nations may turn on each other. Perhaps in the midst of the chaos, they mutually suspect that the other is double-crossing them, and they respond by opening fire on each other. In any event, this will cause innumerable casualties.

The Outbreak of Disease (Ezekiel 38:22)

In phase three of God's execution of enemy forces, many troops will die due to the outbreak of disease. This is not hard to imagine. Following the earthquake, countless dead bodies will be lying around. Transportation will be disrupted, so transferring the wounded or bringing in supplies will be difficult if not impossible. Food and medicine will become scarce. Even more dead bodies will lie exposed after massive friendly fire breaks out. Meanwhile, a myriad of birds and other predatory animals will have a feast on this unburied flesh. All this is a recipe for a pandemic, which according to Ezekiel will take many, many lives.

To understand how disease could take so many lives, consider what scientists are now saying about the lethality of the avian (bird) flu should it become transmittable from human to human. That disease alone could claim multiple millions of lives (perhaps more than 100 million lives in a worst-case scenario). In any event, those among the northern invaders who survive God's judgments thus far will be utterly demoralized—and things are about to get even worse.

Torrential Rain, Hailstones, Fire, and Burning Sulfur (Ezekiel 38:22)

The fourth and final phase of God's execution of enemy forces will involve torrential rain (with heavy flooding), hailstones, fire, and burning sulfur pouring down on the invading troops. The powerful earthquake may set off volcanic deposits in the region, thrusting into the atmosphere a hail of molten rock and burning sulphur (volcanic ash) that then falls on the enemy troops, utterly destroying them. One only need recall the ultimate end of Sodom and Gomorrah to know how destructive all this will be on the northern coalition. By the time God's judgments are complete, virtually no one will be left standing.[4]

What a turn of events all this will be. The invading troops come with the intention of killing, but they themselves are killed. They believe their power to be overwhelming, but they end up being overwhelmed by the greater power of God. They come to take over a new land (Israel) but instead end up being buried in the land. The whole world will surely marvel at this turn of events!

Fire on Magog

As if all this weren't enough, God then promises, "I will rain down fire on Magog and on all your allies who live safely on the coasts" (Ezekiel 39:6 NLT). As we have seen, the term *Magog* seems to refer to the southern part of the former Soviet Union—perhaps including the former southern Soviet republics of Kazakhstan, Kyrgyzstan, Uzbekistan, Turkmenistan, Tajikistan, and possibly even northern parts of modern Afghanistan. This prophetic verse tells us that God will rain fire down on this area of the world, as well as on Magog's "allies who live safely on the coasts." These sobering words have led Joel Rosenberg to make this comment:

> This suggests that targets throughout Russia and the former Soviet Union, as well as Russia's allies, will be supernaturally struck on this day of judgment and partially or completely

> consumed. These could be limited to nuclear missile silos, military bases, radar installations, defense ministries, intelligence headquarters, and other government buildings of various kinds. But such targets could very well also include religious centers, such as mosques, madrassas, Islamic schools and universities, and other facilities that preach hatred against Jews and Christians and call for the destruction of Israel. Either way, we will have to expect extensive collateral damage, and many civilians will be at severe risk.[5]

This judgment will nullify any possible reprisal or future attempts at invasion. No further attack against Israel by these evil forces will be possible!

God's Purpose in Destroying the Coalition

God's primary purpose, as Israel's protector, will be to deliver Israel from harm. This is an outworking of the ancient covenant God made with His friend Abraham. In Genesis 12:3 God promised Abraham, "I will bless those who bless you, and the one who curses you I will curse." Surely the Muslims—those who comprise this vast Islamic invading force—curse Israel and seek Israel's destruction, and God curses the invaders with an annihilating judgment.

Beyond this, however, Scripture also reveals that God in this judgment will openly reveal His glory and power to a watching world:

- God affirms, "I will magnify Myself, sanctify Myself, and make Myself known in the sight of many nations; and they will know that I am the LORD" (Ezekiel 38:23).
- Of the invaders, God says, "They will know that I am the LORD" (Ezekiel 39:6).
- God then affirms, "The nations will know that I am the LORD, the Holy One in Israel" (Ezekiel 39:7).
- Of the Israelites God says, "Then they will know that I am the LORD their God" (Ezekiel 39:28).

In short, God's destruction of the northern military coalition will be a powerful testimony to His power, glory, and majesty. It will be a testament to the one true God, as opposed to the false god of Islam.

This reminds me of God's deliverance of the Israelites from the Egyptians—who worshipped numerous false gods that they considered more powerful than the gods of any other nation. The Egyptians were soon to learn a hard lesson as a result of ten powerful plagues.

Recall God's oft-repeated twofold purpose in inflicting the Egyptians with the ten plagues: to the Jews, "You shall know that I am the LORD your God, who brought you out from under the burdens of the Egyptians" (Exodus 6:7). And to the Egyptians, You "shall know that I am the LORD" (7:17); "...in order that you may know that I, the LORD am in the midst of the land" (8:22); "...so that you may know that there is no one like Me in all the earth" (9:14); "...that you may know that the earth is the LORD's" (9:29); and "...the Egyptians will know that I am the LORD" (14:4,18).

Obviously, the true God did not want anyone to misunderstand His purpose! He wanted to make utterly clear that He is the one and only true God in the universe. The same truth will be clear when the northern military coalition invades Israel. The one true God, whose name is Yahweh, will prevail over this predominantly Islamic invader, thereby proving the impotence of the false god Allah.

Try to imagine the scene. This massive invading force moves across the land like a cloud, and the Muslim invaders shout over and over again, *Allahu-Akbar!*—"Allah is the greatest!" Then, following Yahweh's mighty judgment against the invaders, no one will be found anywhere shouting *Allahu-Akbar.* What an awesome and glorious testimony this will be to the one true God.

Today's Islamic Threat Against Israel

At the time of this writing, Iran's president, Mahmoud Ahmadinejad, is making vitriolic threats that Israel will soon be a thing of the past. He has recently claimed that the world will soon know what it is like to live in an Israel-free and United States–free world. He is promising that Israel will soon be annihilated, "eliminated by one storm." This ominous threat is eye-opening considering that thousands of years ago, the prophet Ezekiel revealed history in advance by predicting that the future invaders will "come like a storm" and "will be like a cloud to cover the land" (Ezekiel 38:16).

As I have stated earlier, I do not believe in date setting (Acts 1:7). Nor do I believe in sensationalism (Mark 13:32-37). But I do believe Jesus calls us to be accurate observers of the times (Matthew 16:1-3; Luke 21:29-33). A studied consideration of the world scene today seems to indicate that things are shaping up for the eventual military invasion Ezekiel envisioned so long ago. One day, it will surely come to pass. God Himself assures everyone, "Behold, it is coming and it shall be done...That is the day of which I have spoken" (Ezekiel 39:8).

The Impending Shift in the Balance of Power

Several Bible prophecy scholars have noted—correctly in my view—that when God destroys this massive invading force, the resulting shift in the balance of power in the world may catapult the Antichrist into global supremacy.

> With Russia out of the way, the head of the revived Roman Empire, in control of the Mediterranean area at that time, will be able to proclaim himself as dictator of the whole world. There will be, accordingly, a fulfillment of the Scriptures which prophesy that the Roman government of that time will not only rule over all the territory of the ancient Roman Empire, but will extend its suzerainty to every people, land, kindred, and tongue (cf. Rev. 13:4-8). Chapters 38 and 39 of Ezekiel may well fit into the prophetic picture, and the defeat of Russia and its military force may be the occasion of the establishment of the world government by the world rulers pictured in Scripture.[6]

In the next chapter, we will examine the broader effects of this catastrophic defeat of the northern military coalition.

11

The Aftermath of the Invasion (Ezekiel 39:9-29)

Ezekiel writes sobering words about what takes place following the complete destruction of the northern military coalition. It is worse than any horror depicted in any Hollywood disaster film. With so much blood, so much rotting flesh, and so much gore, the clean-up effort will be the most repugnant activity imaginable. And yet, following this horror, we are also awed by the many who turn to God as a result of His mighty self-testimony in preserving Israel.

Ezekiel describes the aftermath of the northern invader's defeat in Ezekiel 39:9-29. As you read these verses, pay special attention to the words in bold:

> "Then those who inhabit the cities of Israel will go out and **make fires with the weapons and burn them**, both shields and bucklers, bows and arrows, war clubs and spears, and **for seven years they will make fires of them**. They will not take wood from the field or gather firewood from the forests, for **they will make fires with the weapons**; and **they will take the spoil of those who despoiled them and seize the plunder of those who plundered them**," declares the Lord GOD.
>
> "On that day I will give Gog a burial ground there in Israel,

the valley of those who pass by east of the sea, and it will block off those who would pass by. So **they will bury Gog there with all his horde**, and they will call it the valley of Hamon-gog. **For seven months the house of Israel will be burying them in order to cleanse the land.** Even all the people of the land will bury them; and it will be to their renown on the day that I glorify Myself," declares the Lord GOD. "They will set apart men who will constantly pass through the land, burying those who were passing through, even those left on the surface of the ground, in order to cleanse it. **At the end of seven months they will make a search. As those who pass through the land pass through and anyone sees a man's bone, then he will set up a marker by it until the buriers have buried it** in the valley of Hamon-gog. And even the name of the city will be Hamonah. So they will cleanse the land."

"As for you, son of man, thus says the Lord GOD, '**Speak to every kind of bird and to every beast of the field, "Assemble and come, gather from every side to My sacrifice which I am going to sacrifice for you, as a great sacrifice on the mountains of Israel, that you may eat flesh and drink blood. You will eat the flesh of mighty men and drink the blood of the princes of the earth, as though they were rams, lambs, goats and bulls**, all of them fatlings of Bashan. So **you will eat fat until you are glutted, and drink blood until you are drunk**, from My sacrifice which I have sacrificed for you. **You will be glutted at My table with horses and charioteers, with mighty men and all the men of war**," declares the Lord GOD.

"And I will set My glory among the nations; and all **the nations will see My judgment which I have executed** and My hand which I have laid on them. And **the house of Israel will know that I am the LORD their God** from that day onward. The nations will know that the house of Israel went into exile for their iniquity because they acted treacherously

> against Me, and I hid My face from them; so I gave them into the hand of their adversaries, and all of them fell by the sword. According to their uncleanness and according to their transgressions I dealt with them, and I hid My face from them."'"
>
> Therefore thus says the Lord GOD, "**Now I will restore the fortunes of Jacob and have mercy on the whole house of Israel**; and I will be jealous for My holy name. **They will forget their disgrace and all their treachery which they perpetrated against Me**, when they live securely on their own land with no one to make them afraid. When I bring them back from the peoples and gather them from the lands of their enemies, then I shall be sanctified through them in the sight of the many nations. **Then they will know that I am the LORD their God because I made them go into exile among the nations, and then gathered them again to their own land; and I will leave none of them there any longer. I will not hide My face from them any longer, for I will have poured out My Spirit on the house of Israel**," declares the Lord GOD.

In this chapter, we will look at four events that occur after God's destruction of the northern invaders: the gathering and burning of enemy weapons, the burial of enemy bodies, the flesh-and-blood feast of the animals, and the conversion of multitudes—both Jew and Gentile.

The Gathering and Burning of Enemy Weapons (Ezekiel 39:9-10)

Following God's destruction of the northern military coalition, the Israelites will gather and burn enemy weapons for a period of seven years.* That means a formidable arsenal will be collected! This ongoing task will save the Israelites from having to cut down forest

* How this seven-year period relates to the timing of the invasion—whether before, during, or following the tribulation period—will be covered in chapter 12.

trees for firewood for this extended time (Ezekiel 39:10). Firewood will become a precious commodity during the tribulation period, for after the first trumpet judgment, one-third of the trees of the earth will be burned up (Revelation 8:7).

Commentator William MacDonald suggests that the fact that the Israelites "will not need wood from the field or the forest with which to make campfires would seem to support the view that the abundant and abandoned weapons are indeed made of wood."[1] Perhaps these are indeed old-fashioned weapons. Recall that the first three and a half years of the tribulation period could be so catastrophically destructive that people will need to utilize whatever weaponry they can find, including weapons made of wood.

In any event, Ezekiel's prophecy also tells us that the Israelites will take as spoil what the invaders bring into the land when they come to despoil the Israelites. Israel will plunder those who intended to plunder her and loot those who intended to loot her. God, in His sovereignty, will turn the tables on the invaders.

Some scholars have raised the possibility that the burning of weapons may not be intended to be interpreted literally. They point out that in apocalyptic (prophetic) literature, numbers are often symbolic—and in Scripture, the number seven is often used to indicate completeness.

So, in regard to the burning of weapons, one scholar suggests, "If symbolic, the number [seven] would suggest the completeness and finality of the war. The point here is not that modern armored vehicles must be made of some combustible material. What is emphasized is God's utter destruction of Israel's enemies, despite their having soldiers and weapons so vast as to be humanly invincible."[2] Another scholar suggests that the seven years spent collecting weapons "implies the completeness of the cleansing" of the land from enemy weapons.[3]

The same symbolism might apply to the seven months involved in burying the dead. The *Keil and Delitzsch Commentary on the Old Testament* suggests, "The number seven in the seven years as well as in the seven months of burying (v. 11) is symbolical...[indicating] the completion of a divine judgment."[4] And again, "The number seven (vv. 9,14) signifies the completeness of the cleansing of the land from its enemies,"[5] both in terms of weapons and dead bodies.

Despite the number of scholars who see these references as symbolical, I tend to think that in Ezekiel 38–39, "seven months" is really seven months just as "seven years" is really seven years. Ezekiel's prophecy reads like he is providing the reader with history in advance, and in the process he provides many specific details. Some of these details relate to the timing of end-time events. As we have mentioned, when plain sense makes good sense, seek no other sense. For this reason, I personally do not take the references to the number seven as a metaphor for completion.

The Burial of Enemy Bodies for Seven Months (Ezekiel 39:11-12,14-16)

Normally, when many are slain in a major battle and the battle is over, the invaders bury their own dead. In the present case, however, all the invaders are dead. The task of burial therefore falls to the house of Israel.

The number of slain invaders will be staggering. The number of casualties will be so vast, so innumerable, that nothing but a deep valley would suffice for their corpses (Ezekiel 39:11). And Israel will take a full seven months to accomplish the task of burial in this valley.

From the perspective of the Jews, the dead must be buried because exposed corpses are a source of ritual contamination to the land (Numbers 19:11-22; Deuteronomy 21:1-9).[6] The land must therefore be completely cleansed and purged of all defilement. Neither the enemies nor their belongings (their weapons) can be left to pollute the land!

In the cleanup process, the occupation of interment will engage the entire nation, and all the while the Jewish people will be impressed with the awesome thought that they have been witnesses of God's judgment on His and their enemies. Gog's burial will become a memorable day, for the death of this massive enemy demonstrates God's faithfulness to protect His people forever. God's act of deliverance brings awesome glory to the name of the Lord. Israel will never doubt God's sovereign protection from that day forward (see Ezekiel 39:13).

Ezekiel tells us that following the seven-month period, a secondary burial crew will traverse the land as they engage in a "mopping up" operation, searching with precision for any bones that were missed. This is all part of the concerted effort to cleanse the land perfectly from all uncleanness arising from the bones of the dead. Searchers will place markers wherever bones are found, and gravediggers will follow up by taking the bones to the burial site—the Valley of Hamon Gog (Ezekiel 39:11). Interestingly, the term *Hamon* literally carries the idea of "multitude," so the name of this valley—the "valley of the multitude of Gog"—commemorates the overthrow of the multitudes of the foe. Bible expositor Thomas Constable suggests, "Probably the Esdraelon Valley is in view since it is east of the Mediterranean Sea and since many travelers normally passed and still pass through it."[7]

After the burial, however, no further travelers will be able to make their way through this valley (see Ezekiel 39:11). As Charles Feinberg put it, "The valley will be so clogged with the corpses of Gog's hosts that the way will be impassable for travelers."[8]

Some scholars suggest that the actual burial of bones in this valley will take place only after birds and animals have eaten the flesh off the bones. After all, the burying cannot be effected immediately or all at once. One prophecy expert explains it this way:

> In seeking to harmonize the need for proper burial under Jewish law (verses 12-16) with the devouring of the fallen soldiers by "every...bird and beast of the field" (verses 4,17-20), it may be that two phases of disposal are in view. The first phase of disposal is that performed by wild animals assembled to reduce the corpses to skeletons (verses 18-20). Then the bones of the enemy will be properly buried by "all of the people of the land" (verse 13).[9]

The Flesh-and-Blood Feast of Animals (Ezekiel 39:17-20)

The carnage of enemy bodies will provide a feast of flesh and blood for myriads of birds and animals (Ezekiel 39:17-20; see also Isaiah 34:6; 63:1-6; Jeremiah 46:10; Zephaniah 1:7-8; Revelation 19:17-21). How ironic that the northern invaders were acting as the predators in moving against Israel but are now being eaten by predatory animals.

God metaphorically speaks of these animals as guests at the table He has prepared where they shall enjoy an abundant meal. The menu will be flesh and blood. John F. Walvoord notes that "God will reverse the roles of animals and people. Usually people slaughtered and ate sacrificed animals. Here, however, the men of Gog's armies will be sacrifices; they will be eaten by animals."[10] Moreover, ordinarily the fat and blood—the holiest part of the sacrifice—were offered to the Lord (Leviticus 3:11-17), but here they are offered to beasts. These animals will not just dine well but will gorge themselves on this feast, so plentiful is the meal.

This is a sobering reality: God will judge and kill a huge number of people for their heinous attack against Israel. In the previous chapter I noted that God is not only a God of love but also a God of judgment. God is also absolutely sovereign over the timing of each person's death (Job 14:5; Psalm 31:15; 139:16; Luke 2:29; Acts 17:25-26). God is the One who creates life, and He maintains the right to take life when circumstances call for it. When people rebel against Him or defiantly go against His will (as will be the case with this northern military coalition), God as the divine Judge retains the right to end their lives.

The Conversion of Multitudes—Jew and Gentile (Ezekiel 39:21-29)

A number of verses in Ezekiel 38–39 portray God as giving a mighty testimony of His power and glory in His destruction of the northern invaders.

- "My holy name I will make known in the midst of My people Israel; and I will not let My holy name be profaned anymore. And the nations will know that I am the LORD, the Holy One in Israel" (Ezekiel 39:7).

- "I will magnify Myself, sanctify Myself, and make Myself known in the sight of many nations; and they will know that I am the LORD" (Ezekiel 38:23).
- "I will set My glory among the nations; and all the nations will see My judgment which I have executed and My hand which I have laid on them. And the house of Israel will know that I am the LORD their God from that day onward" (Ezekiel 39:21-22).

Clearly, then, God's destruction of the northern invaders will be a powerful testimony no one can ignore. The whole world will behold God's greatness (Ezekiel 38:22), His holiness (Ezekiel 38:23), and His glory (Ezekiel 39:13,21). And Israel will be utterly awed at God's intervention on her behalf. God's stunning defeat of Gog will force Israel to acknowledge His power and justice.

So both Israel and the nations learn a great lesson about God in all of this. In his book *The Prophecy of Ezekiel,* Charles Feinberg explains this:

> If the people of Israel could discern the working of God among the nations, then it is equally true that the nations of earth could learn the character and will of God from His relationship with His chosen people. In short, both segments of the human family are an object lesson for the other, displaying the infinite holiness and love of the universal God. The visitation of the Lord upon the rebellious nations will first have significance for Israel. Contrariwise, the nations will then realize that Israel suffered captivity and defeat not because of any inherent weakness in God, but because of their sinful ways which He punished in this manner. The withdrawal of God's favor from Israel, far from being a result of any caprice, was occasioned by their unrelieved opposition to the will of their God.[11]

The Expositor's Bible Commentary likewise tells us this:

> When Israel experiences God's marvelous faithfulness in restoration and protection against Gog, she would know without question from that day forward that the Lord was her God, the only true God, and there was none other (vv. 22, 25, 28). In turn the nations would know that the Lord had not been a weak God when he sent Israel into exile; rather they would observe that he cared enough to set his face against Israel because of her sin of unfaithfulness to him (vv. 23-24). Likewise, the nations would observe that it was God's grace and faithfulness that brought Israel back from among the nations, gave her her promised land, and enabled her to live safely on that land without fear of oppression.[12]

As a result of all this, many conversions will occur in that day. Despite the horrific catastrophe God causes against the northern invaders, God's mercy and grace will be more than evident as He draws many to Himself, bringing both Jews and Gentiles to salvation. Particularly in reference to the Jews, God says, "Then they will know that I am the LORD their God because I made them go into exile among the nations, and then gathered them [again] to their own land; and I will leave none of them there any longer. I will not hide My face from them any longer, for I will have poured out My Spirit on the house of Israel" (Ezekiel 39:28-29). Many who turn to God during this time may be among the vast group of the redeemed mentioned in Revelation 7:9-14.[13]

The conversions that take place as a result of God's destruction of the northern invaders will likely supplement the conversions that take place as a result of the ministry of the 144,000 Jewish evangelists who will witness all over the earth (Revelation 7:1-8). They will undoubtedly also supplement the many conversions that will occur as a result of the two witnesses of God mentioned in Revelation 11, who perform mighty miracles just as Moses and Elijah did. Clearly, many will turn to the Lord during the future tribulation period.

As I close this chapter, let us glory in the recognition that once all this comes to pass, never again will the Lord turn His face from Israel and allow another foreign nation to oppress it. Never again will Israel be terrorized (Ezekiel 39:26,29). God will cleanse Israel, remove its shame, and pour out His Spirit upon it. And God will fulfill all the promises He made to Israel in the covenants of the past. Finally, Israel will be completely and irrevocably secure in its land and in fellowship with God. As John Walvoord put it, "The ultimate result of the battle with Gog will be Israel's national repentance and spiritual restoration. This will be fulfilled in the millennial kingdom."[14] It is a day to look forward to.

12

The Timing of the Invasion: General Considerations

When will Russia lead the northern military coalition to invade Israel? Before the tribulation period? During or in the middle of the tribulation period? Toward the end of the tribulation period? After the tribulation period? During the millennial kingdom? This is one of the most controversial questions pertaining to Ezekiel 38–39. In this chapter and the next, we will briefly summarize some the positions and their strengths and weaknesses.

At the outset, remember that to be dogmatic and unbending on this issue is unwise. As one scholar put it, "The plethora of interpretations for this passage caution the student concerning dogmatism in his conclusions."[1] Many fine scholars have debated this issue back and forth through the centuries, and that fact alone calls for humility in the face of this interpretive difficulty. All of us should examine the issue and come to our own conclusions, but we should show grace to those who hold to different positions.

This brings to mind something John F. Walvoord once told me. We were talking about the timing of the rapture, and even though he was a thoroughly convinced pretribulationist (who believed the rapture will occur before the tribulation period), he commented, "Anyone who thinks his or her prophetic position has no problems simply hasn't studied prophecy very carefully." His point was that even our own position has problems (though, in our humble estimation, our position has fewer problems than the other positions).

Knowing that Dr. Walvoord had written one of the greatest defenses of the pretribulational rapture in print *(The Rapture Question),* I decided to ask him, "In the future, what if you discover that you are *in* the tribulation period, and the rapture hasn't happened yet? What will you do?"

He paused for a moment, and with a grin on his face he said: "I think I'll write a new book called *Rethinking the Rapture.*" A great man with a great sense of humor!

Even though much debate exists on the *specific* timing of the Ezekiel invasion, the *general* timing seems rather clear. More specifically, Scriptural clues embedded in the text of Ezekiel's prophecy unmistakably place the fulfillment of these events in the prophetic end times. These are among the important scriptural clues:

1. The invasion will take place in the "latter years" or "latter days," which can only be taken to mean the end times.
2. No invasion on the magnitude of Ezekiel 38–39 has ever taken place in Israel's history, so the invasion must yet be future.
3. A precondition for this invasion is that Israel must first be restored to the land (1948 was a pivotal year in this regard).
4. Israel must be living in security.
5. Certain national developments are to be expected in conjunction with this invasion.

Let's focus some brief attention on these scriptural clues.

The Invasion Takes Place in the "Latter Years" or "Last Days"

The prophet Ezekiel stated that the fulfillment of his prophecy about an invasion of a northern military coalition into Israel would take place in the "latter years." In Ezekiel 38:8 we read God's words to Gog, the leader of the northern coalition: "After many days you will be summoned; in the latter years you will come into the land that is restored from the sword, whose inhabitants have been gathered from many nations to the mountains of Israel." In Ezekiel 38:16 God likewise said to Gog, "You will come up against My people Israel like a cloud to cover the land. It shall come about in the last days that I will bring you against My land."

The question is, what do *latter years* and *last days* mean? In several New Testament passages, *last days, last times,* and *last time* refer to the present church age in which we now live. For example, the writer of Hebrews says, "God, after He spoke long ago to the fathers in the prophets in many portions and in many ways, in these last days has spoken to us in His Son" (Hebrews 1:1-2). We also see this in 1 Peter 1:20, where we are told that Christ, in the incarnation, "has appeared in these last times for the sake of you." Theologians believe such references refer to the current church age, which began in New Testament times. This means that we today are living in the last days, in the sense defined in these New Testament verses. The entire church age is a part of the last days.

However, a critical distinction exists between the way the New Testament uses the term *last days* in reference to the church and how the Old Testament uses the term in reference to Israel. I believe Thomas Ice is correct in his assessment that the Old Testament use of the term *last days* (and similar terms) refers to the time leading up to the coming of the Messiah to set up His millennial kingdom on earth.[2] Ice cites many verses, including Deuteronomy 4:30, where we read, "When you are in distress and all these things have come upon you, in the latter days, you will return to the LORD your God and listen to His voice." The English word *distress* comes from the Hebrew word for *tribulation.* Ice therefore believes this verse equates the future tribulation with the *latter days.* Following his study, Ice concludes that the Old Testament usage of such terms as " 'latter days,' 'last days,' 'latter years,' 'end of time,' and 'end of the age' all refer to a time when Israel is in her time of tribulation."[3] In keeping with this, theologian Charles Ryrie (of *The Ryrie Study Bible*) believes Deuteronomy 4:30 will find its ultimate fulfillment "in the final restoration of Israel at the second coming of Jesus Christ."[4]

Dallas Theological Seminary professor J. Dwight Pentecost, after a much broader examination of Scripture, affirms that the term *last days,* used of Old Testament Jews, "has specific reference to the latter years and days of God's dealing with the nation Israel, which, since it is before the millennial age (Ezek. 40), must place it during God's dealing with Israel in the seventieth week of Daniel's prophecy."[5] This seventieth week is the seven-year tribulation period.

Harold Hoehner likewise affirms that "the familiar expressions 'after many days,' 'in the latter days' (38:8), and 'in the last days' (38:16) refer to the time of the tribulation (Deut. 4:27-30; Dan. 2:28; 8:19, 23; 10:14) and/or the millennial restoration (Isa. 2:2-4; Mic. 4:1-7). The context must determine the setting. Here in Ezekiel 38–39 it must refer to the time of great tribulation for Israel."[6]

Scholar Ralph H. Alexander, in an article published in the *Journal of the Evangelical Theological Society,* confirms that in Ezekiel 38–39 the end times are certainly in view. He notes that "the phrase 'after many days' (*miyamim rabim*) in Ezekiel 38:8 characteristically has the indefinite sense, 'for a long time,' though is employed at times to reach as far as the *eschaton* (cf. Jer. 32:14; Hos. 3:4; Dan. 8:26)" (or end times). He notes that the phrase "after many days" is found in conjunction with Israel's restoration "in the latter years" (Hebrew: *beáaharit hassanim*), a chronological phrase employed only this once in the Old Testament. He then notes that "the expression 'in the last days' (*beáaharit hayyamim*), found in Ezekiel 38:16, places these events at the end time, for this phrase is most frequently employed to designate the time of Israel's final restoration to the land and the period of Messiah's rule (cf. Isa. 2:2; Jer. 23:20; 30:24; Hosea 3:5; Mic. 4:1; Dan. 10:14)."[7]

If these scholars are correct, and I believe they are, then the prophet Ezekiel was pointing to the distant future, the end times, the final phase of Israel's history in preparation for the establishment of the millennial kingdom, when God will finally and completely fulfill His covenant promises to Israel. More specifically, Ezekiel was pointing to the future time of Israel in the tribulation period, which precedes the millennial kingdom.

No Such Invasion Has Happened to Israel

No invasion on the magnitude of Ezekiel 38–39 has ever taken place in Israel's history. To be sure, Israel has encountered innumerable battles and invasions in her history. She has suffered numerous attacks and countless conflicts. But in no invasion has a massive alliance of nations in the territories of modern Russia, Iran, Turkey, Sudan, and Libya attacked Israel. Never has God utterly and horrifically destroyed an invading alliance with a massive earthquake, with fire and brimstone from heaven, with infighting among the troops, and with disease. And never has an invasion resulted in so many casualties that burying the dead required seven months.

> It is obvious from the details given to us in the chapters under consideration that no invasion experienced in Israel's history is sufficient to be the fulfillment of this prophecy. There have been invasions in the past which wrought hardship on the land and the people, but none that answer to the details presented here. This can refer only to some future event in Israel's experience.[8]

If the invasion hasn't happened yet, it will happen in the future. It didn't take place in Ezekiel's days, but it will take place in the last days.

Israel Must Be Restored to the Land

Before the northern coalition's invasion of Israel, Israel must first be restored to the land. Ezekiel 38:8 makes reference to the holy land "whose inhabitants have been gathered from many nations to the mountains of Israel." Ezekiel 36–37 specifically focus on the regathering of Israel to her land in the last days.

Why is this a precondition? Simply put, if Israel is not in the land, the land cannot be invaded. The late 1800s witnessed the beginning of Israel's restoration to the land as many Jews began to migrate to the area. However, 1948 was the pivotal year in which the modern nation of Israel was officially born. For the first time in 19 centuries, Israel was a nation again. With Israel now back in the land after a long and worldwide dispersion of Jews in many nations, a key piece of the puzzle is now in place, setting the stage for the northern military coalition's future invasion of Israel.

We might get even more specific. Ezekiel 39:2,4 indicates that Israel must be in possession of *the mountains* of Israel. Until the Six-Day War in 1967, the Jordanian Arabs were in possession of all the mountains of Israel except for a small corridor of west Jerusalem. Since this war, Israel has been in possession of these mountains.

Israel Must Be Living in Security and at Rest

Another precondition for the northern military invasion into Israel is that Israel must be living in security. Ezekiel makes this quite clear. Pay special attention to the words in bold in the following references in Ezekiel:

- "After many days you will be summoned; in the latter years you will come into the land that is restored from the sword, whose inhabitants have been gathered from many nations to the mountains of Israel which had been a continual waste; but its people were brought out from the nations, **and they are living securely, all of them**" (Ezekiel 38:8).

- "You will say, 'I will go up against the land of unwalled villages. I will go against **those who are at rest, that live securely, all of them living without walls and having no bars or gates'"** (Ezekiel 38:11).
- "Therefore prophesy, son of man, and say to Gog, 'Thus says the Lord GOD, "On that day when **My people Israel are living securely**, will you not know it?"'" (Ezekiel 38:14).

Ezekiel thus tells us that Israel must not only be regathered to the land but also be living in security. Both of these must be true before the invasion of the northern military coalition can take place.

Some Christians today believe Israel is already in a state of relative security. For example, Joel Rosenberg believes Israel's present level of security is based on a number of factors, including the fall of Saddam Hussein's regime, the death of Yasser Arafat, the withdrawal of the Syrians from Lebanon, and Israel's peace treaty with Egypt, peace treaty with Jordan, well-equipped army, first-rate air force, effective missile defense system, strong economy, and strong relationship with the United States.

> Note that the Hebrew prophet does not go so far as to say there will be a comprehensive peace treaty between Israel and all of her neighbors, or that all or even most hostilities in the Middle East will have ceased. But he does make it clear that in "the last days" (Ezekiel 38:16 NASB) before the Russian-Iranian attack, the Jewish people are "living securely" in "the land that is restored from the sword" (Ezekiel 38:8 NASB).[9]

Rosenberg thus feels that present conditions in Israel fulfill the spirit of Ezekiel's prophecy. Arnold Fruchtenbaum also holds this view.

> This is not a security due to a state of peace, but a security due to confidence in their own strength. This...is a good

> description of Israel today. The Israeli army has fought four major wars since its founding and won them swiftly each time. Today Israel is secure, confident that her army can repel any invasion from the Arab states. Hence, Israel is dwelling securely.[10]

Other Christians take a different view. Since Israel became a nation in 1948, she has had to stay on alert because of the danger she is in from all her Arab neighbors (and there are lots of them). Israel has never really been able to let her guard down. Consider today's headlines. Iran's president, Mahmoud Ahmadinejad, says the world will soon know what it is like to live in an Israel-free world. He has openly stated that he wants to push Israel into the sea, and other Muslim leaders around the world have expressed a similar sentiment. The constant conflict and tension in the Middle East have led one Western leader after another to try to broker a peace deal for the region. After all, stability in the Middle East and the Persian Gulf is a high priority for the entire world.

In view of this, many pretribs believe Israel will experience true security when the leader of a revived Roman Empire—a European superstate—signs a peace pact or covenant with Israel, an event that will officially begin the tribulation period (Daniel 9:27).* This leader—the Antichrist—will seemingly accomplish the impossible, solving the Middle East peace puzzle. And, indeed, if he is able to bring peace even among leaders like Mahmoud Ahmadinejad in Iran, who has vowed to destroy Israel, he will surely be hailed the greatest peacemaker ever. From the moment Israel signs the covenant and for the next three and a half years, Israel will enjoy a heightened sense of security, and this security will be backed by the military might of one of the most powerful personages in the world.[11]

Pretribs who hold to this view note that Ezekiel's prophecy tells us that Israel must not only be living in security but also be at rest (Ezekiel

---

* Israel will also experience security at the second coming when Christ destroys Israel's enemies and sets up His millennial kingdom—see Revelation 19:11–20:10. However, I don't think this is what Ezekiel was referring to. More on this later.

38:11). The Hebrew word here carries the idea of being undisturbed or quieted. Israel may presently have a certain sense of security due to her strong military, but she is not at rest in the sense Ezekiel describes. Interpreters suggest that this rest will come when the Antichrist signs the peace pact with Israel—a pact that guarantees protection.

Certain National Developments Will Occur

As a final precondition for the invasion of the northern military coalition into Israel, certain international developments will take place as this coalition emerges. More specifically, we can expect certain nations to rise to power, certain alliances to develop between nations, and the motivation to invade Israel to become clear.

Developments in Russia

Let's begin by considering Russia. At one time, the Soviet Union and the United States were the only two superpowers in the world. We have heard some overtures of democracy in Russia since the fall of the Soviet Union in 1991, but the winds of change are blowing across Russia today. With the rule of President Putin, a former high-level KGB member, things seem to be returning to their old totalitarian ways with a centralized government.* Most of Putin's government officials are also former high-level KGB members. In fact, one report reveals that 78 percent of Russia's government and business elite have a KGB background.[12] Our best information says these government officials would love to see Russia return to its former glory. An invasion into Israel would increase Russia's control of the Middle East.

1967. Russia has long been an expansionist country with designs on extending the power of its influence.[13] Historical records prove, for example, that during the 1967 Six-Day War, the Russians were poised to attack Israel and had been preparing to do so for a substantial time.

---

* It is not healthy for Russians to criticize Putin's centralized government. Indeed, journalists who print articles critical of Putin have a nasty habit of suddenly dying. So far, 130 journalists have been murdered in Russia since 1991, and almost without exception, the victims died because they printed something that challenged the local or national structures of power.

Soviet warships, submarines, bombers, and fighter jets were mobilized and ready for action. However, President Johnson's order for the U.S. Sixth Fleet to steam toward Israel as a show of solidarity with Israel stared down the Russian bear.

1973. In 1973, the Russians again showed military aggression toward Israel. Egypt, Syria, and some other Arab/Islamic countries initially launched an attack against Israel, but Russia was providing the military muscle behind the attack—including weaponry, ammunition, intelligence, and military training to assist this Arabic coalition to destroy Israel. While Russia provided help to the Arabs, the United States provided help to Israel. Things began to heat up between the Russians and the United States. Russian general secretary Leonid Brezhnev fired off a threatening communiqué, couched in diplomatic language, to President Richard Nixon. Both Soviet and U.S. forces were put on high alert. Nixon promptly responded to Brezhnev that his actions could lead to "incalculable consequences." This strongly worded communiqué, combined with the presence of U.S. military forces in the region, again served to stop the Russians.

1982. In 1982, then–Israeli prime minister Menachem Begin revealed that a secret but massive cache of Russian weaponry had been discovered in deep underground cellars in Lebanon, apparently positioned for use in a future Russian invasion into Israel and perhaps other Middle East nations. The cache included massive quantities of ammunition, armored vehicles, tanks, small arms, heavy weapons, communication devices, and other paraphernalia useful to military forces. Much of the equipment was highly sophisticated. Removal of the stash required virtually hundreds of trucks. Israel's leaders admitted they had no idea of such extensive plans for a future ground assault into Israel.

Russia's growing alliance with Iran. Meanwhile, since the 1990s, Russia and Iran have developed strong ties, largely military. This is extremely relevant, for no such alliance has existed in the history of these nations. Previous to recent history, the relationship between Russia and Iran has been full of hate. From 1946 to 1979, Iran—

led by the Shah—was an ally of the United States. Then the Shah was overthrown by radical Muslims. Later, following the Iran-Iraq war (1980–1988), Iran needed to rebuild its military after its years of fighting with Iraq, and Russia needed money from weapons sales. The rest is history.

Iran quickly became the third-largest recipient of Russian arms, now with an estimated annual trade of $500 million. In his book *Tehran Rising,* Ilan Berman tells us, "In late 2000, buoyed by its expanding ties with the Kremlin, the Iranian government announced plans for a massive, twenty-five year national military modernization program—one entailing upgrades to its air defense, naval warfare, land combat capabilities and built almost entirely around Russian technology and weaponry."[14] The modernization program includes the purchase of fighter aircraft for use by the Iranian air force and assistance in constructing military submarines, antiaircraft missile systems, radar stations, infantry fighting vehicles, naval landing craft, and patrol equipment.[15] Moreover, as we have seen, Russia has been assisting Iran in the development of its nuclear program.

Russian alliances with other nations. Russia seems likely to continue to seek political, military, and economic alliances with Muslim nations, even beyond Iran. About 20 million Russians are Muslims, and more than 7000 Muslim mosques are on Russian soil. Russia is presently building ties with other Muslim nations besides Iran, including Syria, Libya, and Turkey, all of whom would like to see Israel destroyed.

Russian military growth. Recent reports reveal that Russia is spending a phenomenal amount of money on a military buildup. An Associated Press report tells us that "a rising tide of oil revenues gave Russia a chance to increase its defense spending following a desperate money shortage that plagued the military throughout the 1990s." Russian leaders concede that "economic growth and the scientific achievements allow us to reach a qualitatively new level in military procurement." In terms of actual money spent, "Russia's defense budget which stood at 214 billion rubles ($8.1 billion) in 2001 nearly quadrupled to 821 billion ($31 billion) this year" (that is, 2007). As part of the military buildup plan, "the navy will get 31 new ships, including eight nuclear submarines carrying intercontinental ballistic missiles."[16]

Developments in Iran

Ezekiel includes Persia, which is modern-day Iran, in his list of nations in the coalition with Russia in the end-time invasion of Israel. Iran today is the mother of Islamic terrorism, and Iran's president, Mahmoud Ahmadinejad, is as anti-Israel as anyone. He is on a messianic mission to destroy the Jews. The Iranians certainly don't lack any motivation for an invasion into Israel.

Ties with former Soviet republics. Iran has been busy building alliances with other nations. One analyst suggests that Iranian officials are busy building strategic ties to former republics of the Soviet Union in order to create a regional coalition to counter Western influence. In other words, Iran is making alliances specifically in order to stand against the influence of the United States in the region.[17]

Certainly the military alliance between Iran and Russia is of great concern. As noted previously, Mahmoud Ahmadinejad has made deals with Russia to purchase military equipment over a 25-year period that will greatly increase the strength of Iran's military. Further, Russia has been assisting Iran in the development of its nuclear program. Today, Iran is making headlines on a daily basis because of the world's concern that Iran will soon have nuclear weapons.

A gas cartel? Iran and Russia may also be forming a gas cartel. "Iran and Russia can establish the structure for an organization of gas cooperation like OPEC as half of the world's gas reserves are in Russia and Iran," Iranian state television quoted supreme leader Ayatollah Ali Khamenei as saying.[18]

The idea is understandably worrisome to Westerners. "At 48 trillion cubic meters, Russia has the world's largest gas reserves, 27 percent of the world's total." This could easily became an anti-Western cartel, which would be extremely troublesome to the U.S. economy.[19] "A gas

OPEC is an interesting idea. We're going to think about it," Putin has affirmed.[20]

Ties with Syria. Iran has also increased cooperation with Syria, another rogue state. Though Syria is not specifically mentioned as one of the nations that participate in the northern military coalition in Ezekiel 38, Ezekiel 38:6 refers to "many peoples with you," which could certainly include such rogue states as Syria.

In recent years, Tehran has transferred both solid-fuel and liquid-fuel technologies to the Baathist state and is assisting it to establish an indigenous missile production plant. Government officials in Jerusalem now estimate that due to Iran's help, the Syrian regime of Bashar Assad has some 100 ballistic missiles that are equipped with the nerve agent VX, and these missiles are directly targeted at Israel. This has reportedly served as a counterbalance to Israel's nuclear advantage.[21]

Ties with Turkey. Iran, surprisingly, has also managed to forge some strategic ties with Turkey, traditionally a regional rival as well as a vital regional ally of the United States. Without going into all the details, Iran and Turkey have taken steps toward alignment in an array of regional security and strategic issues. In 2004, Turkish prime minister Recep Tayyip Erdogan traveled to Tehran for a meeting with the Iranian president—a meeting that yielded accords on economic, political, and security issues. These strategic ties to Turkey may, in the end, be one of many contributing factors to countering American influence in the region.

More recently, observers have noted that a fascistic takeover is under way in Turkey. This takeover is being orchestrated by the Islamist AK Party. Turkey appears to be transitioning from "a secular democracy with a Muslim society into a state governed by a radical Islamic ideology hostile to Western values and freedoms."[22] At the same time, Turkey's traditional secularist educational system is being replaced by madrassa-style "imam hatip" schools, where students are taught only the Koran and its interpretation according to the Islamists. Graduates of these educational institutions, which now begin training as early as age four, are indoctrinated to implement the program of the Islamist AK Party.

The Day Draweth Nigh

What all this means is that, ultimately, the northern military coalition prophesied by Ezekiel is slowly but surely coming together in our day—with alliances or strategic agreements forming between Russia, Iran, Turkey, Libya, Syria, various former Soviet republics, and others. This, combined with the fact that the other preconditions for this invasion (discussed earlier) are either met or could easily be met in the near future, indicates that the stage may indeed be being set for the Ezekiel invasion. As noted previously in the book, the situation in the Middle East could decompress, in which case the invasion could still be a long way off. But if things keep on their present course, we have good reason to suspect that "the day draweth nigh."

13

The Timing of the Invasion: Interpretive Options

When will Ezekiel's northern military coalition invade Israel? Let's briefly summarize the major options and note some of the arguments for and against each one.

Before the Rapture and the Tribulation

Some interpreters believe the invasion of the northern military coalition into Israel takes place before the tribulation *and* before the rapture. This is the scenario portrayed in the popular Left Behind series, by Tim LaHaye and Jerry Jenkins.[1] This view is also held by Joel Rosenberg, who wrote the popular novel *The Ezekiel Option* and the popular nonfiction book *Epicenter*.[2] Rosenberg concedes, however, that no one can be certain of this timing, for Ezekiel does not stipulate precise timing.

Many suggest that a pretribulation and prerapture scenario is feasible for several reasons:

1. This view coincides nicely with the seven-year tribulation period. In other words, the seven years of burying the dead (Ezekiel 39:9) correspond to the seven-year tribulation period. We know the tribulation period lasts seven years because it is the seventieth week of Daniel (see Daniel 9:27). This "week" is a week of years—seven years. And

it begins the moment the Antichrist signs a peace pact with Israel—a pact that is designed to last for "one week" (or seven years).[3] If the Gog invasion takes place prior to the rapture, the seven-year burning of weapons (Ezekiel 39:9) and the seven-year tribulation period parallel each other.

2. This view may best explain why Israel is able to build its new temple. If the Muslims were still in power in the early part of the tribulation period, they would prevent Israel from building its temple on the temple mount in Jerusalem. But if God destroys the Muslim armies prior to the beginning of the tribulation period, Israel would be free to rebuild the temple.[4]

3. Some pretribulationists suggest that this position must be correct because the other suggested scenarios seem unfeasible. David Cooper, for example, commented, "It is utterly impossible for one to locate the fulfillment of this prediction after the Millennial Age. It cannot be placed in the beginning of the Millennium, nor at the end of the tribulation. It must, therefore, be located before the tribulation because there is no other place for it to occur since the three other suggested dates are impossible."[5]

4. Some interpreters suggest that this view is consistent with God's heart for people coming to Christ as well as God's grace and mercy. We have seen that when God destroys the massive northern coalition, He will also give a convincing testimony to His power, majesty, and glory before a watching world. As a result, many Jews and Gentiles will be converted. If this invasion takes place prior to the rapture, many people may come to Christ and be taken out of the world in the rapture, thereby being spared the horrible events of the tribulation.[6]

Despite the arguments in favor of this position, it also has some significant problems:

1. The idea that the invasion takes place before the rapture seems to contradict Ezekiel's indication that the invasion takes place in the "last days" or "latter years" (Ezekiel 38:8,16). As we noted earlier, many pretribulationists believe these phrases, when used of Israel in the Old Testament, point to the tribulation. If this is so, it would

seem to preclude the possibility that the invasion will take place before the rapture and tribulation. Pretribulationist Arnold Fruchtenbaum, however, does not think this is a problem, for he believes "these terms simply apply to the whole period of the end times when prophecy is again being fulfilled, and so it can very easily apply to the closing days of the Church Age as well."[7]

2. Some pretribulationists believe the idea that the invasion takes place before the rapture contradicts Ezekiel's prophecy that the invasion would take place when Israel was living in security and at rest (Ezekiel 38:11). These interpreters believe that Israel will not have this strong sense of security and rest until the leader of the revived Roman Empire (the Antichrist) signs a peace pact, guaranteeing Israel's protection (Daniel 9:27). As John F. Walvoord puts it, "The scene is one of peace which has its best explanation with the seven-year covenant enacted by the ruler of the ten-nation confederacy."[8] Until then, Israel will remain as she presently is—always on alert because of the possibility of attack. At any time, a Muslim suicide bomber could walk into a pizza parlor in Israel and blow up everyone. Palestinian militants could try to sneak in and take sniper shots at Israel's citizens. Missiles could fly in overhead and blow up buildings in Israel. Many believe this will not stop until the peace pact is signed.

3. The New Testament teaches that the rapture is imminent. Nothing must be prophetically fulfilled before the rapture occurs, so we cannot say that this invasion *must* occur before the rapture. In fairness, however, those who believe the invasion may occur before the rapture "carefully avoid saying that it *must* occur before the rapture."[9] In other words, they hold to the doctrine of imminence.

4. Second Thessalonians 2:6-8 indicates that the Antichrist (the "lawless one") cannot emerge until He who restrains is taken out of the way. Many interpret this restrainer as being the Holy Spirit. They explain that the Holy Spirit (or restrainer) will be taken out of the way when the rapture of the church occurs, because the church is the temple of the Holy Spirit (1 Corinthians 3:16). We might summarize this way: (1) Israel will not have security until the Antichrist signs a

peace pact with Israel and the tribulation begins. (2) However, the Antichrist cannot emerge until after the rapture because that is when the restrainer—the Holy Spirit—will be removed. (3) So Israel will not be in security until after the rapture, and (4) the invasion by the northern military coalition cannot occur until after this time.

5. Some have suggested that if the seven years of burning weapons is parallel to the seven-year tribulation period, Israel cannot escape from Jerusalem in the middle of the tribulation. When the Antichrist sets up headquarters in Jerusalem in the middle of the tribulation, Jews will need to flee (Matthew 24:15-16). So the problem is this: How could the Jews continue the task of burning weapons if they had to take flight from Jerusalem in the middle of the tribulation? Arnold Fruchtenbaum avoids this problem by not making the seven years of burning weapons parallel to the seven-year tribulation period. Instead, he suggests that if the Ezekiel invasion takes place at least three and a half years prior to the beginning of the tribulation, Israel will finish burning the weapons by the midpoint of the tribulation period.

After the Rapture but Before the Tribulation

Another possibility is that the northern military coalition's invasion of Israel will take place after the rapture but before the tribulation. As Thomas Ice, an advocate of this position, puts it, "It will be during the interval of days, weeks, months, or years between the rapture and the start of the seven-year tribulation."[10] Several arguments support this view:

1. The world will be in a state of absolute chaos following the rapture. The United States has a heavy population of Christians, so the rapture will have a devastating effect on the United States. Russia and her Muslim allies may well seize the moment and launch a massive attack against Israel, which, up until this time, had been protected by the United States.

2. Once God destroys Russia and the Muslim invaders prior to the tribulation, the Antichrist would be free to rise as the leader of the revived Roman Empire—a European superstate. Thomas Ice writes,

"I have always thought that one of the strengths of this view is the way in which it could set the stage for the biblical scenario of the tribulation. If the tribulation is closely preceded by a failed regional invasion of Israel (by Russia and her Muslim allies), then this would remove much of the Russian and Muslim influence currently in the world today and allow a Euro-centric orientation to arise."[11]

3. If God destroys the Muslim invaders prior to the beginning of the tribulation, the Antichrist could more easily sign a peace pact with Israel (Daniel 9:27), guaranteeing that Israel will be protected. In other words, Israel will be easier to protect if the Muslim forces are already out of the picture.

4. This scenario, like the previous one, may account for Israel's ability to construct the Jewish temple on the temple mount in Jerusalem. With Muslim forces destroyed, Muslim resistance will be greatly minimized.

5. If the invasion takes place after the rapture, and the rapture takes place at least three and a half years prior to the beginning of the tribulation, Israel would have time to burn the weapons for seven years prior to the midpoint of the tribulation, when they take flight from Jerusalem. A significant lapse of time may therefore exist between the rapture and the beginning of the tribulation.

These are the common objections cited against this scenario:

1. Some believe the idea that the northern invasion precedes the tribulation period contradicts the fact that the invasion takes place in the "last days" or "latter years" (Ezekiel 38:8,16). As we saw earlier, some pretribulationists believe these phrases—when used of Israel—point to the tribulation. However, other interpreters, such as Arnold Fruchtenbaum, say that "last days" is a more general term for the end times and could include the time just previous to the tribulation.

2. Some pretribulationists believe the idea that the invasion takes place after the rapture but before the tribulation period contradicts Ezekiel's prophecy that the invasion will take place when Israel is living in security and at rest (Ezekiel 38:11). These believe Israel will not have this strong sense of security and rest until the leader of the

revived Roman Empire (the Antichrist) signs a peace pact, guaranteeing Israel's protection (Daniel 9:27). (The signing of this peace pact begins the tribulation period.) Other interpreters, such as Joel Rosenberg, believe Israel's security (and even peace) is rooted in the strength of her military as well as her peace agreements with certain nations, so Israel can enjoy this peace prior to the tribulation. Much debate exists on all this.

In the First Half or the Middle of the Tribulation

A third possibility is that the northern military coalition's invasion into Israel takes place sometime during the first half of the tribulation, even as late as the middle of the tribulation. This view is held by John F. Walvoord, J. Dwight Pentecost, Charles Ryrie, Herman Hoyt, Mark Hitchcock, and others. Here are some of the arguments in favor of this position:

1. This position easily satisfies the precondition of Israel being secure and at rest prior to the invasion. This state of security and rest will be based on Israel signing the peace pact with the leader of the revived Roman Empire (the Antichrist). Israel will essentially have a guarantee of protection from this world leader. During this time of security and rest, during the first half of the tribulation period, the northern military coalition will invade Israel.

2. When God destroys the northern coalition during the first half of the tribulation, the resulting power vacuum will allow for the quick ascendancy of the Antichrist. With no more Russian and Muslim military forces, the Antichrist will have a much easier time of attaining world domination (see Revelation 13). As John F. Walvoord puts it, "When the invading armies are defeated, the ruler of the ten nations will elevate himself and proclaim himself ruler of the entire world."[12]

3. The destruction of Muslim forces in the first half of the tribulation will also allow for the emergence of a one-world religion. Christians will have already been raptured. Now the Muslim forces will have been destroyed. The emergence of a one-world religion will be much easier in this religious vacuum.

As do the other scenarios, this view has some weaknesses:

1. Any view that has this invasion taking place within the tribulation, especially near the middle of the tribulation, has a hard time explaining how Israel will bury bodies for seven months and burn weapons for seven years. The mid-trib view, in particular...

> would require that the seven months of burying take place during the second half of the Tribulation, a time when the Jews are in flight and are not able to bury their own dead, let alone those of the Russians...Regarding the seven years of burning, this view would require the Jews to be burning weapons during the second half of the Tribulation, when Jews are fleeing out of the Land. They would also have to continue burning them for 3½ years into the Millennium, which is inconsistent with Messiah's cleansing of the Land and the renovation which results.[13]

One proponent of this view suggests that if the invasion takes place at least a year prior to the midpoint of the tribulation, at least the bodies will be buried before the Antichrist takes over Jerusalem. In this scenario, the burning of the weapons would extend beyond the end of the tribulation by a few years and into the millennial kingdom.[14]

2. Closely related to the above, some claim that those who hold to this view may not properly appreciate the level of persecution of the Jews in the second half of the tribulation. Bible expositor Thomas Constable, for example, says that it seems "unlikely that the Jews could bury corpses for seven months and burn weapons as fuel for seven years following an invasion in the middle of the seven-year Tribulation. The last half of the Tribulation will involve unparalleled persecution for the Jews (Dan. 9:27)."[15]

3. Arnold Fruchtenbaum asks why God would intervene on Israel's behalf by destroying the northern intruder near the middle of the tribulation, only to then allow events in the second half of the tribulation that do great damage to Israel.[16] Fruchtenbaum places the invasion some years prior to the tribulation.

4. Professor Harold Hoehner suggests that to cleanse the land at the midpoint of the tribulation by burying the dead (Ezekiel 39:11-16) at the same time as the abomination of desolation (Matthew 24:15)—the ultimate desecration of the Jewish temple, which occurs in the middle of the tribulation when the Antichrist puts a statue of himself in the temple—is highly improbable.[17]

At the End of the Tribulation (Armageddon)

In yet another view, the northern military coalition's invasion takes place at the end of the tribulation and is to be equated with Armageddon. The word *Armageddon* literally means "Mount of Megiddo" and refers to a location about 60 miles north of Jerusalem. This is the location of Barak's battle with the Canaanites (Judges 4) and Gideon's battle with the Midianites (Judges 7). This will be the site for the final horrific battles of humankind just prior to the second coming (Revelation 16:16). Some interpreters equate Armageddon with the Ezekiel invasion for several reasons:

1. Armageddon takes place during the tribulation, and Ezekiel's invasion is in the "last days" and "latter years"—terms which some believe indicate the tribulation—so these events must be the same.

2. Birds and predatory animals will feast on dead bodies following God's destruction of the northern coalition (Ezekiel 39:4,17-20) and following Armageddon (Revelation 19:17-18), so the northern invasion and Armageddon must be one and the same.

3. Zechariah 12:10 tells us that many Jews will turn to the Lord at the end of the tribulation (following Armageddon). And in Ezekiel 39:22 God affirms that after He defeats the northern coalition "the house of Israel will know that I am the LORD their God from that day onward." In Ezekiel 39:29 He says, "I will have poured out My Spirit on the house of Israel." The time of salvation in both instances seems to line up.

Despite such arguments, this view also has a number of problems:

1. Armageddon involves all the nations of the earth (Joel 3:2; Zephaniah 3:8; Zechariah 12:3; 14:2), whereas the northern military

coalition is made up of specific nations such as Russia, Iran, Sudan, Turkey, Libya, and some other Muslim nations (see Ezekiel 38:1-6).

2. The locations are different. In Armageddon the destruction takes place at the Mount of Megiddo, about 60 miles north of Jerusalem, whereas the destruction depicted by Ezekiel takes place on the mountains of Israel.

3. The casualties of the wicked at Armageddon result from the personal appearance of Jesus Christ at the second coming (Revelation 19:15), whereas the casualties of the northern military coalition result from a great earthquake, infighting among the troops, the outbreak of disease, torrential rain, and fire and brimstone falling upon the troops (Ezekiel 38:20-22).

4. The Jews at the end of the tribulation (when Armageddon will occur) will not be living in security and at rest, for they will be enduring great persecution at the hands of the Antichrist. By contrast, the Jews during the first half of the tribulation will be living in relative security and rest, which is when many believe Ezekiel's invasion takes place.[18]

5. In the Ezekiel invasion, some nations protest the invasion (Ezekiel 38:13), whereas no one protests the campaign of Armageddon because all the nations are involved.

6. If Ezekiel's invasion is equated with Armageddon, this means that following this time, Israel will bury bodies for seven months and burn weapons for seven years, well into the millennial kingdom. Some interpreters do not see a problem here because they see this as compatible with other prophetic statements, such as beating swords into plowshares and spears into pruning hooks at the beginning of the millennium (Isaiah 2:4; Micah 4:3).

7. At Armageddon the Beast is the head of the invasion campaign (Revelation 19:19), whereas Gog is the head of the invading force in Ezekiel's prophecy (Ezekiel 38:7).

8. The armies gathered at Armageddon array themselves against Jesus Christ (Revelation 19:19), which is not true of Ezekiel's northern military coalition.

Between the Tribulation and the Millennium

A few interpreters place the invasion by the northern military coalition between the end of the tribulation and the beginning of the millennial kingdom. They say Ezekiel 38–39 is fulfilled during an interlude.

In support of this position, some claim that if an interlude could exist between the rapture and the beginning of the tribulation, to be consistent, an interlude could exist between the end of the tribulation and the beginning of the millennial kingdom. An interlude of sufficient time would allow for the burial of dead bodies over a seven-month period.

These interpreters also suggest that Israel will truly be living in security and rest following the second coming, so the invasion must take place at this point.

The big problem with this view is not that an interlude of *some* length exists between the end of the tribulation and the beginning of the millennial kingdom, but that the interlude will be long enough to accommodate all the details of Ezekiel 38–39. All expositors acknowledge an interlude of at least some length so Christ can (among other things) judge the nations (Matthew 25:31-46). However, the interlude would need to be at least seven years long in order to satisfy all the details of Ezekiel 38–39. Scripture gives no evidence of such a lengthy interlude.

Of course, one could argue that the interlude is shorter and that the burial of bodies for seven months and burning of weapons for seven years continue into the millennial kingdom. Such a view, however, is less than satisfactory. Many expositors believe Daniel 12:12 limits the interlude to just 75 days.[19]

At the Beginning of the Millennium

Arno Gaebelein and others say the invasion by the northern military coalition takes place at the beginning of the millennial kingdom. The primary argument in favor of this viewpoint is that Israel will certainly be at peace and at rest in Christ's millennial kingdom. There are, however, a number of problems with this view:

1. Isaiah 2:4 excludes the possibility of war in Christ's millennial kingdom. The only war that breaks out is at the end of the millennium when Satan is loosed (Revelation 20:7-9).

2. An invasion into Israel early in the millennium would be virtually impossible because after the second coming of Christ, God will judge the nations and execute the unbelievers (Matthew 25:31-46). Jeremiah 25:32-33 flatly affirms that the Lord will destroy all the wicked of the earth at His return. This is echoed in Revelation 19:15-18. Only believers enter into Christ's millennial kingdom. And believers would never launch an invasion from the north into Israel![20]

3. Ezekiel 39:12 tells us that the land will be defiled for seven months until all the dead bodies are buried. It is difficult to believe the land will be defiled for seven months during the inaugural period of Christ's millennial kingdom.

4. Isaiah 9:4-5 tells us that all weapons of war will be destroyed following the beginning of Christ's millennial kingdom, so the northern military coalition would have no weapons.[21]

5. Many today view the Muslim hatred of the Jewish people to be satanically inspired. But God will bind Satan during the millennium (Revelation 20:1-3). Therefore, Satan could not stir up hatred against Jewish believers during the early part of the millennium.

6. No nation would try to launch an attack against Israel when Christ is ruling in His kingdom. Such would be the height of madness.

At the End of the Millennium

Still other interpreters believe the Ezekiel invasion takes place at the end of the millennial kingdom. This view has been predominant among non-evangelicals.[22] These are among the arguments for this view:

1. Revelation 20:7-10 tells us that...

> when the thousand years are completed, Satan will be released from his prison, and will come out to deceive the nations which are in the four corners of the earth, Gog and Magog, to gather them together for the war; the number of them is like the sand of the seashore. And they came up on the broad plain of the earth and surrounded the camp of the saints and the beloved city, and fire came down from heaven and devoured them. And the devil who deceived them was thrown into the lake of fire and brimstone, where the beast and the false prophet are also; and they will be tormented day and night forever and ever.

Revelation 20:7-10 refers to Gog and Magog, so this must be the same invasion as described in Ezekiel 38–39. Therefore, the Gog and Magog invasion takes place at the end of the millennial kingdom.

2. Both cases include a large number of soldiers. In the Ezekiel invasion, we read of "a great company" (Ezekiel 38:4), "many peoples with you" (38:6), and "a great assembly" (38:15). Likewise, the invasion force mentioned in Revelation is massive: "The number of them is like the sand of the seashore" (Revelation 20:8).[23]

3. This view best explains the tremendous prosperity of Israel when this invasion occurs (Ezekiel 38:12). This prosperity is in fulfillment of God's promise of millennial blessings on Israel.

4. In both cases, God Himself defeats the invaders (Ezekiel 39:3-6; Revelation 20:9).

Of course, as expected, many have cited problems with this interpretation.

1. The chronology is all wrong. The invasion of Ezekiel 38–39 is part of a larger section of Ezekiel's book that deals with the restoration of Israel (chapters 33–39). This is followed by another large section of Ezekiel's book that describes the Jewish millennial temple and the restoration of sacrifices (chapters 40–48). In other words, Ezekiel's invasion is before the millennial kingdom. By contrast, the invasion described in Revelation 20:7-10 takes place at the end of the millennial kingdom, and so the invasions are separated by a thousand years.

2. In keeping with the above, the invasion in Ezekiel is immediately followed by the millennial kingdom (Ezekiel 40–48), whereas the invasion prophesied in Revelation 20:7-10 is immediately followed by the eternal state (Revelation 21).[24]

3. The seven months required to bury dead bodies doesn't make sense at the end of the millennial kingdom. The Israelites would spend seven hard months burying the dead who invaded them, and immediately following this, according to the book of Revelation, these same wicked dead are resurrected in order to take part in the Great White Throne judgment and be thrown into the lake of fire. This doesn't make sense. Besides, Revelation 20:9 (NKJV) tells us that "fire came down from God out of heaven and devoured them." There won't be any bodies left to bury since they'll all be incinerated.

4. The next event in the book of Revelation after the Great White Throne judgment is the beginning of the eternal state (Revelation 21). This naturally brings up the problem of the burning of the weapons for seven years. If this invasion takes place at the end of the millennial kingdom, the burning of weapons would have to go beyond the millennial kingdom and into the eternal state, which doesn't make any sense at all. In fairness, some proponents of this view, such as J. Paul Tanner, suggest that perhaps an interlude exists between the end of the millennium and the beginning of the eternal state. How long would the interlude be? "In all honesty we do not know how much time there may be, but there is nothing in the text that would preclude a period of seven years in which the weapons of war could be burned."[25]

5. In the Ezekiel invasion, a coalition of localized nations (Russia and a number of Muslim nations) invade from the north. In the invasion at the end of the millennium, an international army—"the nations which are in the four quarters of the earth"—participates in this battle (Revelation 20:8 KJV).

6. The invasion mentioned in Revelation 20:9 is "up on the broad plain" and against "the camp of the saints." By contrast, the invasion prophesied by Ezekiel takes place on the mountains of Israel (Ezekiel 39:2; 38:16).

7. The invasion prophesied by Ezekiel occurs relatively soon after Israel's rebirth and the ingathering of Jewish people from around the world (Ezekiel 36–37). The invasion mentioned in Revelation 20:7-10, by contrast, occurs after Jesus has been reigning on earth for a thousand years.[26]

8. Scholar Charlie Dyer notes that "in Ezekiel the battle is the catalyst God will use to draw Israel to Himself (cf. Ezek. 39:7, 22-29) and to end her captivity. But the battle in Revelation 20 will occur after Israel has been faithful to her God and has enjoyed His blessings for 1,000 years."[27]

9. The apostle John was likely using the terms *Gog* and *Magog* as a shorthand metaphor. His readers no doubt immediately drew the right connection and understood that this invasion at the end of the millennium would be similar to what Ezekiel described in that a confederation of nations will attack Israel but not succeed.[28] In other words, this was to be a Gog-Magog-like invasion.

10. In his book *The Millennial Kingdom,* John F. Walvoord helps us to understand what is really going on in the Gog-Magog battle at the end of the millennial kingdom. Citing Revelation 20:7-9, he notes that at the end of the millennium, Satan will be loosed to deceive the nations as he has always done throughout human history. "Those who will be deceived evidently are those who will be born in the millennial kingdom whose parents previously entered the millennium [as Christians] in their natural bodies. Some of the children born no doubt will become true children of God, whereas others will merely profess to follow Christ under the compulsion of the absolute reign of the Lord."[29] Under Satan's prompting, some of these "professors" will align themselves against the Lord and the earthly city of Jerusalem. In this connection, Satan goes out to "deceive the nations which are in the four quarters of the earth, Gog and Magog, to gather them together to battle" (Revelation 20:8 KJV).

My Assessment

I close this chapter by reemphasizing that we should not be

dogmatic and unbending on the issue of the precise timing of the Ezekiel invasion. Many fine scholars have debated this issue through the centuries, and that fact alone is enough to cause one to be humble in the face of this interpretive difficulty. Yes, we should examine the issue and come to our own conclusion. But we should show grace to those who hold to a different position.

Having said that, allow me now to give my personal assessment of the matter:

I respectfully reject both millennial views. That is, I reject the view that the invasion takes place at the beginning of the millennium and I reject the view that the invasion takes place at the end of the millennium. The problems with these positions are, in my view, far too substantial for them to be viable options.

I respectfully reject the idea that the invasion will take place during an interlude between the end of the tribulation and the beginning of the millennium. I see virtually no evidence for such a view.

I respectfully reject the views that the invasion takes place at the midpoint of the tribulation or at the end of the tribulation. To me, these views are more difficult to fit into what the larger corpus of Bible prophecy reveals about the tribulation period.

The two positions that I think stand the greatest chance of being correct are that the invasion takes place prior to the tribulation and that the invasion takes place in the early part of the tribulation. If the invasion takes place prior to the tribulation, it would make good sense to place it at least three and a half years prior to the tribulation. This view solves one of the primary dilemmas—the burning of the weapons for seven years prior to Israel taking flight from Jerusalem in the middle of the tribulation, after which the Jews will be the targets of severe persecution by the Antichrist.

I also resonate with the possibility that the invasion takes place after the rapture but before the tribulation (though Scripture really does not reveal how long an interval this might be). Though this view has a few problems, overall it fits very well with other elements of Bible prophecy.

One possible weakness of this position is that it may not deal as effectively with the precondition of Israel being secure and at rest when the invasion takes place. In this scenario, Israel has not yet signed the peace pact with the leader of the revived Roman Empire—the Antichrist. However, Rosenberg may be correct in saying that Israel's security may be based on factors that are already in place (prior to the tribulation), including the fall of Saddam Hussein's regime, the death of Yasser Arafat, the withdrawal of the Syrians from Lebanon, and Israel's peace treaty with Egypt, peace treaty with Jordan, well-equipped army, first-rate air force, effective missile-defense system, and strong economy.

If the invasion takes place in the early part of the tribulation, Israel would obviously be secure and at rest—she would have signed a peace pact with the leader of a revived Roman Empire (the Antichrist).

The big weakness of this position pertains to how Israel will be able to continue to burn weapons at the midpoint of the tribulation (and beyond) when the Jews take flight from Jerusalem and suffer severe persecution under the Antichrist. Will the Jews take some of these burnable weapons with them when they flee Jerusalem? (Firewood will be a precious commodity during those years because one-third of the trees will be destroyed at the first trumpet judgment [Revelation 8:7.] The Jews will need burnable items to survive.) Will the Jews plan ahead and stash these burnable weapons in secret hidden bins that they can access by stealth throughout the rest of the tribulation period, unbeknownst to the forces of the Antichrist? Will some kind of Jewish underground distribute these weapons as well as food and survival supplies throughout the tribulation? As long as some Jews (perhaps even a minority) continue to burn the remaining weapons throughout the second half of the tribulation, the prophecy of Ezekiel 39:9 would be fulfilled. My point is that I don't think this problem necessarily deals a deathblow to the idea that the Ezekiel invasion could occur early in the tribulation.

All things considered, my first preference is for the idea that the invasion follows the rapture but precedes the tribulation period by at least three and a half years. But I'm open to the possibility of it occurring early in the tribulation. It's just a bit harder to fit there.

Some problems remain with such views, but I think these scenarios have the fewest substantial problems of all those I've discussed. And these are easiest to fit within the broader scope of what Bible prophecy reveals about the end times.

Whichever view is correct, I urge all my readers to *pray for the peace of Jerusalem.*

14

How Then Should We Live?

Polls indicate that Americans are steadily becoming more interested in biblical prophecy.

- In 1999, 40 percent of all Americans—including 71 percent of evangelical Protestants—said they believed the world would end just as the Bible predicts.
- In 2002, 59 percent of Americans said they believed the prophecies in the book of Revelation would come true.
- Since the terrorist attacks on September 11, 2001, 35 percent of Americans have said they are now paying closer attention to the news and to specific events that might relate to the end of the world.[1]
- According to a 2006 poll, 42 percent of Americans said they agreed that Israel's rebirth as a nation, the instability of the Middle East, and other such events are indications that we are living in what the Bible calls "the last days." Moreover, 52 percent of Americans agreed that the rebirth of Israel as a nation in 1948 and the return of millions of Jews to the Holy Land is a direct fulfillment of biblical prophecies.[2]

What is your opinion? Does a studied examination of biblical prophecies alongside a thorough and rational survey of the world scene today indicate we may be living in the last days? Personally, I believe we have good reason to suspect this.

Some current events certainly seem to be setting the stage for the eventual fulfillment of Ezekiel's prophecy of a northern military coalition invading Israel.

- The Jews have been regathered to their homeland in a state of unbelief (Ezekiel 36–37). At present, more Jews live in Israel than anywhere else in the world.
- The nations mentioned in Ezekiel 38 as part of this military coalition are identifiable (for example, Russia, Iran, Turkey, Sudan, and Libya), have a strong motive to attack Israel (most are Muslim nations who would love to see Israel annihilated), and even now have developed significant alliances among themselves (Iran, for example, has a strong weapons agreement with Russia).
- Russia seems to be returning to her totalitarian ways and is apparently seeking increased influence in the Middle East. With its well-documented past aggressions against Israel in 1967, 1973, and 1982, we have every reason to believe the Russian bear will once again rise to move against Israel.
- Mahmoud Ahmadinejad, the president of Iran, is on a messianic mission to invoke the coming of the Twelfth Imam (Islamic ruler) through various means, including conflict and hostility toward Israel. Ahmadinejad assures his followers that the Twelfth Imam may appear within the next two years.
- Israel's enemies know that Israel is not only a strategic land to conquer but also a land of wealth, with vast gas and oil reserves beneath its soil. With the oil/energy crisis that will inevitably occur in the not-too-distant future, Israel's oil will increasingly become an enticement to enemy nations.

- In Matthew 24 and Luke 21, Jesus said the last days would be characterized by the rise of false prophets and false messiahs, wars and rumors of wars, revolutions, famines, earthquakes, persecution of believers, and the worldwide spread of the gospel.

Everything seems to be lining up—indeed, converging—for the eventual fulfillment of Ezekiel 38–39. As one prophetic scholar put it, "Never before in the history of the world has there been a confluence of major evidences of preparation for the end."[3] Another prophecy expert writes, "Today, for the first time in two thousand years, we are seeing all of these signs come true, and the rebirth of Israel is the most dramatic sign of them all. We can, therefore, have confidence that Jesus' return is closer than ever."[4]

How Then Should We Live?

We have focused detailed attention on Ezekiel's prophecy of an impending northern military coalition invading Israel in the end times. Now we should ask ourselves, how then shall we live? Should we change the way we live our lives? Should we be worried about the future? Should we be discouraged about world events? What should be our attitude as we live in the end times?

To be sure, extremists have taken unhealthy paths as a result of their understanding of prophecy. To avoid such extreme decisions, I've always advised people to live their lives as if the rapture could happen today but to plan their lives as if they'll be here their entire lifetime expectancy. That way they are prepared for time and eternity.

Beyond this, Scripture gives us several helpful exhortations that clarify what our attitude should be as we live in the end times. We will see that Scripture does not in any way advise extreme changes or policies. Rather, Scripture takes a sound approach that Christians can live by. I urge you to meditate on these scriptural truths so that when storms come, you'll have an anchor to keep you from being blown and tossed.

Be an Accurate Observer of the Times

Scripture says we should seek to be accurate observers of the times. Of course, some people today utterly ignore biblical prophecy. Other people have been misled by anti-prophecy Christians (preterists) who teach that most biblical prophecies were fulfilled in the first century and that we should not look for any future fulfillments of Bible prophecies relating to the tribulation or the rapture. This viewpoint is as unfortunate as it is unbiblical. Scripture indicates that just as biblical prophecies about the first coming of Christ were fulfilled in a quite literal way (see, for example, Isaiah 7:14; Micah 5:2; Zechariah 12:10), so the prophecies about the second coming (and related events, like the Ezekiel invasion) will also be literally fulfilled. In view of this, we do well to stay aware of what Scripture teaches about the end times, and to be accurate observers of the times. We shouldn't be sensationalists or alarmists, for such behavior is not becoming of our God (1 Peter 4:7-10). But we should be accurate observers of the times. Consider Jesus' words in Matthew 16:1-3:

> The Pharisees and Sadducees came up, and testing Jesus, they asked Him to show them a sign from heaven. But He replied to them, "When it is evening, you say, 'It will be fair weather, for the sky is red.' And in the morning, 'There will be a storm today, for the sky is red and threatening.' Do you know how to discern the appearance of the sky, but cannot discern the signs of the times?"

What a rebuke! These guys—the religious elite of the time—were supposed to know the teachings of Scripture, and yet they were completely unable to properly discern the times. The Pharisees and Sadducees had been surrounded by spiritual signs of Jesus' identity and they had missed them all. They were blinded to the reality that the Messiah was with them. Jesus' miracles pointed to His divine identity just as surely as dark clouds signal rain. The Old Testament prophesied about the Messiah's miracles (Isaiah 35:5-6), and the Pharisees and Sadducees—experts in the Old Testament—should have realized

Jesus fulfilled these messianic verses. But in their blindness, they could not "discern the signs of the times." Let's not follow their example.

Jesus also urged, "Now learn the parable from the fig tree: when its branch has already become tender and puts forth its leaves, you know that summer is near; so, you too, when you see all these things, recognize that He is near, right at the door" (Matthew 24:32-33). Jesus indicates in this verse that God has revealed certain things in prophecy that ought to cause people who know the Bible to understand that a fulfillment of prophecy is taking place (or perhaps the stage is being set for a prophecy to eventually be fulfilled). Jesus is thus informing His followers to be accurate observers of the times so that they will take note when biblical prophecies are fulfilled (see also Luke 21:25-28).

Prophecy Should Lead to Purity in Our Lives

God doesn't just tell us the future to show off. He doesn't give us prophecy to teach us mere intellectual facts about eschatology. Many verses in the Bible that deal with prophecy include an exhortation to personal purity. This means that studying Bible prophecy should change the way we live. It ought to have an effect on our behavior.

In Romans 13:11-14, for example, the apostle Paul—speaking in a context of prophecy—provides this exhortation:

> Do this, knowing the time, that it is already the hour for you to awaken from sleep; for now salvation is nearer to us than when we believed. The night is almost gone, and the day is near. Therefore let us lay aside the deeds of darkness and put on the armor of light. Let us behave properly as in the day, not in carousing and drunkenness, not in sexual promiscuity and sensuality, not in strife and jealousy. But put on the Lord Jesus Christ, and make no provision for the flesh in regard to its lusts.

Another passage that teaches that prophecy should lead to purity is 2 Peter 3:10-14:

> The day of the Lord will come like a thief, in which the heavens will pass away with a roar and the elements will be destroyed with intense heat, and the earth and its works will be burned up. Since all these things are to be destroyed in this way, what sort of people ought you to be in holy conduct and godliness, looking for and hastening the coming of the day of God, because of which the heavens will be destroyed by burning, and the elements will melt with intense heat! But according to His promise we are looking for new heavens and a new earth, in which righteousness dwells. Therefore, beloved, since you look for these things, be diligent to be found by Him in peace, spotless and blameless.

Finally, we read this in 1 John 3:2-3:

> Beloved, now we are children of God, and it has not appeared as yet what we will be. We know that when He appears, we will be like Him, because we will see Him just as He is. And everyone who has this hope fixed on Him purifies himself, just as He is pure.

This last passage is referring to the rapture. And what a glorious day that will be. One scholar put it this way: "The hope of the rapture, when we will meet the Savior, should be a sanctifying force in our lives. We will be made completely like Him then; so we should endeavor with His help to serve Him faithfully now and to lead lives of purity."[5]

Be Sober Minded, Maintain Sound Judgment, Pray, and Be Loving

First Peter 4:7-10 is jam-packed with wisdom for how we ought to live in view of biblical prophecy.

> The end of all things is near; therefore, be of sound judgment and sober spirit for the purpose of prayer. Above all, keep fervent in your love for one another, because love covers

> a multitude of sins. Be hospitable to one another without complaint. As each one has received a special gift, employ it in serving one another as good stewards of the manifold grace of God.

Many people tend to become sensationalistic and alarmist about end-time prophecies. But God tells us to be sober minded. God instructs us to maintain sound judgment. The best way to be sober minded and maintain sound judgment is to regularly feed our minds with the Word of God. Keeping our minds focused on the Scriptures will keep us on track in our thinking and in our life choices in the light of biblical prophecy.

Never Set Dates

The timing of end-time events is in God's hands, and He hasn't given us the details. In Acts 1:7 we read of Jesus' words to the disciples before He ascended into heaven: "It is not for you to know times or epochs which the Father has fixed by His own authority." This means that we can be accurate observers of the times, as Jesus instructed (Matthew 24:32-33; Luke 21:25-28), but we don't have precise details on the exact timing. We must simply resolve to trust God with those details.

Christians who get caught up in date setting (like setting a date for the rapture) can damage the cause of Christ. Unbelievers enjoy scorning Christians who have put stock in end-time predictions—especially when they attach specific dates to specific events. Why give ammunition to the enemies of Christianity? We can be excited about events that appear to be setting the stage for the eventual fulfillment of prophecy without engaging in such sensationalism. Remember, Christ calls His followers to live soberly and alertly as they await His coming (Mark 13:32-37).

Do Not Be Troubled

In John 14:1-3 Jesus talks to His disciples about the rapture:

> Do not let your heart be troubled; believe in God, believe also in Me. In My Father's house are many dwelling places; if it were not so, I would have told you; for I go to prepare a place for you. If I go and prepare a place for you, I will come again and receive you to Myself, that where I am, there you may be also.

John F. Walvoord has a great insight on this passage:

> These verses are the Bible's first revelation of the rapture, in which Christ will come back to take His own to heaven. He exhorted the disciples not to be troubled. Since they trusted the Father, they also should trust Christ, whose power was demonstrated in His many miracles. Having referred to Himself as the Source of peace, Jesus spoke of His coming to take them to heaven. They need not be anxious about His leaving because later He would return for them.[6]

So regardless of what happens in this world, we do not need to be troubled. Why not? Because we know the Prince of Peace, Jesus Christ. He is the source of peace, and the peace He gives does not depend on circumstances (John 14:27). We need not worry. We need not fear. Besides, as Jesus said, He's now preparing our eternal homes (14:1-3). That future reality is enough to strengthen us through any present difficulties.

Bible Prophecy Points to the Awesome Greatness of God

We should ever keep in mind that Bible prophecy constantly and relentlessly points to the awesome greatness of God. Consider these verses:

> Behold, the former things have come to pass, now I declare new things; Before they spring forth I proclaim them to you (Isaiah 42:9).

> Thus says the LORD, the King of Israel and his Redeemer,

> the Lord of hosts: "I am the first and I am the last, and there is no God besides Me. Who is like Me? Let him proclaim and declare it; yes, let him recount it to Me in order, from the time that I established the ancient nation. And let them declare to them the things that are coming and the events that are going to take place. Do not tremble and do not be afraid; have I not long since announced it to you and declared it? And you are My witnesses. Is there any God besides Me, or is there any other Rock? I know of none" (Isaiah 44:6-8).
>
> Remember this, and be assured; recall it to mind, you transgressors. Remember the former things long past, for I am God, and there is no other; I am God, and there is no one like Me, declaring the end from the beginning, and from ancient times things which have not been done, saying, "My purpose will be established, and I will accomplish all My good pleasure" (Isaiah 46:8-10).
>
> Daniel said, "Let the name of God be blessed forever and ever, for wisdom and power belong to Him. It is He who changes the times and the epochs; He removes kings and establishes kings; He gives wisdom to wise men and knowledge to men of understanding. It is He who reveals the profound and hidden things; He knows what is in the darkness, and the light dwells with Him" (Daniel 2:20-22).

Our God is an awesome God! The Bible reveals some phenomenal facts about this awesome God. Let's meditate on these truths as they relate to the unfolding of God's prophetic plan on earth.

God is eternal. One theologian describes God as "the eternal without beginning, He who is above the whole course of time, He who in harmony beyond explanation possesses unity and life, the Father, the Son, and the Holy Spirit, the basis of eternity, the Living One, the only God."[7]

God transcends time altogether. He is above the space-time universe. As an eternal being, He has always existed. He is the King eternal (1 Timothy 1:17), who alone is immortal (6:16). He is the

Alpha and Omega (Revelation 1:8), the first and the last (Isaiah 44:6; 48:12). He exists from eternity (Isaiah 43:13) and from everlasting to everlasting (Psalm 90:2). He lives forever from eternal ages past (Psalm 41:13; 102:12,27; Isaiah 57:15). Events transpire on a daily basis on the earth, and prophecies are fulfilled temporally, but God Himself is beyond time altogether.

A comforting ramification of God's eternal nature is the absolute confidence that God will never cease to exist. He will always be there for us. His continued providential control of our lives is thereby assured. Human leaders come and go, countries come and go, but God is eternal and is always there!

God is everywhere-present. This does not mean that God in His divine nature is diffused throughout space as if part of Him were here and part of Him were there. Rather, God in His whole being is in every place. No one can go where God is not (Psalm 139:7-8; Jeremiah 23:23-24; Hebrews 1:3; Acts 17:27-28). Whether one is in the United States, Iran, Russia, Sudan, Libya, or anywhere else in the entire universe, God is there.

Things so often seem to us to be spinning out of control. How comforting to know that regardless of where we go, we will never escape the presence of our beloved God. Because He is everywhere-present, we can be confident of His real presence at all times. We will always know the blessing of walking with Him in every trial and circumstance of life.

God is all-knowing. Because God transcends time—because He is above time—He can see the past, present, and future as a single intuitive act. God's knowledge of all things is from the vantage point of eternity, so that the past, present, and future are all encompassed in one ever-present "now" to Him.

God knows all things, both actual and possible (Matthew 11:21-23). He knows all things past (Isaiah 41:22), present (Hebrews 4:13), and future (Isaiah 46:10). Because He knows all things, His knowledge can never increase or decrease. Psalm 147:5 affirms that God's understanding has no limit. His knowledge is infinite (Psalm 33:13-15; 139:11-12;

147:5; Proverbs 15:3; Isaiah 40:14; 46:10; Acts 15:18; Hebrews 4:13; 1 John 3:20). This is why we can trust God when He communicates prophecies about the future to us. God knows all!

God is all-powerful. Scripture portrays God as all-powerful (Jeremiah 32:17). He has the power to do all that He desires and wills. Some 56 times Scripture declares that God is almighty (for example, Revelation 19:6). God is abundant in strength (Psalm 147:5) and has incomparably great power (2 Chronicles 20:6; Ephesians 1:19-21). No one can hold back His hand (Daniel 4:35). No one can reverse Him (Isaiah 43:13) and no one can thwart Him (Isaiah 14:27). Nothing is impossible with Him (Matthew 19:26; Mark 10:27; Luke 1:37), and nothing is too difficult for Him (Genesis 18:14; Jeremiah 32:17,27). The Almighty reigns (Revelation 19:6). This means that none of the nations of the world are beyond God's control. Regardless of any threat one nation might make against another—such as Iran threatening Israel—we must remember that our God, who is all-powerful, is in control. No one can thwart His plans.

God is sovereign. Scripture portrays God as absolutely sovereign. He rules the universe, controls all things, and is Lord over all (see Ephesians 1). Nothing can happen in this universe that is beyond the reach of His control. All forms of existence are within the scope of His absolute dominion. Psalm 50:1 (NIV) refers to God as the Mighty One who "speaks and summons the earth from the rising of the sun to the place where it sets." Psalm 66:7 (NIV) affirms that "He rules forever by his power." Psalm 93:1 assures us that "the Lord reigns" and "is armed with strength."

God asserts, "My purpose will stand, and I will do all that I please" (Isaiah 46:10). He assures us, "Surely, as I have planned, so it will be, and as I have purposed, so it will stand" (Isaiah 14:24). Proverbs 16:9 tells us, "In his heart a man plans his course, but the LORD determines his steps." Proverbs 19:21 says, "Many are the plans in a man's heart, but it is the LORD's purpose that prevails."

Every believing soul can enjoy supreme peace knowing that God is sovereignly overseeing all that comes into our lives. Regardless of what we may encounter, and even though we may fail to understand why certain things happen in life, and even as horrible as the headlines in newspapers may seem to be, the knowledge that our sovereign God is in control is like a firm anchor in the midst of life's storms.

God is holy. Because God is holy, He is not only entirely separate from all evil but also is absolutely righteous (Leviticus 19:2). He is pure in every way. The Scriptures lay great stress on this attribute of God:

- "Who is like You—majestic in holiness?" (Exodus 15:11).
- "There is no one holy like the LORD" (1 Samuel 2:2).
- "The LORD our God is holy" (Psalm 99:9 NIV).
- "Holy and awesome is His name" (Psalm 111:9).
- "Holy, holy, holy is the LORD Almighty" (Isaiah 6:3 NIV).
- "You alone are holy" (Revelation 15:4).

A key ramification of God's holiness is that God will not allow persons or nations to get away with sinful actions. When the northern military coalition launches a massive invasion into Israel, God will respond by utterly destroying them.

God is just. God carries out His righteous standards justly and with equity. He never deals with people in partiality or unfairness (Genesis 18:25; Psalm 11:7; Zephaniah 3:5; John 17:25; Romans 3:26; Hebrews 6:10). The fact that God is just is both a comfort and a warning. It's a comfort for those who have been wronged in life. They can rest assured that God will right all wrongs in the end. But it's a warning for those who think they have been getting away with evil. Justice will prevail in the end!

The relevance of God's justice to this book is obvious: Justice will prevail, so the massive northern military coalition will be destroyed, even as it seeks to destroy Israel, the apple of God's eye.

Maintain an Eternal Perspective

God's awesome greatness creates an excitement in our hearts—an excitement that we, as Christians, will live for all eternity in heaven with our wondrous God. Whatever takes place on this earth, we each have a splendorous destiny ahead. I never tire of saying that daily pondering the incredible glory of the afterlife is one of the surest ways to stay motivated to live faithfully during our relatively short time on earth. We are but pilgrims on our way to another land—to the final frontier of heaven, where God Himself dwells.

J.I. Packer once said that the "lack of long, strong thinking about our promised hope of glory is a major cause of our plodding, lackluster lifestyle."[8] Packer points to the Puritans as a much-needed example for us, for they believed that "it is the heavenly Christian that is the lively Christian." The Puritans understood that we "run so slowly, and strive so lazily, because we so little mind the prize...So let Christians animate themselves daily to run the race set before them by practicing heavenly meditation."[9]

A daily habit of Puritan Richard Baxter was to "dwell on the glory of the heavenly life to which one was going." Baxter daily practiced "holding heaven at the forefront of his thoughts and desires."[10] The hope of heaven brought him joy, and joy brought him strength. Baxter once said, "A heavenly mind is a joyful mind; this is the nearest and truest way to live a life of comfort...A heart in heaven will be a most excellent preservative against temptations, a powerful means to kill thy corruptions."[11]

■ ■ ■ ■

I assume all my readers are Christians, but there is a possibility that you are not. You may have picked up this book because the title intrigued you or because you are interested in Middle East tensions. If you are not a Christian and you would like to come into a personal relationship with the God I have described above, I urge you to read appendix 2. I wrote it specifically for you!

Appendix 1

Messianic Prophecies Fulfilled in Christ

From the book of Genesis to the book of Malachi, the Old Testament abounds with anticipations of the coming Messiah. Numerous predictions—fulfilled to the crossing of the *t* and the dotting of the *i* in the New Testament—relate to His birth, life, ministry, death, resurrection, and glory.

Some liberal scholars argue that these prophecies were made after Jesus lived, not before. They suggest that the books of the Old Testament were written close to the time of Christ and that the messianic prophecies were merely Christian inventions. But to make this claim is to completely ignore the historical evidence, as Norman Geisler and Ron Brooks point out:

> Even the most liberal critics admit that the prophetic books were completed some 400 years before Christ, and the Book of Daniel by about 167 BC. Though there is good evidence to date most of these books much earlier (some of the psalms and earlier prophets were in the eighth and ninth centuries BC), what difference would it make? It is just as hard to predict an event 200 years in the future as it is to predict one that is 800 years in the future. Both feats would require nothing less than divine knowledge.[1]

God's ability to foretell future events is one thing that separates Him from all the false gods. God addressed the polytheism of Isaiah's time:

- "Who then is like me? Let him proclaim it. Let him declare and lay out before me what has happened since I established my ancient people, and what is yet to come—yes, let him foretell what will come" (Isaiah 44:7 NIV).
- "Do not tremble, do not be afraid. Did I not proclaim this and foretell it long ago? You are my witnesses. Is there any God besides me? No, there is no other Rock; I know not one" (Isaiah 44:8 NIV).
- "Who foretold this long ago, who declared it from the distant past? Was it not I, the LORD? And there is no God apart from me" (Isaiah 45:21 NIV).
- "I foretold the former things long ago, my mouth announced them and I made them known; then suddenly I acted, and they came to pass...Therefore I told you these things long ago; before they happened I announced them to you so that you could not say, 'My idols did them; my wooden image and metal god ordained them'" (Isaiah 48:3,5 NIV).

Of course, anyone can make predictions—that's easy. But having them fulfilled is another story altogether. "The more statements you make about the future and the greater the detail, the better the chances are that you will be proven wrong."[2] But God was never wrong; all the messianic prophecies in the Old Testament were fulfilled specifically and precisely in the person of Jesus Christ.

Jesus often indicated to listeners that He was the specific fulfillment of messianic prophecy.

- "Do not think that I have come to abolish the Law or the Prophets; I have not come to abolish them but to fulfill them" (Matthew 5:17 NIV).
- "But this has all taken place that the writings of the prophets might be fulfilled" (Matthew 26:56 NIV).
- "And beginning with Moses and all the Prophets, he explained to them what was said in all the Scriptures concerning himself" (Luke 24:27 NIV).
- "This is what I told you while I was still with you: Everything must be fulfilled that is written about me in the Law of Moses, the Prophets and the Psalms" (Luke 24:44 NIV).
- "You diligently study the Scriptures because you think that by them you possess eternal life. These are the Scriptures that testify about me, yet you refuse to come to me to have life" (John 5:39-40 NIV).
- "If you believed Moses, you would believe me, for he wrote about me. But since you do not believe what he wrote, how are you going to believe what I say?" (John 5:46-47 NIV).
- "Then he rolled up the scroll, gave it back to the attendant and sat down. The eyes of everyone in the synagogue were fastened on him, and he began by saying to them, 'Today this scripture is fulfilled in your hearing'" (Luke 4:20-21 NIV).

An in-depth study of the messianic prophecies in the Old Testament is beyond the scope of this appendix. However, the chart below lists some of the more important messianic prophecies Jesus Christ directly fulfilled.

Messianic Prophecies Fulfilled by Jesus Christ

Topic	Old Testament Prophecy	New Testament Fulfillment in Christ
Seed of woman	Genesis 3:15	Galatians 4:4
Line of Abraham	Genesis 12:2	Matthew 1:1
Line of Jacob	Numbers 24:17	Luke 3:23,34
Line of Judah	Genesis 49:10	Matthew 1:2
Line of Jesse	Isaiah 11:1	Luke 3:23,32
Line of David	2 Samuel 7:12-16	Matthew 1:1
Virgin birth	Isaiah 7:14	Matthew 1:23
Birthplace: Bethlehem	Micah 5:2	Matthew 2:6
Forerunner: John	Isaiah 40:3; Malachi 3:1	Matthew 3:3
Escape into Egypt	Hosea 11:1	Matthew 2:14
Herod kills children	Jeremiah 31:15	Matthew 2:16
King	Psalm 2:6	Matthew 21:5
Prophet	Deuteronomy 18:15-18	Acts 3:22-23
Priest	Psalm 110:4	Hebrews 5:6-10
Judge	Isaiah 33:22	John 5:30
Called "Lord"	Psalm 110:1	Luke 2:11
Called "Immanuel"	Isaiah 7:14	Matthew 1:23
Anointed by Holy Spirit	Isaiah 11:2	Matthew 3:16-17
Zeal for God	Psalm 69:9	John 2:15-17
Ministry in Galilee	Isaiah 9:1-2	Matthew 4:12-16
Ministry of miracles	Isaiah 35:5-6	Matthew 9:35
Bore world's sins	Psalm 22:1	Matthew 27:46
Ridiculed	Psalm 22:7-8	Matthew 27:39,43
Stumbling stone to Jew	Psalm 118:22	1 Peter 2:7
Rejected by own people	Isaiah 53:3	John 7:5,48
Light to Gentiles	Isaiah 60:3	Acts 13:47-48

Taught parables	Psalm 78:2	Matthew 13:34
Cleansed the temple	Malachi 3:1	Matthew 21:12
Sold for 30 shekels	Zechariah 11:12	Matthew 26:15
Forsaken by disciples	Zechariah 13:7	Mark 14:50
Silent before accusers	Isaiah 53:7	Matthew 27:12-19
Hands and feet pierced	Psalm 22:16	John 20:25
Heart broken	Psalm 22:14	John 19:34
Crucified with thieves	Isaiah 53:12	Matthew 27:38
No bones broken	Psalm 22:17	John 19:33-36
Soldiers gambled	Psalm 22:18	John 19:24
Suffered thirst on cross	Psalm 69:21	John 19:28
Vinegar offered	Psalm 69:21	Matthew 27:34
Christ's prayer	Psalm 22:24	Matthew 26:39
Disfigured	Isaiah 52:14	John 19:1
Scourging and death	Isaiah 53:5	John 19:1,18
His "forsaken" cry	Psalm 22:1	Matthew 27:46
Committed self to God	Psalm 31:5	Luke 23:46
Rich man's tomb	Isaiah 53:9	Matthew 27:57-60
Resurrection	Psalm 16:10	Matthew 28:6
Ascension	Psalm 68:18	Luke 24:50-53
Right hand of God	Psalm 110:1	Hebrews 1:3

Any reasonable person who examines these Old Testament prophecies in an objective manner must conclude that Jesus was the promised Messiah. "If these Messianic prophecies were written hundreds of years before they occurred, and if they could never have been foreseen and depended upon factors outside human control for their fulfillment, and if *all* of these prophecies perfectly fit the Person and life of Jesus Christ, then Jesus had to be the Messiah."[3]

Indeed, Christ on three different occasions directly claimed in so many words to be the Christ. (Note that the word *Christ* is the

Greek equivalent of the Hebrew word *Messiah.*) For example, in John 4:25-26 Jesus encountered a Samaritan woman who said to Him, "I know that Messiah is coming." Jesus replied, "I who speak to you am He." Later, Jesus referred to Himself in the third person, in His high priestly prayer to the Father, as "Jesus Christ, whom You have sent" (John 17:3). In Mark 14:61-62 we find the high priest asking Jesus, "Are you the Christ, the Son of the Blessed One?" Jesus declared unequivocally, "I am."

Others also recognized that Jesus was the prophesied Messiah. In response to Jesus' inquiry concerning His disciples' understanding of Him, Peter confessed: "You are the Christ" (Matthew 16:16). When Jesus said to Martha, "I am the resurrection and the life. He who believes in me will live, even though he dies; and whoever lives and believes in me will never die. Do you believe this?" Martha answered, "Yes, Lord...I believe that you are the Christ" (John 11:25-27 NIV).

Some may ask why Jesus didn't explicitly claim more often to be the prophesied Messiah. Robert L. Reymond offers us some keen insights in answering this question.

> Jews of the first century regarded the Messiah primarily as Israel's national deliverer from the yoke of Gentile oppression...Had Jesus employed uncritically the current popular term as a description of Himself and His mission before divesting it of its one-sided associations and infusing it with its richer, full-orbed Old Testament meaning, which included the work of the Messiah as the Suffering Servant of Isaiah, His mission would have been gravely misunderstood and His efforts to instruct the people even more difficult. Consequently, the evidence suggests that He acknowledged He was the Christ only where there was little or no danger of His claim being politicized—as in the case of the Samaritan woman, in private conversation with His disciples (at the same time, demanding that they tell no one that He was the Messiah), in semi-private prayer, or before the Sanhedrin when silence no longer mattered or served His purpose.[4]

Even if Jesus had never verbally claimed to be the prophesied Messiah, the very fact that He was the precise fulfillment of virtually hundreds of messianic prophecies cannot be dismissed, as some liberal critics have attempted. The odds against one person fulfilling all these prophecies is astronomical; indeed, it is impossible to calculate. But Jesus did fulfill these prophecies, and then He added proof upon proof of His identity by the many astounding miracles He performed. Truly, Jesus is the Messiah.

Of course, it is fashionable today to claim that the New Testament writers manipulated things to give the appearance that Jesus fulfilled messianic prophecy. One critic asserts, "The biblical authors went to great lengths to pound Jesus into the mold of Jewish messianic expectation. In their enthusiasm, however, they resorted to blatant distortions."[5]

This allegation does not fit the biblical facts. First, note that the biblical writers were God-fearing Jews who gave every evidence of possessing the highest moral character, each having been raised since early childhood to obey the Ten Commandments (including the commandment against bearing false witness—Exodus 20:16). To say that these men were deceitful and sought to fool people into believing Jesus was the Messiah when He really was not breaches all credulity. Also these men would never have chosen to suffer and give up their lives in defense of what they knew to be untrue.

Further, Jesus fulfilled many prophecies that the biblical writers could not have manipulated, such as His birthplace in Bethlehem (Micah 5:2), His direct descent from David (2 Samuel 7:12-16) and from Abraham (Genesis 12:2), being born of a virgin (Isaiah 7:14), the identity of His forerunner, John the Baptist (Malachi 3:1), the Sanhedrin's gift of 30 pieces of silver to Judas, the betrayer (Zechariah 11:12), the soldiers gambling for His clothing (Psalm 22:18), and His legs remaining unbroken (Psalm 22:17).

Still further, concerning prophecies related to Jesus' resurrection from the dead (Psalm 16:10), the biblical writers could not have stolen the body in order to give the appearance of a resurrection. The tomb had a huge stone weighing several tons blocking it, it had a seal of the Roman government (with an automatic penalty of death for anyone who broke it), and it was guarded by brawny Roman guards trained to defend and kill. Jesus' Jewish followers could not overcome these guards, move the stone, and steal the body.

The evidence is massive. Jesus is the fulfillment of virtually hundreds of messianic prophecies. Critics may continue to make their claims against the biblical account, but they have an uphill battle.

Appendix 2

If You Are Not a Christian

Choosing to begin a personal relationship with Jesus is the most important decision you could ever make. It is unlike any other relationship. If you go into eternity without this relationship, you will spend eternity apart from Him.

If you will allow me, I would like to tell you how you can come into a personal relationship with Jesus.

God Desires a Personal Relationship with You

God created you (Genesis 1:27). And He did not create you to exist all alone and apart from Him. He created you to have a personal relationship with Him.

God had face-to-face encounters and fellowship with Adam and Eve, the first couple (Genesis 3:8-19). Just as God fellowshipped with them, so He desires to fellowship with you (1 John 1:5-7). God loves you (John 3:16). Never forget that fact.

Humanity's Sin Blocks a Relationship with God

When Adam and Eve chose to sin against God in the garden of Eden, they catapulted the entire human race—to which they gave birth—into sin. Since that time, every human being has been born into the world with a propensity to sin.

The apostle Paul affirmed that "sin entered the world through one man, and death through sin" (Romans 5:12 NIV). We are told that "through the disobedience of the one man the many were made sinners" (Romans 5:19 NIV). Ultimately this means that "death came through a man...in Adam all die" (1 Corinthians 15:21-22 NIV).

Jesus often spoke of sin in metaphors that illustrate the havoc sin can wreak in one's life. He described sin as blindness (Matthew 23:16-26), sickness (Matthew 9:12), slavery (John 8:34), and darkness (John 8:12; 12:35-46). Moreover, Jesus taught that this is a universal condition and that all people are guilty before God (Luke 7:37-48).

Jesus also taught that both inner thoughts and external acts render a person guilty (Matthew 5:28). He taught that from within the human heart come evil thoughts, sexual immorality, theft, murder, adultery, greed, malice, deceit, envy, slander, arrogance, and folly (Mark 7:21-23). He affirmed that God is fully aware of every person's sins, both external acts and inner thoughts; nothing escapes His notice (Matthew 22:18; Luke 6:8; John 4:17-19).

Of course, some people are more morally upright than others. However, we all fall short of God's infinite standards (Romans 3:23). In a contest to see who can throw a rock to the moon, a muscular athlete would be able to throw the rock much farther than I could. But all human beings would fall short of the task. Similarly, all of us fall short of measuring up to God's perfect holy standards.

Jesus Died for Our Sins and Made Salvation Possible

God's absolute holiness demands that sin be punished. The good news of the gospel, however, is that Jesus has taken this punishment on Himself. God loves us so much that He sent Jesus to bear the penalty for our sins!

Jesus affirmed that He came into the world for the very purpose of dying (John 12:27). He saw His death as a sacrificial offering for the sins of humanity (Matthew 26:26-28). Jesus took His sacrificial mission with utmost seriousness, for He knew that without Him, humanity would certainly perish (Matthew 16:25; John 3:16) and spend eternity apart from God in a place of great suffering (Matthew 10:28; 11:23; 23:33; 25:41; Luke 16:22-28).

Jesus therefore described His mission this way: "The Son of Man did not come to be served, but to serve, and to give his life as a ransom for many" (Matthew 20:28 NIV). "The Son of Man came to seek and to save what was lost" (Luke 19:10 NIV). "God did not send his Son into the world to condemn the world, but to save the world through him" (John 3:17 NIV).

Believe in Jesus Christ the Savior

By His sacrificial death on the cross, Jesus took the sins of the entire world on Himself and made salvation available for everyone (1 John 2:2). But this salvation is not automatic. Only those who personally choose to believe in Christ are saved. This is Jesus' consistent testimony.

- "For God so loved the world that he gave his one and only Son, that whoever believes in him shall not perish but have eternal life" (John 3:16 NIV).
- "For my Father's will is that everyone who looks to the Son and believes in him shall have eternal life, and I will raise him up at the last day" (John 6:40 NIV).
- "I am the resurrection and the life. He who believes in me will live, even though he dies" (John 11:25 NIV).

Choosing *not* to believe in Jesus, by contrast, leads to eternal condemnation: "Whoever believes in him is not condemned, but whoever does not believe stands condemned already because he has not believed in the name of God's one and only Son" (John 3:18 NIV).

Free at Last: Forgiven of All Sins

When you believe in Christ the Savior, a wonderful thing happens. God forgives you of all your sins. All of them! He puts them completely out of His sight. Ponder for a few minutes the following verses, which speak of the forgiveness of those who have believed in Christ:

- "In him we have redemption through his blood, the forgiveness of sins, in accordance with the riches of God's grace" (Ephesians 1:7 NIV).
- "Their sins and lawless acts I will remember no more" (Hebrews 10:17-18 NIV).
- "Blessed is he whose transgressions are forgiven, whose sins are covered. Blessed is the man whose sin the LORD does not count against him and in whose spirit is no deceit" (Psalm 32:1-2 NIV).
- "For as high as the heavens are above the earth, so great is his love for those who fear him; as far as the east is from the west, so far has he removed our transgressions from us" (Psalm 103:11-12 NIV).

Such forgiveness is wonderful indeed, for none of us can possibly work our way into heaven or be good enough to warrant God's good favor. Because of what Jesus has done for us, we can freely receive the gift of salvation. It is a gift provided solely through the grace of God (Ephesians 2:8-9). It becomes ours when we place our faith in Jesus.

Don't Put It Off

Putting off a decision to turn to Christ for salvation is dangerous, for you do not know the day of your death. What if it happens this evening? "Death is the destiny of every man; the living should take this to heart" (Ecclesiastes 7:2 NIV).

If God is speaking to your heart, now is your door of opportunity to believe. "Seek the LORD while he may be found; call on him while he is near" (Isaiah 55:6 NIV).

Would you like to place your faith in Jesus for the forgiveness of sins, thereby guaranteeing your eternal place in heaven along His side? If so, pray the following prayer with me. Keep in mind that the prayer itself does not save you. The faith in your heart saves you. So let the following prayer be a simple expression of the faith that is in your heart:

> *Dear Jesus, I want to have a relationship with You. I know I cannot save myself, because I know I am a sinner. Thank You for dying on the cross on my behalf. I believe You died for me, and I accept Your free gift of salvation. Thank You, Jesus. Amen.*

Welcome to God's Forever Family

On the authority of the Word of God, I can now assure you that you are a part of God's forever family. If you prayed the above prayer with a heart of faith, you will spend all eternity by the side of Jesus in heaven. Welcome to God's family!

What to Do Next

1. Purchase a Bible and read from it daily. Read at least one chapter a day and then spend some time in prayer. I recommend starting with the Gospel of John.
2. Join a Bible-believing church immediately. Get involved in it. Join a Bible study at the church so you will have regular fellowship with other Christians.
3. Please write to me at Ron Rhodes, P.O. Box 2526, Frisco, TX 75034. I would love to hear from you.
4. Please visit my website, where you'll find materials that will help you: www.ronrhodes.org.

Bibliography

Ankerberg, John, and Dillon Burroughs. *Middle East Meltdown*. Eugene, OR: Harvest House, 2007.

Ansari, Ali. *Confronting Iran*. New York: Basic Books, 2006.

Berman, Ilan. *Tehran Rising*. New York: Rowman & Littlefield, 2005.

Block, Daniel. *The Book of Ezekiel: Chapters 25–48*. Grand Rapids: Eerdmans, 1998.

Corsi, Jerome. *Atomic Iran*. Nashville: WND, 2005.

Demar, Gary. *End Times Fiction*. Nashville: Thomas Nelson, 2001.

Feinberg, Charles. *The Prophecy of Ezekiel*. Eugene, OR: Wipf and Stock, 2003.

Fruchtenbaum, Arnold. *The Footsteps of the Messiah*. San Antonio: Ariel, 2004.

Gaffney, Frank. *War Footing*. Annapolis: Naval Institute Press, 2006.

Gold, Dore. *The Fight for Jerusalem*. Washington: Regnery, 2007.

Hitchcock, Mark. *Bible Prophecy*. Wheaton: Tyndale, 1999.

Hitchcock, Mark. *The Coming Islamic Invasion of Israel*. Sisters, OR: Multnomah, 2002.

Hitchcock, Mark. *Iran*. Sisters, OR: Multnomah, 2006.

Hitchcock, Mark. *Is America in Bible Prophecy?* Sisters, OR: Multnomah, 2002.

Hitchcock, Mark. *The Second Coming of Babylon*. Sisters, OR: Multnomah, 2003.

Hoyt, Herman. *The End Times*. Chicago: Moody, 1969.

Ice, Thomas, and Randall Price. *Ready to Rebuild*. Eugene, OR: Harvest House, 1992.

Ice, Thomas, and Timothy Demy. *Prophecy Watch*. Eugene, OR: Harvest House, 1998.

Ice, Thomas, and Timothy Demy. *When the Trumpet Sounds*. Eugene, OR: Harvest House, 1995.

LaHaye, Tim. *The Beginning of the End*. Wheaton: Tyndale, 1991.

LaHaye, Tim. *The Coming Peace in the Middle East*. Grand Rapids: Zondervan, 1984.

LaHaye, Tim, ed. *Prophecy Study Bible*. Chattanooga: AMG, 2001.

LaHaye, Tim, and Ed Hindson, eds. *The Popular Bible Prophecy Commentary*. Eugene, OR: Harvest House, 2006.

LaHaye, Tim, and Ed Hindson, eds. *The Popular Encyclopedia of Bible Prophecy*. Eugene, OR: Harvest House, 2004.

LaHaye, Tim, and Jerry Jenkins. *Are We Living in the End Times?* Wheaton: Tyndale, 1999.

LaHaye, Tim, and Thomas Ice. *Charting the End Times.* Eugene, OR: Harvest House, 2001.

Leeb, Stephen. *The Coming Economic Collapse.* New York: Warner Business Books, 2006.

Pentecost, J. Dwight. *Things to Come.* Grand Rapids: Zondervan, 1964.

Pollack, Kenneth. *The Persian Puzzle.* New York: Random House, 2005.

Phares, Walid. *Future Jihad.* New York: Palgrave MacMillan, 2005.

Price, Randall. *Fast Facts on the Middle East Conflict.* Eugene, OR: Harvest House, 2003.

Price, Randall. *Unholy War.* Eugene, OR: Harvest House, 2001.

Reid, T.R. *The United States of Europe.* New York: Penguin Books, 2004.

Rosenberg, Joel. *Epicenter.* Carol Stream: Tyndale, 2006.

Ruthven, Jon Mark. *The Prophecy That Is Shaping History.* Fairfax: Xulon, 2003.

Timmerman, Kenneth. *Countdown to Crisis.* New York: Three Rivers, 2006.

Venter, Al. *Iran's Nuclear Option.* Philadelphia: Casemate, 2005.

Walvoord, John F. *End Times.* Nashville: Word, 1998.

Walvoord, John F. *The Millennial Kingdom.* Grand Rapids: Zondervan, 1975.

Walvoord, John F. *The Prophecy Knowledge Handbook.* Wheaton: Victor, 1990.

Walvoord, John F. *The Return of the Lord.* Grand Rapids: Zondervan, 1979.

Walvoord, John F., and John E. Walvoord. *Armageddon, Oil, and the Middle East Crisis.* Grand Rapids: Zondervan, 1975.

Yamauchi, Edwin. *Foes from the Northern Frontier.* Eugene, OR: Wipf and Stock, 1982.

Notes

Chapter 1—The Threat from the North

1. See Jon Mark Ruthven, *The Prophecy That Is Shaping History* (Fairfax: Xulon, 2003), pp. 4-5.

Chapter 2—The Rise of Radical Islam

1. Geoffrey Parrinder, *World Religions* (New York: Facts on File, 1971), p. 462.
2. Charles Adams, ed., *A Reader's Guide to the Great Religions* (New York: The Free Press, 1965), p. 287.
3. Harold Berry, *Islam* (Lincoln: Back to the Bible, 1992), p. 4.
4. Frank Gaffney, *War Footing* (Annapolis: Naval Institute Press, 2006), p. 220.
5. Ibid., p. 222.
6. Reza Safa, *Inside Islam* (Lake Mary, FL: Charisma House, 1996), p. 34.
7. Ibid.
8. George Braswell, *What You Need to Know About Islam and Muslims* (Nashville: Broadman and Holman, 2000), p. 45.
9. Berry, p. 5.
10. Braswell, p. 2.
11. Ibid., p. 45.
12. Ibid.
13. Russell Chandler, *Racing Toward 2001* (Grand Rapids: Zondervan, 1992), p. 184.
14. William Miller, *A Christian's Response to Islam* (Phillipsburg, NJ: Presbyterian and Reformed, 1976), p. 94.
15. David Goldmann, *Islam and the Bible* (Chicago: Moody, 2004), p. 18.
16. Based on Goldmann, p. 19.
17. Jamal Elias, *Islam* (Upper Saddle River, NJ: Prentice Hall, 1999), p. 73.
18. Frederick Denny, *An Introduction to Islam* (New York: Macmillan, 1985), p. 136.

19. Elias, p. 73.
20. John Ankerberg and John Weldon, *Fast Facts on Islam* (Eugene, OR: Harvest House, 2001), p. 105.
21. Ergun Mehmet Caner and Emir Fethi Caner, *Unveiling Islam* (Grand Rapids: Kregel, 2002), p. 49.
22. Goldmann, p. 22.
23. Ankerberg and Weldon, p. 19.
24. Quoted in Caner and Caner, pp. 183-84.
25. Cited in Gaffney, p. 222.
26. Ibid., pp. 5-6.
27. Ali Ansari, *Confronting Iran* (New York: Basic Books, 2006), p. 3.
28. Cited in Mark Hitchcock, *Iran* (Sisters, OR: Multnomah, 2006), p. 57.
29. Dore Gold, *The Fight for Jerusalem* (Washington: Regnery, 2007), p. 22.
30. Gold, pp. 231-32.
31. Cited in Gold, p. 232.
32. Gold, p. 232.
33. Joshua Yasmeh, "Ahmadinejad: The Next Hitler?" *Tribe,* February 2, 2007.
34. Iranian officials have sought to do damage control following Mahmoud Ahmadinejad's threats to wipe Israel off the map. In mid-2007, Mohammad Larijani, Iran's national security chief, claimed his country was not intending to wipe Israel off the map. He claimed Ahmadinejad was merely speaking of "erasing the practices" followed by Israel against the Palestinians, rather than erasing Israel itself. He also claimed the Western media deliberately distorted Ahmadinejad's words to make him look bad. Of course, government leaders around the world know better than to believe this spin. See Luan Shanglin, "Iran: No Intention to Wipe Israel Off the Map," *China View,* May 19, 2007.
35. "Iran's Ahmadinejad: Israel, U.S. Soon Will Die," NewsMax.com, January 24, 2007.
36. Jack Kinsella, "A World Without Ahmadinejad," *The Omega Letter Daily Intelligence Digest,* vol. 64, no. 18, January 20, 2007.
37. See Joel C. Rosenberg, "State of the Union," *Flash Traffic,* January 23, 2007.
38. Quoted in Kenneth Timmerman, *Countdown to Crisis* (New York: Three Rivers, 2006), p. 325.
39. Ibid., p. 325.

40. Ibid.
41. Hitchcock, p. 87.

Chapter 3—The Emerging Nuclear Nighmare

1. Some of this data is derived from atomicarchive.com. See also Graham Allison, *Nuclear Terrorism* (New York: Owl Books, 2005), pp. 1-4, 87, 107, 128; Joel Rosenberg, *Epicenter* (Carol Stream, IL: Tyndale, 2006), p. xii; "Effects of Nuclear Explosions," *Wikipedia;* "Avoiding Nuclear D-Day," special edition of *NewsMax* magazine.
2. Cited in Ryan Mauro, "Paul Williams Details 'American Hiroshima,'" *WorldNetDaily,* September 3, 2005.
3. "Bush Strategy Doctrine Calls Iran Great Challenge," Bloomberg.com, March 16, 2006.
4. Ilan Berman, *Tehran Rising* (New York: Rowman & Littlefield, 2005), p. ix.
5. Joel Rosenberg, "Nuclear Terrorism," *Flash Traffic,* April 30, 2007.
6. Rosenberg, *Epicenter,* p. 111.
7. Kenneth Pollack, *The Persian Puzzle* (New York: Random House, 2005), p. 377.
8. Jerome Corsi, *Atomic Iran* (Nashville: WND, 2005), p. 25.
9. Cited in Rosenberg, *Epicenter,* p. xii-xiii.
10. Kenneth Timmerman, "Iran's Nuclear Weapons," *NewsMax,* February 2007, p. 41.
11. Al Venter, *Iran's Nuclear Option* (Philadelphia: Casemate, 2005), p. xiv.
12. "A World Without Zionism or America," *E-Zion Israel News,* October 27, 2005.
13. Venter, pp. xvii-xviii.
14. Walid Phares, *Future Jihad* (New York: Palgrave MacMillan, 2005), p. 243.
15. Phares, p. 244.
16. George W. Bush, "The National Security Strategy," part 5, March 2006. Available online at www.whitehouse.gov.
17. Corsi, p. 26.
18. Cited in Mark Hitchcock, *Iran* (Sisters, OR: Multnomah, 2006), p. 18.
19. Frank Gaffney, *War Footing* (Annapolis: Naval Institute Press, 2006), p. 153.
20. Rosenberg, *Epicenter,* p. 119.
21. Venter, p. 85.

22. Quoted in Rosenberg, *Epicenter,* p. xiv.

23. See Hitchcock, pp. 16-17.

24. Quoted in Venter, pp. 12-13.

25. Venter, p. 207.

26. Ibid.

27. Quoted in Berman, p. 49.

28. Berman, pp. 57-58.

29. Ibid.

30. JoAnne Allen, "Iran Says Always Ready for Nuclear Talks," Reuters, February 13, 2007.

31. Ali Akbar Dareini, "Iran Says It's Installing Centrifuges," Associated Press, January 27, 2007.

32. Patrick Goodenough, "Take Ahmadinejad Seriously, Bolton Urges," CNSNews.com, December 15, 2006.

33. Venter, p. 113.

34. Cited in Corsi, pp. 34-35.

35. Quoted in Gaffney, p. 212.

36. Ibid.

37. Berman, p. 88.

38. Ibid., p. 44.

39. Ibid.

40. Quoted in Corsi, p. 56.

41. Corsi, pp. 116-17.

42. Ibid., p. 117.

43. Hitchcock, p. 108.

44. Cited in Moshe Yaalon, "Confronting Iran," The Washington Institute for Near-East Policy, March 7, 2006.

45. Hitchcock, p. 70.

46. Farhad Pouladi, "Iran Warns Will Hit Back at US if Attacked," *AFP,* February 8, 2007. See also "Iran's Ahmadinejad Warns of 'Severe' Retaliation if U.S. Attacks," AHN Media, May 14, 2007.

47. Rosenberg, *Epicenter,* pp. xiii-xiv.

48. Quoted in Pouladi, "Iran Warns Will Hit Back at US if Attacked."

49. Hitchcock, p. 112.
50. "US Incapable of Confronting Iran—Ahmadinejad," *Kuwait Today Magazine,* January 24, 2007.
51. "Excerpts of Reuters Interview with Ahmadinejad," Reuters, April 23, 2007.
52. Quoted in Pouladi, "Iran Warns Will Hit Back at US if Attacked."
53. Quoted in Parisa Hafezi, "Iran Ready for Anything in Nuclear Dispute," Reuters, February 24, 2007.
54. Hafezi, "Iran Ready for Anything in Nuclear Dispute." See also "Iran Would Respond Militarily to U.S. Attack," Reuters, March 14, 2007.
55. "Iran Would Respond Militarily To U.S. Attack."
56. See Corsi, p. 33.
57. Corsi, p. 219.
58. Ibid., p. 42.
59. Ibid., pp. 41-42.
60. Quoted in Goodenough, "Take Ahmadinejad Seriously, Bolton Urges."

Chapter 4—The Addiction to Black Gold (Oil)

1. Joel Bainerman, "Is the World Running Out of Oil?" *The Middle East,* April 1, 2004.
2. Warren Brown, "We're Running Out of Oil," *The Washington Post,* May 28, 2006.
3. Mark Hitchcock, *Iran* (Sisters, OR: Multnomah, 2006), p. 100.
4. Hitchcock, p. 98.
5. Richard Vodra, "The Next Energy Crisis," *Financial Planning,* October 1, 2005.
6. George Jahn, "The End of Oil," *The Cincinnati Post,* September 17, 2005. Estimates vary as to how much oil is recoverable through proven oil reserves. Oil industry journal *World Oil* puts it at 1.1 trillion barrels. British Petroleum estimates it at 1.2 trillion barrels. The *Oil and Gas Journal* estimates 1.3 trillion barrels. IHS Energy estimates it between 1.3 trillion and 2.4 trillion barrels. See Ronald Bailey, "Peak Oil Panic," *Reason,* May 1, 2006.
7. Hitchcock, pp. 100-101.
8. Vodra, "The Next Energy Crisis."
9. Bainerman, "Is the World Running Out of Oil?"

10. Gail Luft and Anne Korin, "Provide for U.S. Energy Security," in Frank Gaffney, *War Footing* (Annapolis: Naval Institute Press, 2006), p. 46.

11. Cited in Gaffney, p. 46.

12. Cited in Bainerman, "Is the World Running Out of Oil?"

13. Ibid.

14. Stephen Leeb, *The Coming Economic Collapse* (New York: Warner Business, 2006), p. 19.

15. Adam Porter, "Running on Empty," *New Internationalist,* October 1, 2003.

16. Leeb, p. 131.

17. Edward L. Morse and James Richard, "The Battle for Energy Dominance," *Foreign Affairs,* March/April 2002.

18. Morse and Richard, "The Battle for Energy Dominance."

19. Leeb, p. 22.

20. Jahn, "The End of Oil." See also Charles Arthur, "Oil and Gas Running Out Much Faster than Expected, Says Study," *The Independent,* October 2, 2003.

21. Quoted in Bainerman, "Is the World Running Out of Oil?"

22. Jane Bryant Quinn, "The Price of Our Addiction," *Newsweek,* April 24, 2006.

23. Vodra, "The Next Energy Crisis."

24. Quoted in Jahn, "The End of Oil."

25. Quoted in Ronald Bailey, "Peak Oil Panic," *Reason,* May 1, 2006.

26. Bailey, "Peak Oil Panic."

27. Jahn, "The End of Oil."

28. Bailey, "Peak Oil Panic."

29. Porter, "Running on Empty."

30. Ibid.

31. Ibid.

32. Matt Crenson, "Is the World Running Out of Gas?" *Wisconsin State Journal,* May 29, 2005.

33. Bainerman, "Is the World Running Out of Oil?"

34. Quinn, "The Price of Our Addiction."

35. Bainerman, "Is the World Running Out of Oil?"

36. Bailey, "Peak Oil Panic."

37. Quinn, "The Price of Our Addiction."

38. Al Venter, *Iran's Nuclear Option* (Philadelphia: Casemate, 2005), p. 326.

39. Venter, p. 326.

40. Ali Ansari, *Confronting Iran* (New York: Basic Books, 2006), p. 2.

41. Jerome Corsi, *Atomic Iran* (Nashville: WND, 2005), p. 180.

42. Ilan Berman, *Tehran Rising* (New York: Rowman & Littlefield, 2005), p. 79; see also Gaffney, p. 42.

43. Berman, p. 79.

44. Ansari, p. 2.

45. Berman, p. 79.

46. Venter, p. 326.

47. Leeb, pp. 129-30.

48. Quoted in Thomas D. Kraemer, "Addicted to Oil," May 2006. Available online at www.StrategicStudiesInstitute.army.mil/.

49. Ibid.

50. See Kraemer.

51. Leeb, p. 2.

52. Corsi, p. 179.

53. Gaffney, p. 42.

54. Kraemer.

55. Gaffney, p. 47.

56. Kraemer.

57. Hitchcock, p. 103.

58. Kraemer.

Chapter 5—Land Battles: To Whom Does the Holy Land Really Belong?

1. Randall Price, *Fast Facts on the Middle East Conflict* (Eugene, OR: Harvest House, 2007), p. 45.

2. Gleason Archer, "Confronting the Challenge of Islam in the 21st Century," *Contend for the Faith* (Chicago: EMNR, 1992), p. 97.

3. Cited in Josh McDowell and Don Stewart, *Handbook of Today's Religions* (San Bernardino: Here's Life, 1989), p. 387.

4. Alhaj Ajijola, *The Essence of Faith in Islam* (Lahore: Islamic Publications, 1978), p. 79.

5. Gerhard Nehls, *Christians Answer Muslims.* Accessed in *The World of Islam* CD-ROM (Global Mapping International, 2000).

6. Maurice Bucaille, *The Bible, The Quran, and Science* (Pakistan: Darulfikr, 1977), p. 9.

7. Larry A. Poston with Carl F. Ellis Jr., *The Changing Face of Islam in America* (Camp Hill, PA: Horizon, 2000), p. 183.

8. W. St. Clair Tisdall, *Christian Reply to Muslim Objections* (London: Society for Promoting Christian Knowledge, 1904). Accessed in *The World of Islam* CD-ROM.

9. William J. Saal, *Reaching Muslims for Christ* (Chicago: Moody, 1993). Accessed in *The World of Islam* CD-ROM.

10. L. Bevan Jones, *Christianity Explained to Muslims* (Calcutta: YMCA Publishing, 1938). Accessed in *The World of Islam* CD-ROM.

11. Cited in Price, pp. 44-55.

12. John F. Walvoord, *The Prophecy Knowledge Handbook* (Wheaton: Victor, 1990), p. 44.

13. Donald K. Campbell, "Joshua," in John F. Walvoord and Roy B. Zuck, *The Bible Knowledge Commentary: Old Testament* (Wheaton: Victor, 1985), pp. 364-65.

14. Walter C. Kaiser Jr., "An Assessment of 'Replacement Theology,'" *Mishkan,* no. 21, 1994, p. 17.

15. Thomas Ice, "Modern Israel's Right to the Land." Available online at www.pre-trib.org/.

16. Tim LaHaye, *The Beginning of the End* (Wheaton: Tyndale, 1991), pp. 44-45.

17. Price, pp. 45-55.

18. Joel Rosenberg, *Epicenter* (Carol Stream, IL: Tyndale, 2006), p. 27.

19. This information about the gradual return of Jews to their homeland is based on James Combs, "Israel in Two Centuries," in Tim LaHaye, ed., *Prophecy Study Bible* (Chattanooga: AMG, 2001), p. 970.

20. Walid Phares, *Future Jihad* (New York: Palgrave MacMillan, 2005), pp. 93-94.

21. Ilan Berman, *Tehran Rising* (New York: Rowman & Littlefield, 2005), p. 115.

Chapter 6—Interpreting Ezekiel 38–39

1. Harold Hoehner, "The Progression of Events in Ezekiel 38–39," in Charles Dyer

and Roy Zuck, eds., *Integrity of Heart, Skillfulness of Hands* (Grand Rapids: Baker, 1994), p. 82.

2. Jon Mark Ruthven, *The Prophecy That Is Shaping History* (Fairfax: Xulon, 2003), p. 33.
3. Charles Feinberg, *The Prophecy of Ezekiel* (Eugene, OR: Wipf and Stock, 2003), pp. 218-19.
4. Feinberg, pp. 218-19.
5. James Orr, ed., *The International Standard Bible Encyclopedia* (Albany, OR: Ages Software, 1999), s.v. "Gog."
6. Ruthven, p. 28.
7. Tim LaHaye and Ed Hindson, eds., *The Popular Encyclopedia of Bible Prophecy* (Eugene, OR: Harvest House, 2004), p. 150.
8. Mark Hitchcock, *Iran* (Sisters, OR: Multnomah, 2006), pp. 29-30.
9. See Ruthven, p. 31. Note that "from Jerome to our day, Gog has been variously identified as the Babylonians, the Scythians, Cambyses king of Persia, Alexander the Great, Antiochus the Great, Antiochus Epiphanes, Antiochus Eupator, the Parthians, Mithridates king of Pontus, Suleiman's Turks, the Turks and the Christians, the Armenian descendants of the Scythians, and a confederation of northern European powers including Russia (Rosh; Meshech and Tubal as Moscow and Tobolsk) and Germany (Gomer)." Charles F. Pfeiffer, *The Wycliffe Bible Commentary: Old Testament* (Chicago: Moody Press, 1962), q.v. Ezekiel 38:1. Accessed on Logos Bible software.
10. John Walvoord, *End Times* (Nashville: Word, 1998), p. viii.
11. LaHaye and Hindson, *The Popular Encyclopedia of Bible Prophecy*, p. 150.
12. Norman Geisler, *Explaining Hermeneutics* (Downers Grove: InterVarsity, 1988), pp. 14-15.
13. Graham Stanton, "Presuppositions in New Testament Criticism," in Harold Marshall, ed., *New Testament Interpretation* (Grand Rapids: Eerdmans, 1977), p. 68.
14. Bernard Ramm, *Protestant Bible Interpretation* (Grand Rapids: Baker, 1978), p. 105.
15. J.I. Packer, *"Fundamentalism" and the Word of God* (Grand Rapids: Eerdmans, 1958), p. 102, italics added.
16. LaHaye and Hindson, *The Popular Encyclopedia of Bible Prophecy*, p. 150.
17. Feinberg, pp. 218-19.

18. Walvoord, p. 10.
19. LaHaye and Hindson, *The Popular Encyclopedia of Bible Prophecy*, p. 150.
20. Thomas Ice, "The Literal Fulfillment of Bible Prophecy." Available online at www.pre-trib.org.
21. Arnold Fruchtenbaum, *The Footsteps of the Messiah* (San Antonio: Ariel, 2004), p. 108.

Chapter 7—Identifying the Nations of Ezekiel 38

1. See, for example, Mark Hitchcock, *Iran* (Sisters, OR: Multnomah, 2006), p. 175.
2. Clyde Billington, "The Rosh People in History and Prophecy," part 3, *Michigan Theological Journal*, 4:1, Spring 1993, p. 44.
3. Thomas Ice, "Ezekiel 38 and 39," part 2. Available online at www.pre-trib.org. Tim LaHaye and Ed Hindson, eds., *The Popular Encyclopedia of Bible Prophecy* (Eugene, OR: Harvest House, 2004), p. 119.
4. Mark Hitchcock, *Bible Prophecy* (Wheaton: Tyndale, 1999), p. 128.
5. See, for example, Earl D. Radmacher, Ronald Barclay Allen, and H. Wayne House, eds., *Nelson's New Illustrated Bible Commentary* (Nashville: Nelson Publishers, 1999), q.v. "Ezekiel 38:1–39:29"; see also Tim LaHaye, ed., *Prophecy Study Bible* (Chattanooga: AMG, 2001), p. 971.
6. Frank Gaebelein and J. D. Douglas, eds., *Expositor's Bible Commentary*, vol. 6, *Isaiah–Ezekiel* (Grand Rapids: Zondervan, 1992). Accessed in Oak Tree Software.
7. Thomas Constable Bible Study Notes, "Ezekiel." Available online at www.soniclight.com/constable.
8. Mark Hitchcock, *The Coming Islamic Invasion of Israel* (Sisters, OR: Multnomah, 2002), pp. 31-32.
9. Flavius Josephus, *Antiquities of the Jews*, book 1, chapter 6, "How Every Nation was Denominated from Their First Inhabitants."
10. Charles Feinberg, *The Prophecy of Ezekiel* (Eugene, OR: Wipf and Stock, 2003), pp. 220-21.
11. Matthew George Easton, *Easton's Bible Dictionary*, q.v. "Magog." Accessed in Logos Bible Software.
12. Hitchcock, *Iran*, p. 160.

13. Edwin Yamauchi, *Foes from the Northern Frontier* (Eugene, OR: Wipf and Stock, 1982), p. 64.
14. James D. Price, "Rosh: An Ancient Land Known to Ezekiel," in *Grace Theological Journal,* 6:1, 1985, p. 88.
15. Clyde Billington, "The Rosh People in History and Prophecy," part 1, *Michigan Theological Journal,* 3:1, Spring 1992, p. 65.
16. Billington, "The Rosh People in History and Prophecy," part 1, pp. 61-62.
17. G.A. Cook, *A Critical and Exegetical Commentary on the Book of Ezekiel* (Edinburgh: T&T Clark, 1936), pp. 408-409.
18. Thomas Ice, "Ezekiel 38 and 39," part 4, *Pre-Trib Perspectives,* vol. VIII, no. 44, April 2007, p. 6.
19. Randall Price, "Ezekiel" in Tim LaHaye and Ed Hindson, eds., *The Popular Bible Prophecy Commentary* (Eugene, OR: Harvest House, 2007), p. 190.
20. Billington, "The Rosh People in History and Prophecy," part 1, p. 56.
21. D.R.W. Wood et al., eds., *New Bible Dictionary* (Downers Grove: InterVarsity, 1996), p. 423.
22. Daniel Block, *The Book of Ezekiel: Chapters 25–48* (Grand Rapids: Eerdmans, 1998), p. 434.
23. Yamauchi, pp. 20-21.
24. Cited in Jon Mark Ruthven, *The Prophecy That Is Shaping History* (Fairfax: Xulon, 2003), p. 7.
25. Cited in Ruthven, *The Prophecy That Is Shaping History,* p. 16.
26. Billington, "The Rosh People in History and Prophecy," part 1, p. 63.
27. Ibid., pp. 63-64.
28. C.F. Keil and F. Delitzsch, *Keil and Delitzsch Commentary on the Old Testament,* vol. 9, *Ezekiel and Daniel* (Grand Rapids: Eerdmans, 1969), pp. 159-60.
29. Thomas Ice, "Ezekiel 38 and 39," part 4, p. 6.
30. Jon Ruthven, "Ezekiel's Rosh and Russia: A Connection?" *Bibliotheca Sacra* (Dallas: Dallas Theological Seminary, 1996). Accessed in Logos Bible Software.
31. Clyde Billington, "The Rosh People in History and Prophecy," part 2, *Michigan Theological Journal,* 3:2, Fall 1992, p. 172.
32. Ice, "Ezekiel 38 and 39," part 4, p. 6.
33. LaHaye and Hindson, *The Popular Bible Prophecy Commentary,* p. 190.

34. Ice, "Ezekiel 38 and 39," part 4, p. 6.

35. Billington, "The Rosh People in History and Prophecy," part 3, p. 49.

36. John Walvoord, *The Nations in Prophecy* (Grand Rapids: Zondervan, 1967), p. 106. See also Arnold Fruchtenbaum, *The Footsteps of the Messiah* (San Antonio: Ariel, 2004), p. 107.

37. Ruthven, *The Prophecy That Is Shaping History,* pp. 99-100.

38. Hitchcock, *Iran,* p. 164.

39. Gaebelein and Douglas, eds., *Expositor's Bible Commentary,* vol. 6, *Isaiah–Ezekiel.*

40. Thomas Constable Bible Study Notes, "Ezekiel."

41. Yamauchi, p. 25.

42. James Orr, ed., *The International Standard Bible Encyclopedia* (Albany: Ages Software, 1999).

43. Merrill Unger, R.K. Harrison, and Howard Frederic Vos, eds., *The New Unger's Bible Dictionary* (Chicago: Moody, 1988). Accessed in Logos Bible Software.

44. Charles Pfeiffer, Howard Vos, and John Rea, eds., *The Wycliffe Bible Encyclopedia* (Chicago: Moody, 2005). Accessed in Logos Bible Software.

45. Wood, *New Bible Dictionary,* p. 753.

46. Tim LaHaye, *The Beginning of the End* (Wheaton: Tyndale, 1991), pp. 71-72.

47. Joel Rosenberg, *Epicenter* (Carol Stream, IL: Tyndale, 2006), p. 129.

48. Rosenberg, p. 129.

49. Ronald Youngblood, F.F. Bruce, and R.K. Harrison, eds., *Nelson's New Illustrated Bible Dictionary* (Nashville: Nelson, 1995), q.v. "Gomer." Accessed in Logos Bible Software.

50. Wood, *New Bible Dictionary,* q.v. "Gomer."

51. Pfeiffer, Vos, and Rea, *The Wycliffe Bible Encyclopedia,* q.v. "Gomer."

52. Rosenberg, p. 129.

53. Fruchtenbaum, p. 108.

54. Hitchcock, *The Coming Islamic Invasion of Israel,* p. 46.

55. See Rosenberg, pp. 129-30. See also Radmache, Allen, and House, *Nelson's New Illustrated Bible Dictionary,* "Beth-togarmah."

56. Credit for these insights goes to Hitchcock, *Iran,* pp. 167-69.

Chapter 8—Is America Involved?

1. These facts are derived from Mark Hitchcock, *Is America in Bible Prophecy?* (Sisters, OR: Multnomah, 2002), pp. 19-20.
2. Stephen Leeb, *The Coming Economic Collapse* (New York: Warner Business, 2006), p. 30.
3. Michael Shermer, "Why ET Hasn't Called," *Scientific American,* August 2002.
4. Jared Diamond, *Collapse* (New York: Penguin 2005); Joseph Tainter, *The Collapse of Complex Societies* (Cambridge: Cambridge University Press, 1990).
5. Leeb, p. 36.
6. These views are representative of a number of different prophecy writers. Hitchcock has concisely summarized most of them in his book *Is America in Bible Prophecy?* pp. 52-53, 80. See also Mark Hitchcock, *Bible Prophecy* (Wheaton: Tyndale, 1999), pp. 172-74.
7. Thomas Ice, "Is America in Bible Prophecy?" Available online at www.pre-trib.org.
8. Hal Lindsey, "Where Is America in Bible Prophecy?" posted at hallindseyoracle.com.
9. Ibid.
10. See Ice, "Is America in Bible Prophecy?"
11. Lindsey, "Where Is America in Bible Prophecy?"
12. Ice, "Is America in Bible Prophecy?"
13. Ibid.
14. "Morality Continues to Decay," The Barna Group. Available online at www.barna.org/flexpage.aspx?Page=BarnaUpdate&BarnaUpdateID=152.
15. Jerome Corsi, *Atomic Iran* (Nashville: WND, 2005), p. 57.
16. David Gates, "The New Prophets of Revelation," *Newsweek,* May 24, 2006.
17. Quoted in Kenneth Timmerman, "U.S. Threatened with EMP Attack," *Insight on the News,* May 28, 2001.
18. Frank Gaffney, Curt Weldon, and Roscoe Bartlett, "Counter the Mega-Threat: EMP Attack," in *War Footing* (Annapolis: Naval Institute Press, 2006), pp. 100-101.
19. "The EMP Threat Is Real," United Press International, October 28, 2004.
20. Timmerman, "U.S. Threatened with EMP Attack."
21. Ibid.

22. Gaffney, Weldon, and Bartlett, pp. 103-104.
23. Timmerman, "U.S. Threatened with EMP Attack."
24. Gaffney, Weldon, and Bartlett, p. 104.
25. "The EMP Threat Is Real," United Press International.
26. Ibid.
27. Gaffney, Weldon, and Bartlett, p. 108.
28. Timmerman, "U.S. Threatened with EMP Attack."
29. Ibid.
30. Ibid.
31. Cited in George Jahn, "The End of Oil," *The Cincinnati Post,* September 17, 2005.
32. Leeb, p. 31.
33. Ibid., pp. 127-28.
34. Ibid., pp. 121-22.
35. Hitchcock, *Is America in Bible Prophecy?* p. 69.
36. Mark Hitchcock, *Iran: The Coming Crisis* (Sisters, OR: Multnomah, 2006), p. 128.

Chapter 9—The Final Jihad: The Coalition Invades

1. Thomas Ice, "Ezekiel 38 and 39," part 2, Pre-Trib Perspectives. Available online at www.pre-trib.org.
2. Earl D. Radmacher, Ronald Barclay Allen, and H. Wayne House, eds., *Nelson's New Illustrated Bible Commentary* (Nashville: Thomas Nelson, 1999), q.v. Ezekiel 38:1–39:29. Accessed in Logos Bible Software.
3. Cited in Mark Hitchcock, *Iran* (Sisters, OR: Multnomah, 2006), p. 95.
4. Arnold Fruchtenbaum, *The Footsteps of the Messiah* (San Antonio: Ariel, 2004), pp. 111-12.
5. Joel Rosenberg, *Epicenter* (Carol Stream, IL: Tyndale, 2006), p. 63.
6. Fruchtenbaum, pp. 111-12.
7. "Israel Strikes Black Oil Deposit," IsraelNationalNews.com, May 6, 2004.
8. Hitchcock, *Iran,* pp. 186-87.
9. John F. Walvoord and Roy B. Zuck, eds., *The Bible Knowledge Commentary* (Wheaton: Victor, 1985). Accessed in Logos Bible Software.

10. John F. Walvoord and John E. Walvoord, *Armageddon, Oil, and the Middle East Crisis* (Grand Rapids: Zondervan, 1975), p. 125.

11. Mark Hitchcock, *The Coming Islamic Invasion of Israel* (Sisters, OR: Multnomah, 2002), p. 106.

12. Hitchcock, *Iran,* pp. 186-87.

13. Charles Feinberg, *The Prophecy of Ezekiel* (Eugene, OR: Wipf and Stock, 2003), pp. 220-21.

14. Fruchtenbaum, pp. 111-12.

Chapter 10—The Defeat of the Invading Forces

1. J.I. Packer, *Knowing God* (Downers Grove: InterVarsity, 1983), p. 126.

2. John F. Walvoord and Roy B. Zuck, eds., *The Bible Knowledge Commentary* (Wheaton: Victor, 1985). Accessed in Logos Bible Software.

3. Mark Hitchcock, *Iran* (Sisters, OR: Multnomah, 2006), pp. 172-73.

4. The King James Version indicates that all will be destroyed save one-sixth of the invaders. This is a faulty rendering. As Arnold Fruchtenbaum puts it: "The King James Version indicates that one-sixth of the invading army is left alive. This is not found in the Hebrew text and has not been translated that way by subsequent translations. It is not true that one-sixth of the invading army will be left alive. The entire invading army will be destroyed when they invade Israel and nothing will remain, not even one-sixth." See Arnold Fruchtenbaum, *The Footsteps of the Messiah* (San Antonio: Ariel, 2004), p. 115.

5. Joel Rosenberg, *Epicenter* (Carol Stream, IL: Tyndale, 2006), pp. 163-64.

6. John F. Walvoord, *The Return of the Lord* (Grand Rapids: Zondervan, 1979), pp. 139-40.

Chapter 11—The Aftermath of the Invasion

1. William MacDonald, *Believer's Bible Commentary,* ed. Arthur Farnstad (Nashville: Thomas Nelson, 1997). Accessed in Logos Bible Software.

2. Earl D. Radmacher, Ronald Barclay Allen, and H. Wayne House, eds., *Nelson's New Illustrated Bible Commentary* (Nashville: Thomas Nelson, 1999). Accessed in Logos Bible Software.

3. Robert Jamieson, A.R. Fausset, et al., *A Commentary, Critical and Explanatory, on the Old and New Testaments* (Peabody, MS: Hendrickson, 1997). Accessed in Logos Bible Software.

4. C.F. Keil and F. Delitzsch, *Keil and Delitzsch Commentary on the Old Testament,*

vol. 9, *Ezekiel and Daniel* (Grand Rapids: Eerdmans, 1977). Accessed in Logos Bible Software.

5. Charles F. Pfeiffer, ed., *The Wycliffe Bible Commentary* (Chicago: Moody, 1962). Accessed in Logos Bible Software.

6. The ancient Jews believed there were a number of things that could quickly render a person unclean. For example, a woman was rendered ceremonially unclean during menstruation and following childbirth (Leviticus 12:2-5; Ezekiel 16:4). Touching a dead animal rendered one unclean (Leviticus 11:24-40), as did touching any dead body (Numbers 19:11). A person with a skin infection was considered unclean (Leviticus 13:3). Sexual discharges rendered one unclean (Leviticus 15:2). The Samaritans of New Testament times were considered unclean because they were a mixed breed, with Israelite and Assyrian ancestry (see John 14:9). Of course, Jesus taught that true uncleanness was in the human heart, and the only possible cleansing for this condition comes by following Him (Mark 7:14-23; John 15:3) and being reborn (John 3:1-5; Titus 3:5).

7. Thomas Constable Bible Study Notes, "Ezekiel." Available online at www.soniclight.com/constable/.

8. Charles Feinberg, *The Prophecy of Ezekiel* (Eugene, OR: Wipf and Stock, 2003), p. 230.

9. Tim LaHaye and Ed Hindson, eds., *The Popular Bible Prophecy Commentary* (Eugene, OR: Harvest House, 2006), pp. 193-94.

10. John F. Walvoord and Roy B. Zuck, eds., *The Bible Knowledge Commentary* (Wheaton: Victor, 1985). Accessed in Logos Bible Software.

11. Feinberg, pp. 231-32.

12. Frank E. Gaebelein, ed., *Expositor's Bible Commentary* (Grand Rapids: Zondervan, 1978). Accessed in Logos Bible Software.

13. Mark Hitchcock, "The Battle of Gog and Magog." Available online at www.pre-trib.org.

14. Walvoord and Zuck, eds., *The Bible Knowledge Commentary* (Wheaton: Victor, 1985). Accessed in Logos Bible Software.

Chapter 12—The Timing of the Invasion: General Considerations

1. Ralph H. Alexander, "A Fresh Look at Ezekiel 38 and 39," *Journal of the Evangelical Theological Society,* 1974, pp. 157-69.

2. Thomas Ice, "Are We Living in the Last Days?" Available online at www.pre-trib.org.

3. Ibid.

4. Charles Caldwell Ryrie, ed., *The Ryrie Study Bible* (Chicago: Moody, 1994), p. 269.
5. J. Dwight Pentecost, "Where Do the Events of Ezekiel 38–39 Fit into the Prophetic Picture?" *Bibliotheca Sacra* (Dallas Theological Seminary, 1955–1995). Accessed in Logos Bible Software.
6. Harold Hoehner, "The Progression of Events in Ezekiel 38–39," in Charles Dyer and Roy Zuck, eds., *Integrity of Heart, Skillfulness of Hands* (Grand Rapids: Baker, 1994), p. 84.
7. Alexander, "A Fresh Look at Ezekiel 38 and 39."
8. Pentecost, "Where Do the Events of Ezekiel 38–39 Fit into the Prophetic Picture?"
9. Joel Rosenberg, *Epicenter* (Carol Stream: Tyndale, 2006), pp. 68-69.
10. Arnold Fruchtenbaum, *The Footsteps of the Messiah* (San Antonio: Ariel, 2004), p. 121.
11. Some have wondered how Israel's construction of a security fence that acts as a barrier to Palestinian terrorists relates to Ezekiel's prophecy that Israel would be a land of "unwalled villages" prior to the invasion. Actually, the fence does not surround a village or a city. It is primarily a chain-link fence at strategic points. It does not constitute a wall by any stretch of the imagination. Nevertheless, it is possible that this fence may come down after the leader of the revived Roman empire signs a peace pact with Israel. See Mark Hitchcock, "The Battle of Gog and Magog." Available online at www.pre-trib.org.
12. Dana Garrett, "Former KGB Operatives Dominate Russian Government and Business," *Delaware Watch,* December 16, 2006.
13. This is well documented in Rosenberg, *Epicenter,* pp. 144-49. See also Joel C. Rosenberg, "How the Six Day War Almost Led to Armageddon," *Flash Traffic,* May 17, 2007.
14. Ilan Berman, *Tehran Rising* (New York: Rowman and Littlefield, 2005), pp. 57-58.
15. Ibid.
16. "Russia's Defense Minister Lays Out Ambitious Plans for New Weapons Purchases," Associated Press, February 7, 2007.
17. Berman, p. xvii.
18. Sergei Blagov, "Iran Pressing Russia over Plan for OPEC-like Gas Body," CNSNews.com, January 31, 2007.
19. Blagov, "Iran Pressing Russia Over Plan for OPEC-Like Gas Body."

20. Sebastian Smith, "Putin Hints at Gas Cartel, Defends Russian Democracy," Associated Press, February 1, 2007.
21. Berman, p. 50.
22. Frank Gaffney, *War Footing* (Annapolis: Naval Institute Press, 2006), p. 164.

Chapter 13—The Timing of the Invasion: Interpretive Options

1. In earlier years, prior to the publication of the Left Behind series, Tim LaHaye commented, "I risk the criticism of colleagues when I suggest that Christ may rapture His church *after* the destruction of Russia—particularly because there is no conclusive biblical teaching for this view. I may be influenced by my yearning to see the mighty soul harvest...But I caution the reader not to be dogmatic. We know Russia will be destroyed, but we cannot determine exactly when in the scenario it will happen." (See Tim LaHaye, *The Coming Peace in the Middle East* [Grand Rapids: Zondervan, 1984], p. 150.) More recently, Thomas Ice has reported, "Tim LaHaye has told me personally that even though they represented a pre-rapture position on Ezekiel 38 and 39 in their novel, he tends to place it after the rapture but before the tribulation." (See Thomas Ice, "Ezekiel 38 and 39," part 1, *Pre-Trib Perspectives*).
2. Joel Rosenberg, *Epicenter* (Carol Stream: Tyndale, 2006), p. 229.
3. It is important to be clear on the fact that the tribulation period begins the moment the Antichrist signs the peace pact, not the moment following the rapture. LaHaye is correct in his assertion that "the biggest misconception of some pretribulationists is that the second coming of Christ for His church (the rapture) and the beginning of the Tribulation period are simultaneous. They may be, but no passage of Scripture requires it. We must remember that the Tribulation is not started by the rapture of the church but by the signing of the covenant between the Antichrist and Israel." See Tim LaHaye, *The Coming Peace in the Middle East* (Grand Rapids: Zondervan, 1984), p. 145.
4. Mark Hitchcock, *Iran* (Sisters, OR: Multnomah, 2006), pp. 181-82.
5. Cited in J. Dwight Pentecost, *Things to Come* (Grand Rapids: Zondervan, 1964), p. 345.
6. Rosenberg, p. 251.
7. Arnold Fruchtenbaum, *The Footsteps of the Messiah* (San Antonio: Ariel, 2004), p. 121.
8. John F. Walvoord, *The Prophecy Knowledge Handbook* (Wheaton: Victor, 1990). Accessed in Logos Bible Software.

9. Mark Hitchcock, "The Battle of Gog and Magog." Available online at www.pre-trib.org.
10. Ice, "Ezekiel 38 and 39," part 1.
11. Ibid.
12. John Walvoord, *End Times* (Nashville: Word, 1998), p. 124.
13. Fruchtenbaum, pp. 118-19.
14. Hitchcock, "The Battle of Gog and Magog."
15. Thomas Constable Bible Study Notes, "Ezekiel." Available online at www.soniclight.com/constable.
16. Fruchtenbaum, pp. 118-19.
17. Harold Hoehner, "The Progression of Events in Ezekiel 38–39," in Charles Dyer and Roy Zuck, eds., *Integrity of Heart, Skillfulness of Hands* (Grand Rapids: Baker, 1994), pp. 85-86.
18. Hitchcock, *Iran,* pp. 182-84.
19. See, for example, Fruchtenbaum, p. 120.
20. Walvoord, *The Prophecy Knowledge Handbook.*
21. J. Dwight Pentecost, "Where Do the Events of Ezekiel 38–39 Fit into the Prophetic Picture?" *Bibliotheca Sacra* (Dallas Theological Seminary, 1955-1995). Accessed in Galaxie Software.
22. Ralph H. Alexander, "A Fresh Look at Ezekiel 38 and 39," *Journal of the Evangelical Theological Society.* Accessed in Galaxie Software.
23. J. Paul Tanner, "Rethinking Ezekiel's Invasion by Gog," *Journal of the Evangelical Theological Society.* Accessed in Galaxie Software.
24. Pentecost, *Things to Come,* p. 352.
25. Tanner, "Rethinking Ezekiel's Invasion by Gog."
26. Rosenberg, p. 254.
27. Cited cited in Tanner, "Rethinking Ezekiel's Invasion by Gog."
28. Mark Hitchcock, *Bible Prophecy* (Wheaton: Tyndale, 1999), pp. 214-15.
29. John F. Walvoord, *The Millennial Kingdom* (Grand Rapids: Zondervan, 1975), p. 331.

Chapter 14—How Then Should We Live?

1. See Jon Mark Ruthven, *The Prophecy That Is Shaping History* (Fairfax: Xulon, 2003), pp. 1-2.

2. Joel Rosenberg, *Epicenter* (Carol Stream: Tyndale, 2006), p. 50.
3. Cited in Mark Hitchcock, *Iran* (Sisters, OR: Multnomah, 2006), p. 189.
4. Rosenberg, pp. 252-53.
5. John F. Walvoord, *End Times* (Nashville: Word, 1998), p. 219.
6. Ibid., p. 218.
7. Erich Sauer, *From Eternity to Eternity* (Grand Rapids: Eerdmans, 1979), p. 13.
8. J.I. Packer, ed., *Alive to God* (Downers Grove: InterVarsity, 1992), p. 162.
9. Ibid., p. 171.
10. Ibid., p. 165.
11. Cited in Packer, p. 167.

Appendix 1—Messianic Prophecies Fulfilled in Christ

1. Norman Geisler and Ron Brooks, *When Skeptics Ask* (Wheaton: Victor, 1990), p. 115.
2. John Ankerberg, John Weldon, and Walter C. Kaiser, *The Case for Jesus the Messiah* (Chattanooga: The John Ankerberg Evangelistic Association, 1989), p. 16.
3. Ankerberg, Weldon, and Kaiser, p. 91.
4. Robert L. Reymond, *Jesus, Divine Messiah* (Phillipsburg, NJ: Presbyterian and Reformed, 1990), p. 47.
5. George Smith, *Atheism* (New York: Prometheus, 1989), p. 207.

If you have any questions or comments, feel free to contact Reasoning from the Scriptures Ministries.

RON RHODES

Reasoning from the Scriptures Ministries

Phone: 214-618-0912
Email: ronrhodes@earthlink.net
Web: www.ronrhodes.org

Free newsletter available upon request

Other Great Harvest House Reading

by Ron Rhodes

Find It Quick Handbook on Cults and New Religions

Find It Fast in the Bible

The 10 Things You Should Know About the Creation vs. Evolution Debate

The 10 Most Important Things You Can Say to a Catholic

The 10 Most Important Things You Can Say to a Jehovah's Witness

The 10 Most Important Things You Can Say to a Mormon

The 10 Things You Need to Know About Islam

Reasoning from the Scriptures with Catholics

Reasoning from the Scriptures with the Jehovah's Witnesses

Reasoning from the Scriptures with the Mormons

Reasoning from the Scriptures with Muslims

Quick Reference Guides

Angels Among Us

The Complete Guide to Christian Denominations

Answering the Objections of Atheists, Agnostics, and Skeptics

Christianity According to the Bible

The Truth Behind Ghosts, Mediums, and Psychic Phenomena

What Does the Bible Say About...?

To learn more about books by Ron Rhodes
or to read sample chapters, log on to our website:

www.harvesthousepublishers.com